# New Guinea Problems & Prospects

## Peter Hastings

**Cheshire**
Published for the
Australian Institute of
International Affairs

SBN 7015 0465 x cased edition
SBN 7015 0466 8 paperback edition
© 1969 P. Hastings
First published 1969
Printed in Australia for
F. W. Cheshire Publishing Pty Ltd
346 St Kilda Road, Melbourne
142 Victoria Road, Marrickville, NSW
by Halstead Press

Registered in Australia
for transmission by post as a book

To Jan and Olive Hastings

# Contents

# 1 Geography, People and Culture

*And there the great island lies, with its archaic bird-reptile shape. The smoking mountains speak low thunder, the earth shakes lightly, the sun glares down on the impenetrable dark-green mantle of forest with its dark baroque folds, the cloud shadows pass over the green, a white cockatoo rises off the tree tops like a torn scrap of paper . . . like an unread message.*

James McAuley, 'My New Guinea',
*Quadrant*, No. 19, Winter, 1961

## Geography

New Guinea and its adjacent islands form part of the 'Pacific Fire Ring', an area of unstable, volcanic activity encircling the Pacific Ocean that includes in the Western Pacific the Kuriles, Japan, Eastern Indonesia, New Guinea, Bougainville, the Solomons and New Zealand. Along the line of New Guinea's northern mainland and island ranges there are twenty-three volcanoes of which eleven are active and twelve are dead. Further east a second volcanic chain of three dormant and two active volcanoes (both on Bougainville) extend from the Solomons to the New Hebrides. Another six volcanoes in the Owen Stanleys in Eastern Papua have all been active in historical times. One of them, Mt Lamington, exploded in 1951 (clearly audible in Port Moresby) killing several thousand people in a matter of minutes. The island's ranges, particularly those of the outliers, were formed in the middle and late Tertiary period and as a result the New Guinea area is still in the process of subsiding and settling which causes frequent if only mildly intense earthquake shocks.

Measuring approximately 2,000 miles west from the Bird's Head (Vogelkop) to the easternmost tip of the tail of Papua and 450 miles north to south at its broadest point, the Irian boundary, New Guinea is the word's largest island next to Greenland. Lying entirely within the sub-equatorial tropics between 1 and 12 degrees south latitude and between 130 and 156 degrees of east longitude, its total area is approximately 335,000 square miles of which the eastern, or Australian, region of the Territory of Papua and New Guinea comprises about 183,000 square miles—about the same area as Thailand.

The island lies on the eastern perimeter of the vast monsoon area extending from the Asian mainland to northern Australia. This greatly affects New Guinea's climate and rainfall pattern, that of the hot, wet tropics. New Guinea's most striking physical factor, profoundly affecting environment and the pattern of human settlement, is the huge central cordillera that stretches 1500 miles from the Bird's Head in West Irian throughout the length of the island to the Owen Stanley ranges in eastern Papua to appear again, further east across the Coral Sea, in the Louisiade and D'Entrecasteaux archipelagos. This mountainous central spine of New Guinea is one of the world's great cordilleras. Range upon range of mountains, their jagged, serrated peaks blue and purple in the sunlight, black and sullen in the rain or their tops shrouded in early morning mist, run in parallel layers from north-west to south-east. Rising steeply from the narrow valley floors they reach an average height of about 10,000 feet, although in the central cordillera many peaks are higher, including Mt Wilhelm which rises nearly 15,000 feet. Two peaks in West Irian reach above 16,000 feet, one has a permanent snow cap.

On New Guinea's north-eastern outlying islands the pattern is much the same. Mountains rise steeply to about 8,000 feet offering extremely difficult terrain and affording only sparse habitation. In Western New Britain the folds are probably an extension of the formidable 12,000 feet ranges of the Huon Peninsula, while in the Gazelle Peninsula of New Britain and the other outliers the ranges again tend north-west to southeast. These comprise a series of folds rising from the Pacific Ocean floor from depths ranging from 12,000 feet to 30,000 feet in the Planet Deep off the Solomons.

On the main island, the southern walls of the cordillera, in which limestone is predominant, have folded and faulted to create a series of ranges descending in tiers to the southern, swampy lowlands. The northern flanks of the cordillera by contrast, are often fantastically steep, dropping abruptly for 8,000 feet with few mountain passes below 10,000 feet. In other places the descent is much less severe. In the central highlands, heavily eroded by streams, the cordillera bulges enclosing a number of comparatively broad valleys and plateaus between 5,000 and 6,000 feet in altitude in which live some 800,000 or approximately one-third, of New Guinea's 2,200,000 indigenous population. They were found by gold prospectors and government patrols as recently as the early 1930s. Before their discovery it was thought that the central peaks were a mass of steep mountains and massive gorges in which few if any humans lived. The highlands valley systems vary considerably. The largest is the famous Wahgi which runs east-west, parallel with the adjacent ranges. The smaller Chimbu and Asaro valleys lie at right angles and run north-south as do the Wau and Bulolo valleys in the Owen Stanleys.

Other important topographical features of New Guinea are its rivers and swamps which almost as much as the rugged mountain ranges have proved formidable barriers to human communications. A number of the great river systems originate in the central mountain chain; some like the famous Sepik River and the Ramu, flow north to the Bismarck Sea; others, like the Fly-Strickland and Purari, flow south to the Gulf of Papua. These rivers, like the Idenburg-Mamberamo, Digoel and Eilanden Rivers of West Irian, create large swamplands. Muddy, yellow with tannin from decayed vegetable matter, they eventually meander over their own floodplains while their courses and mouths appreciably shift over the years, making the siting and building of bridges impossible. At times some, like the Sepik, are navigable for surprising distances by shallow draught vessels. For the most part the swamps they drain are poor in vegetation and sparse in population. Occasionally, as in the Sepik and the Asmat area of West Irian, they support sizeable populations. In other places human settlement is extremely thin as in the Lake's Plain (*Meervlakte*) of West Irian, an area of hundreds of square miles of rotting vegetation. Viewed from an aircraft it appears as an extensive plain of trees and vegetation, but reflected sunlight in the coppery sheen of underlying water proclaims it a swamp. The area south and east of Kaimana, on the far west coast of West Irian, extends in an ever-broadening belt until it reaches the Fly-Strickland area of Western Papua to comprise one of the largest and most desolate swamps in the world—an area of approximately 100,000 square miles. Its westernmost boundary is the long, rough shoreline of the Casuarina Coast which, it may be remembered, was the scene of one of the greatest searches in modern times—that for Michael Rockefeller in 1961.

In general the northern rivers are more navigable than those of the south which make their way to the coastal swamps through a series of formidable gorges and waterfalls sometimes at a speed of twenty miles an hour rising and falling dramatically from the effects of sudden cloudbursts. On reaching the coastal plains the northern rivers are frequently blocked by parallel layers of coastal ranges, some of considerable height. These tend to trap the water into low lying swamps which are constantly filled by alluvium from the coastal and central ranges. However, areas like the Sepik plains are grass covered and the soils more fertile than those of the south which account in general for the heavier population distribution of north New Guinea's coastal areas as compared with the southern and western lowlands.

There are also marked differences between the island's northern and southern coastlines. That of northern New Guinea is rising, as is the west coast of West Irian. The southern coast is sinking. The northern coast consists of a long, relatively straight shoreline with few natural bays, harbours or major indentations. The coastal mountain ranges afford protection from the prevailing winds to the few anchorages available. The western region of the south coast, as we have seen, is extremely swampy. East of Kikori in the Gulf of Papua there are good anchorages although they are subject to the prevailing south-easterly gales for six months of the year, making conditions hazardous for small craft. Nevertheless, in earlier days great fleets of *lakatois*—large canoes made by people on the south Papuan coast—used the south-easterlies to make their way to Western Papua where they exchanged pottery for sago and waited for the seasonal change in winds to take them home again.

New Guinea's dramatic, concentrated contrasts in landscape between the central cordillera, intermontane grassed valleys, fast-flowing streams, deep gorges, great river systems draining vast coastal swamps and densely jungled shoreline are also the results of unremitting erosion. An extremely high mean annual rainfall together with high temperatures wreak constant changes on an already varied landscape. From an aircraft one can see in all parts of New Guinea the effects of constant weathering through the interaction of rain and heat—peaks sliced hundreds of feet deep by gigantic landslides, torrential rivers eating ever lower into mile deep gorges with 45 degree slopes and scarred, near vegetationless landscapes where the soil's tenuous balance of chemical properties has been fatally upset through excessive leaching or over-cultivation and in some places where there has been a combination of both.

## Climate

With few exceptions New Guinea's climate is uniformly hot and wet. Nevertheless, because of its insular nature and the effects of the central cordillera, there are surprising variations in the weather pattern from one place to another and according to the time of the year, the alignment of the mountain systems and altitude. The most consistent element in New Guinea's climate is the temperature pattern. At sea level daytime temperatures remain in the eighties the year round. Night time temperatures are generally 10 to 15 degrees cooler. Temperatures fall with altitude and above 4000–5000 feet the climate is cool and invigorating and although relative humidity remains high it is less distressing to human comfort.

At Aitape on New Guinea's north coast, approximately 3 degrees south latitude, the 9 a.m. temperature in July, the coolest month, is 75 degrees and in February, the hottest month, 85 degrees at 3 p.m. Mean year round 3 p.m. humidity is 75 per cent. For Port Moresby the equivalent figures are 77 degrees, 88 degrees and 71 per cent, and for Goroka, 5000 feet high, they are 63 degrees, 77 degrees and 56 per cent. In general the highlands valleys are about 10 to 15 degrees cooler than the lowlands although like the lowlands the annual range is slight.

Two other climatic factors are of consequence, both in terms of human comfort and in those of man's relation to his environment. New Guinea has a considerable cloud cover, greatest in the hottest months when it builds up in the early afternoon—incidentally providing one of the major obstacles to flying—which tends to reduce the daily maximum temperature. The relative absence of cloud cover in the cooler months tends to raise the daily maximum, although the averages still correspond to seasonal changes. Human comfort is considerably affected by the alternate wet and dry seasons. Variations in rainfall and humidity are caused by monsoonal winds blowing from reverse directions throughout the year. From April to September the dominant winds are the south-east trades which bring maximum rain to parts of Papua and the south coasts of New Britain and the Huon Peninsula. The north-west winds from October to March bring rain to the northern coasts and lowlands and to the northern flanks of the central mountain system. But even within this system there are considerable variations due to the alignment of the major mountain ranges so that parts of New Guinea get their wet season in mid-year while other parts including the northern islands and some southern highlands valleys get two wet seasons due to exposure to both wind systems. Other variations of alignment, orientation and altitude in the central mountain spine have combined to produce a range of micro-climates. Frosts are rare below 6000–7000 feet.

New Guinea's average rainfall is well above 75 inches annually except for a few isolated areas along Papua's south-east coast, the middle Markham Valley, the Bulolo Valley and Goodenough Bay where it is below 40 inches. In many parts of the island it reaches several hundred inches per annum. At least 85 per cent of New Guinea receives more than 100 inches yearly, making it one of the largest consistently wet lands in the world. But while it has a high number of rainy days per annum this is offset by a high number of sunny hours because rain falls mostly in the afternoons and evenings.

## Flora

Lying between Australia and mainland Asia, New Guinea has a vegetation cover with distinct affinity to both continents. Most of the island is covered with dense, tropical, rain or creeper forests, in which plant life is related principally to the flora of Malaya, Indonesia and other South-East Asian countries. In the dry areas of Port Moresby and the Fly-Strickland basin extending west to the south-west coast of West Irian, the mixed savanna-monsoon forest cover is very similar to that of the northern Australian coastal belts while the high altitude vegetation of the central cordillera has a close affinity to that of Tasmania and New Zealand.

It remains one of the commoner fallacies of popular thinking that tropical soils are richer and more fertile than those of temperate latitudes. Tropical soils, with the exception of favoured volcanic areas, are generally poor in quality. In New Guinea there are some notable exceptions to the general rule. Some soils are as rich as any in Java, but in nearly every instance they possess limited capacity for exploitation because of associated problems of steep slope, over-abundant rainfall, and erosion. New Guinea's heavy rainfall dislodges millions of tons of top soil each year into the river systems which carry it either into useless alluvial swamps or to the sea. The high rainfall coupled with high temperature has another effect. Rain leaches the surface rocks creating chemical changes by penetrating and breaking up the sub-surface rocks and carrying plant nutrients well below the level of tree root systems. High heat-humidity also affects the level of soil fertility. The composition of soils exposed to consistently heavy rainfall becomes increasingly poorer as soluble organic minerals necessary to plant growth are successively drained away.

New Guinea's dense tropical rain forests cover about 85 per cent of the island and are comparable with those of the Amazon, large parts of South-East Asia and central Africa. Average tree height is perhaps 120 feet. Many trees are considerably higher and their top branches form a dense canopy under which are graded storeys of smaller trees. All are covered by vines, ferns and parasitic growths striving fiercely for existence in the dim, fervent rain forest. Nearer ground level are creepers, orchids, staghorns in luxuriant profusion. While tropical soils in general are relatively poor in chemical nutrient properties, those that support tropical rain forests are poorer still. As we have noted the constant heavy rainfall carries nutrient minerals necessary to plant growth to depths well below those of the forest root systems which are generally shallow. These must therefore depend for their sustenance on successive layers of humus created by dead and rotted trees and plants. The high humidity-rainfall combination produces rapid growth of new trees which reach maturity and die relatively quickly. In short, the tropical rain forest lives not on the soil beneath it but on itself. The greater the heat-humidity factor the faster the growth-death cycle. Needless to say the rain forests are a formidable barrier to human settlement and communications as well as to modern commercial exploitation.

Coastal growth is characterised by dense mangrove swamps and strand forests of distinctively different type and of possible use for commercial exploitation. Inland swamps often contain huge areas of sago palm, which furnishes the swamp dwellers' staple diet, and in some places valuable timbers. There are also dry areas of low altitude grassland, like the Markham and Ramu valleys, which are probably the result of past suppression of natural forest growth by frequent firing, both for land cultivation and hunting of game. Above about 2,500 feet the forest decreases in height and the hoop and *klinkii* pine, New Guinea's two most valuable timbers, become dominant among red cedars, oaks and beeches which replace the taun, kwila (used in building), and nutmeg trees of the lower altitudes and the New Guinea rosewoods and mahoganies. With further increase in altitude oaks become more common giving away to magnificent stands of beech in the silent mossy forests between 6,500 and 10,000 feet. Here, in the cloud forests, the environment is cold, dripping and perpetually misty; a land of mosses, lichens, ferns and fungi, some of which are wierdly luminous. Above 10,000 feet the climate becomes quite abruptly sunny again and drier. The montane cloud forest gives way to limited high alpine forests of conifers, shrubs, tree daisies and many types of fern. True alpine grassland areas appear at 12,000 feet on which are found tussock grasses, buttercups, gentians and the equatorial alpine representatives of the snapdragon, fuschia and rose families. Above 14,000 feet is sparse rock-crevice vegetation only, as on Mts Wilhelm (14,790) and Giluwe (14,370), the former receiving occasional snow falls at its summit.

## Fauna

While the jungles, forests and montane vegetation covers of New Guinea are principally Asian in species—standing tribute over aeons of time to the vagaries of ocean currents and the passage of countless generations of birds—the wide variety of fauna living in them is predominantly Australian. The elephant, tiger, rhinoceros, monkey and deer of Asia penetrated no further east along the ancient land bridges than what is now Indonesia. New Guinea's animals, like Australia's, are mainly marsupials of which the island has more than 100 species, some of which have become extinct on the Australian mainland. The largest New Guinea animal is the tree kangaroo, but there are also opossum, wallaby and bandicoot. The island abounds in reptile life—there are plenty of crocodiles, various sizeable lizards and seventy species of snake, many of which are poisonous—and myriad forms of insect life. The mosquito is ubiquitous, including the malaria-bearing Anopheles species. While inland rivers have few fish they are plentiful in the reef-studded seas and estuarine waters where they provide a valuable source of protein for coastal natives.

The island's range of bird species is considerable. The largest bird is the cassowary which resembles the Australian emu. Other species include many kinds of parrot and cockatoo, some spectacular pigeons and many kingfishers and thrushes. New Guinea is the home of the legendary Birds of Paradise which live mostly in the damp, cool cloud forests, their magnificent tail feathers much prized by natives as decoration just as they were in pre-European times by the sultans and courts of the Indo-Malay world to the west who frequently sent trading expeditions to New Guinea's north-west coasts to barter for them.

## The people

Over the last 1500 years or so, New Guinea and its outliers constituted a formidable barrier to the eastward extension of the great rice and religious civilisations of Asia. To the east of New Guinea lay the unknown—the trackless expanses of the Pacific. To the south was the vast, dry continent of Australia sparsely inhabited by nomadic, palaeolithic hunters. New Guinea's forbidding terrain was inhabited by a seemingly barbarous neolithic garden-agriculture people and neither it— other than as the occasional source of slaves and bird of paradise plumes—nor Australia's inhospitable, northern shores proved attractive to Indo-Malay settlers. If they had there would have been evidence of their penetration for many Malay fishing fleets must have fetched up on the shores of Western New Guinea and northern Australia only to disappear or return thankfully to their rich and civilised islands to the west.

In pre-historic times the reverse was true. New Guinea was the land bridge by which the first of the Australian aboriginal races made their way into the continent of Australia and, across yet another land bridge, into Tasmania. It was almost certainly the departure point for the Melanesian races which settled the Solomons, the New Hebrides and the distant Fiji islands. Just when man arrived in New Guinea is unknown and speculation on his arrival and his culture is only educated guess work. Much more archaeological excavation, carbon dating and blood grouping needs to be done before we shall know with reasonable certainty anything about the circumstances of his arrival.

It was certainly a very long time ago, perhaps as much as 40,000 to 50,000 years ago, when South-East Asia contained a number of land bridges remaining from the quaternary ice age.[1] Some experts think that early New Guinea man was probably a frizzy-haired, stocky, short Negrito, although they are not sure what culture he brought with him. It is believed that his descendants exist today in the high valleys of the central cordillera comprising a people markedly different from those in other parts of New Guinea. Perhaps many thousands of years after the Negrito invasion there was a second migration wave of people related to those of the south-west Pacific into New Guinea. They do not appear to have stayed in New Guinea but to have left there some aspects of a stone age culture and the increasingly rare native Papuan dog which is closely related to the Australian dingo.

After this second Australian aboriginal migration there appears to have been another long time gap until about four or five thousand years before the earliest European explorers made their way into the area of New Guinea and the East Indies, when a neolithic, agricultural revolution seems to have taken place in the general region of Asia. It slowly diffused southwards and eastwards until it reached the Melanesian peoples of the Pacific and turned them from hunters and gatherers into subsistence gardeners.

In more recent times it is believed that there was a large influx of proto-Malays into New Guinea. These were the so-called primitive Malays, forefathers of the contemporary *Sakai* people, or *orang asli* of Malaya and Sumatra. They were good seamen who spread in successive waves throughout Indonesia, the Philippines and the Pacific Islands. They brought with them pig and fowl as meats and yam and taro as cultivated root crops, thus establishing subsistence New Guinea farming as it was to be when Europeans came to the island.

Some ethnologists believe that they also brought with them New Guinea's most widespread root crop—the sweet potato.

[1] In the Kiowa rock shelter, near Chuave in the Eastern Highlands, carbon estimates of ash layers fourteen feet below the surface date a highlands culture at 8000 BC. Stone tools at the site and the lower jaw bone of a carnivorous animal (a Tasmanian wolf) suggest a hunting and gathering culture and that animals were more plentiful than in recent times. More recent archaeological findings near a Port Moresby quarry may reveal that early Papuans lived there as long ago as 16000 BC.

Others do not. There is one theory that the sweet potato was originally restricted to Central and South America and that it was brought to the Philippines by the Spanish as recently as the sixteenth century. From there it spread to the South Pacific and eventually to New Guinea where it first established itself on the coast. Over a relatively short period of time it was bartered tribe by tribe through the ancient, mysterious trade routes until it reached the highlands. There, in a congenial combination of climate and soils, the sweet potato ran riot, its increasing availability providing a bulky, if over-carbohydrated, diet.

The new crop, combined with the comparative absence of disease in the high altitudes, particularly malaria, is thought to have been responsible for the population explosions of parts of the highlands in relatively recent times. In the Chimbu, for example, through intensive cultivation of more fertile soils population density reaches between 300 to 4000 people to the square mile of usable land. This is the highest in New Guinea. In the highlands (23,000 sq. miles) overall density is 37 to the square mile while for Western Papua and Gulf Districts (55,000 sq. miles) the figure is approximately 2.5 per square mile.

The proto-Malay migrants brought with them not only garden root crops but also great dug-out canoes, prototypes of the latter day lakatois, polished stone tools, coiled pottery, stone carvings and quadriangular axes. They venerated their dead, sometimes ate them 'with honour', and in some places erected dolmens to house them and menhirs to commemorate them. What happened to them is unknown. They may have died from disease, particularly malaria, or intermarried to the point of breeding out their racial characteristics.

The New Guinea peoples of today divide into three broad groups.

In the first group are the short, muscular Negrito types characterised by prognathous jaws, round heads, broad noses, dark brown skins and short fuzzy hair who live in isolated groups in the Highlands of East and West New Guinea.

The second group comprises the Papuans, a mixed race of

Negrito, Australoid and Melanesian characteristics, who are long-haired and of medium stature. Highlands Papuans tend to be compact, well muscled and frequently hairy. Lowlands Papuans tend to be taller. Intermarriage of Papuans with Melanesians produces a more coppery brown skin colour in offspring.

The third group comprises the Melanesians who vary considerably in physical appearance. Many of them are taller and lighter than the Papuans but these classifications are extremely arbitrary at best. Within them exists a bewildering variety of characteristic exceptions. Although many Melanesians are tall and light toned in skin, the Melanesian people of Buka are almost blue-black in appearance. Confusion in classification arises not only from the wide number of deviations in racial attributes, but also from the fact that the words Papuan and Melanesian are used to describe language groups. New Guinea's racial and cultural fragmentation has been accompanied by an equal fragmentation of languages. There are thought to be between 700 and 1000 different languages throughout the entire island. While most are mutually unintelligible many are related. Many are also of quite singular structural complexity.

## Language

Melanesian languages are chiefly spoken in the islands and along parts of the coast, while Papuan or non-Melanesian languages are found chiefly in the Highlands where they comprise the island's largest linguistic groups. A peculiarity of both is that in a broad spectrum Melanesian languages are restricted to matrilineal societies where descent is reckoned through the female line and Papuan languages belong to patrilineal societies where descent is determined through the male line. Of the sixty language groups in the Highlands fifty-two are related in varying degrees and forty-seven sufficiently closely related to group into five main language families. In 1960, Dr Stephen Wurm, the ethno-linguist, listed sixty Highlands languages spoken by nearly 800,000 people—many of the languages being of considerable complexity in grammar, structure and phonology.[2]

Most of New Guinea's languages are spoken by very small groups, mere handfuls of several hundred people, sometimes only 100 people, separated from other tribes by only a few miles of very rough mountain terrain, swamp or shifting rivers. Some language groups are comparatively very large like the Enga and Chimbu which together have 200,000 speakers. The multiplicity of New Guinea's languages, like its fractured landscapes, has made the tasks of pacification and administration exceedingly difficult.

New Guinea has no *lingua franca* and its absence led to the emergence of pidgin English or neo-Melanesian as it is now somewhat dubiously called. All pidgins arise from the same basic need to create a mutually comprehensible language between peoples speaking different and unrelated languages. It is by no means certain how Pidgin got to New Guinea. Stephen Wurm maintains that it started in Queensland in the last half of the nineteenth century with the importation of blackbirded labour into the cane fields from the Solomons and from New Britain. Over the years of contact between white overseer and black labourer the latter learned English words from the former which he then fitted into a context of Melanesian grammar, word order and phonology, just as in 'Queensland Pidgin' the aboriginal had grafted English words on to his own language structure. The resultant language was also used by the labourers themselves, most of whom came from different places in New Britain and the Solomons, in order to overcome their own language difficulties. According to Wurm, the new Pidgin was taken back to the islands by returning Kanaka labourers at the end of the last century. As many of them were Tolai from New Britain, and Rabaul

---

[2] More recently, in *New Guinea*, No. 2, 1969, Professor Wurm says that, continuing from Dr Capell's pioneering work, he established the East New Guinea Highlands Phylum containing sixty-nine languages and comprising 900,000 speakers. Professor Wurm also maintains that on the basis of recent studies in prehistory, the people who brought the ancestral forms of present day Papuan or non-Melanesian languages into the New Guinea area probably arrived there 60,000 years ago.

was the capital of German New Guinea, the German administrative officers also learned Pidgin and adopted it as the language of administration and contact. As the years went by, the language expanded absorbing a great number of German words and some Malay although its vocabulary became predominantly English.

Richard F. Salisbury, a noted anthropologist, disputes this interpretation of Pidgin's origin, maintaining that very few of Queensland's Kanaka labourers came from New Britain, 100 in all, and that even fewer returned. In his opinion, the beginnings of Pidgin pre-dated the establishment of the German Administration in 1884 and arose out of the early contact of European traders and whalers with the Melanesians of New Britain and the Louisiades. According to Salisbury, Pidgin 'derived from the trading *lingua franca* developed earlier in the Indies (hence the Malay content) and in Polynesia (and that) it has had from the start a quasi-Malayo-Polynesian grammatical structure.'[3] He maintains that the Tolai (New Britain) structure came later. Since then of course Pidgin has spread, expanded and altered. At present it claims more than 500,000 speakers of whom, significantly, 10,000 would know it as their only language, the others having in addition to Pidgin their own local languages. It has also moved extensively into Papua where it has made considerable inroads on the usage of Police Motu, a creolised form of the Motu spoken near and around Port Moresby. Pidgin's implications as a vehicle for New Guinean proto-nationalism are discussed in a later chapter.

## The culture

Throughout the island then, as we have seen, there spread several successive waves of people representing a profusion of racial origins, languages and micro-cultures. Over the millennia they crossed the swamps, climbed the great ranges and forded the large rivers to settle where they could, on the edge of the rain forests, in high valleys and on higher slopes, near lagoons

[3] See *New Guinea*, No. 2, 1967.

and on large and small offshore islands. They formed small communities of between 300 and 500 people (except in the Highlands and we do not know how recently these communities became relatively large) which lived almost completely cut off from each other, in mutual suspicion and fear and in constant apprehension of attack.

This almost complete dependence of each group on its own resources, at best upon an uneasy pattern of shifting alliances with neighbours, probably helped crystallise the New Guinean's magico-religious beliefs and his tiny worlds. Tribal boundaries were strictly demarcated and observed, generally with a no-man's land between, and to pass beyond them was to venture not only into unknown country but among unknown people, to risk death either directly or through the workings of enemy sorcery which were invariably powerful and cunning and whose effects included, because mortality was rarely attributable to natural causes, death from malaria, hookworm, respiratory diseases and the cumulative effects of malnutrition. The New Guinean was, by and large, a chronically sick person of relatively short life span, for the rigours of subsistence living were severe indeed. He is only comparatively healthier today, when male life expectancy is 45 years and female, 44 years but slowly increasing.

The harsh environment, the poor diet, the sheer struggle to live and the high toll taken by disease meant that the number of people living in New Guinea was relatively small in relation to available land so that, even though the soils were generally poor, the technology was adequate so that there was room for most to pursue subsistence gardening. The method of gardening was that of shifting agriculture of yam and taro, broadly restricted to the coast, and in the Highlands, sweet potato. Other root crops supplemented the diet together with bananas, fish and coconut on the mainland coasts and islands and the occasional flesh of small marsupial animals and that of the domesticated pig which was reserved for ceremonial feasts. Swamp dwellers relied principally on crude sago flour while all villages supplemented their extremely protein-short diet with mosses, bulbs, bamboo shoots, certain grasses, creepers and ferns and wild sugarcane.

New Guinean agriculture was very efficient in relation to soils, climate and available technology. Virgin bush was cleared by felling the trees with stone axes and burning the cut timber. The staple crop was then planted in the ashy soil of the cleared area which was enclosed with rough fences of wooden stakes to keep out pigs and any other marauders. Men undertook the heavy labour such as clearing timber, but their main job was to make war, hunt supplementary game and guard the village from attack. Women were beasts of burden who weeded, watered and dug the garden beds with heavy digging sticks.[4] After a few years, or longer periods in some areas, the soil's fertility was exhausted and the garden abandoned to weeds and secondary growth and a new 'slash and burn' garden created. After another period it too was abandoned and yet another garden created, sometimes on the site of an old garden after years of fallowing. New Guinea's terrain is covered with the scars of former gardens. In the highlands, the soils had a higher fertility and some peoples devised surprisingly effective means of terracing, irrigating and composting with mounds of vegetable matter. In some areas of the highlands, however, there is evidence to suppose that at the time of the arrival of the European the native populations were well on their way to destroying the natural environmental balance by overcutting timber and overworking soils as in parts of the Baliem Valley in West Irian.

In this uncompromising microcosm, the New Guinean lived in close relationship with his natural environment of which he felt an integral part and in which he did not need to distinguish between the 'objectively' real and unreal. It was first of all a cosmos of unchanging conditions ordered by immutable forces; by the struggle for existence and the fear of attack, by the important events of birth, marriage and death and by the intricate systems of inheritance and land tenure, by the great

[4] Possibly in no other society in the world was male supremacy so determinedly emphasised as in New Guinea, where in every conceivable activity male superiority was formalised in dress, ritual and speech.

ceremonial gift exchanges and by the bonds of kinship and obligation. In this closed universe the spirits of the living and dead existed side by side in tolerant communion.

Above it were the great deities which had created, because there was no other, this best of all possible worlds, and all therein contained—the forests, swamps, mountains, rivers, and crops, as well as the tools and implements by which the crops were tilled. In many societies each specific resource had a creator deity. Only the help of these deities could ensure that crops properly ripened, that enemies were confounded or that the *lakatois* safely reached their destination. In turn this help could only be enlisted by properly invoking it through the correct rituals and incantations taught to men by the deities in the far gone past. The proper use of magic secured the safe conduct of man's affairs and a successful outcome of his endeavours. The spirits of the ancestors, unlike the deities, had created nothing but acted as guardians of the living, watching over their vital interests, warning them of dangers in war and peace, aiding them in the search for forest foods or in the trapping of game, guiding their enterprise and occasionally killing one of their number for some slight to prestige. Those who sought the aid of the gods or the spirits through slovenly or perfunctory ritual invited retribution in the form of failure or even personal disaster.

The world was full of hostile forces, for even when all ritual had been faithfully observed there was the possibility that successful attainment of its ends might be frustrated through the effects of sorcery emanating, perhaps, from the evil activities of a nearby tribe or those of an immediate personal enemy in one's own tribe. For this reason the New Guinean jealously guarded the disposal of his own personal effects. Locks of his hair, his finger or toe nail clippings, bits of his skin, even his excreta, in an enemy's possession, whether near or distant, could perhaps work mortally against him.

The working of sorcery and numerous other injuries, real or imagined, invariably led to the 'pay-back' by which all injuries were precisely if impersonally avenged. Thus a man of one tribe whose wife was stolen by a man from another might not kill the actual offender, but just someone from the same tribe. More often than not his kinsmen undertook the task for him. For example, in the days of early European contact many whites killed natives in necessary or too hasty self-defence. It has then happened that the first Europeans to return to the area some time afterwards were in turn killed in revenge although they themselves had behaved in exemplary fashion and were in no way responsible for the original killings.

The explosive chain of offence and retribution, sometimes lasting over generations, ended only with restitution in the form of the gift exchange which bound offenders and offended once again in uneasy acceptance of one another according to the relative power of their positions. The gift exchange itself was firmly ordained by tradition and status and varied according to whether the society was patrilineal or matrilineal, coastal or highlands, seafaring or sago gathering. There were precise conditions governing the nature and value of the gifts as there were for the bride price. Thus one party might traditionally offer pig or cowrie and gold-lip shell, another canoes or pottery and yet another dog's or boar's teeth. The gift exchange also had an economic significance, for it was not merely a traditional mode of ensuring or of repaying obligation but also a means of activating the exchange of excess implements, food or ornaments which were the end results of production and skills.

The most fascinating example of this exchange is perhaps Malinowski's 'Kula Ring' which comprised a trading circle located over hundreds of square miles of small islands, including the Trobriands, Woodlarks, D'Entrecasteaux and Engineers groups, off North-East Papua, in which shell armbands (*mwali*) were sent clockwise for perpetual exchange with shell necklaces (*bagi*) travelling in the opposite direction.[5] Other examples were the trade routes of the mainland by which, despite savage tribal enmities and the fearful observance of tribal boundaries, the excess products of local skills, perhaps special foods like sago and prized commodities like salt, pottery and bamboo water containers, wood and bone ornaments and

[5] B. Malinowski, *Argonauts of the Western Pacific*, Routledge, London, 1922.

a variety of shells, were exchanged by innumerable hands for other delicacies or finished products. In the Highlands, shell 'money' and ornaments which are possessions of great prestige have made their long journey from the coast, exchanged at every turn for products or personal services, until they hang about the necks and arms of men who have never seen the ocean and cannot comprehend its existence.[6] Inland from the Casuarina coast of West Irian in the remote villages of the Asmat—a sea of tidal mud in which there are no stones—live New Guinea's most skilful wood carvers. In pre-contact times, even possibly today in some parts, they obtained their axes, chisels and scrapers of stone by trading their intricately carved spears, sago pounders and platters to distant foothill tribes who in turn traded sago and coastal shell for the bird of paradise plumes of the Highlands.

Mostly, production in New Guinea was for local use in a society which probably remained largely unchanged over thousands of years because of the island's isolation from outside influence. Most food was gathered and eaten immediately, because there was no means of lengthy storage, otherwise it spoiled. Excess food in the form of root crops, sago or pigs was eaten in great ceremonial feasts which were organised on a complicated basis of ritual observance and the claims of obligation and kinship. In a society such as this there were probably few technological breakthroughs arising of their own volition. Closed off from the outside world—and to some extent from that of their neighbours—New Guinea's village cultures were not exposed to the ideas and change that cultural pollination brought to Asia. Because of its isolated nature New Guinean society laid great emphasis on each individual within it being able to perform a variety of tasks. The skills needed for them were learned by observation of others and by trial and error, but were secondary to what Peter Lawrence has called 'true

[6] Indeed, some Highlanders, having no knowledge of how shell reached them or where it came from, believed it to be supernatural in origin and created cults around it aimed at increasing its supply-cults which were surely the precursors of the cargo cults of the post-contact period?

knowledge'—the proper observance of the magic and ritual needed to ensure the success of those skills.[7]

In this necessarily inward-looking world the vital personal relationships were those of marriage, descent and kinship. Outside these relationships the New Guinean's interest in his fellows declined to the point where he might feel it his duty to do actual harm to someone outside his clan or village. Within his own tiny group he sought friendly relations with his fellows and showed affection for his kinsmen. He confirmed these relationships by gifts which in turn created obligation on the part of the recipients. If the gifts could not be exactly returned in quality or value they could at least be worked out in personal services of one kind or another. All New Guinean men relentlessly sought personal prestige, and capable and ambitious men, more acutely intuiting their society than their fellows, thus managed the gift exchange in such a way that their friends and kinsmen owed them an unpaid debt of obligations. By these means and through their own natural capacity they became the 'big men' of the tribe or clan whose wealth was determined by the number of pigs (food and prestige) and wives (labour assets and prestige) they owned. Their pre-eminence might arise from their skills in a particular field—although male prestige was particularly bound up with being a good gardener, especially in the yam-competitive cultures of the Trobriands and the Sepik for example. One man might be a big fight leader, another skilled in hunting and yet another in making rain in the dry season. Others were famed for their sorcery or their knowledge of the proper magic which constitutes the vital difference between the making of a bad canoe and good one. These men, and those grown old and sage, formed the 'council of elders' which mainly settled by long discussion the many disputes that arose within tribe or clan.

In principle the system was similar to the Indonesian custom of *musjawarah* (consultation) which leads to *mufakat* (agreement) thus forming the process of *gotong royong* (all together). The primary aim of all consultation was to restore village

[7] See *New Guinea*, No. 1, 1967.

harmony, without which the security of everyone was in jeopardy, rather than mete out an abstract justice. Throughout New Guinea, society was relatively 'egalitarian' in structure. Lacking excess wealth and the rationalising elements of a great religion there were no chieftainly societies, like those in Africa, except in the Trobriands—and in a few other places—where the society was matrilineal and the Paramount Chief, possessing considerable wealth in the form of tribute, reckoned his descent through his mother—his uncle's eldest sister.

Elsewhere in New Guinea there was no inherited status, although it seems reasonable to suppose that the sons of big men obviously had a better chance of becoming big men in turn than those who were not.[8] But even big men or famed sorcerers or influential elders were subject to the inbuilt sanctions of society. Personal arrogance, the assumption and organisation of personal power away from group interests, was subject to a series of complicated social checks and balances. There are arrogant men in all societies, ('bigheads' or *bighets*), and no less so in New Guinea's, but restraints could be invoked including the most powerful social sanction in the hands of the group or of individuals, shame, the reverse side of the coin called prestige. Wives hanged themselves, returned to their own clans and sought death by entering enemy territory in order to shame their husbands.

The role of the individual in New Guinea's primitive societies was probably neither as restricted nor as anonymous as some anthropologists and sociologists once thought it. Adrian Gerbrands, the noted Dutch author on ethno-aesthetics, relates that in the Asmat the wood carvers contrived, quietly and unobtrusively, to form a distinct élite in their society within which they recognised and criticised one another as 'artists'.[9] In 'public', however, they were as reticent about their skills as an Asmat headhunter asked to recount his exploits at a public feast. In any New Guinea society men grew up reasonably proficient in the skills of making implements and the arts of

[8] The fact that many contemporary New Guinean politicians are the sons or nephews of 'big men' seems to suggest this.
[9] See *Eight Woodcarvers of the Asmat*, Mouton Bros, The Hague, 1967.

creating personal adornments, but some were better at it than others and some peoples more talented as groups than others at specific tasks. Traditional group skills depended in any case as much on the availability of materials as upon some eccentricity of culture.

We have seen that the Asmatters became highly skilled wood-carvers in an area in which timber was the sole workable material. In other parts of New Guinea there were other examples of similar virtuosity—people who wove cunning designs in bark fibres, made great pottery bowls, carved elaborate spears and bows and arrows and fashioned intricately designed necklaces of shell and dogs' teeth. In the Sepik, men raised enormous, elaborately-constructed *haus tambarans* seventy feet in height, their facia boards covered with brightly painted faces in ochre that looked like sad Byzantine Christs. In the Highlands, some tribes created fanciful, gorgeously coloured headdresses and in other parts constructed intricate wigs of human hair—that of their relatives, friends and deceased enemies. Masks of every shape and size were worn to honour the spirits, to celebrate the yams or to terrify enemies in battle. In coastal areas men built enormous long houses, sometimes on stilts, in which most adult men lived. In the Highlands they were round and simple, while in the swamps they were occasionally built in high trees. All of these peoples used simple domestic utensils of wood or pottery—sometimes even these were lacking—and cooked their fish, pig and root-crops over open fires or in deep ash. They made music of primitive rhythm on drums and slit gongs, hollowed from logs covered at the opening with dried lizard skin, on conch shells and on bamboo or reed flutes and by blowing over the edge of a leaf. Their dances were frequently elaborate, if formless, except in south-east Papua, where there may have been a certain Polynesian influence.

By and large, cultural anthropologists have tended to rate the cultures of New Guinea as socially and technologically less complex than those of Africa, but even in this there are current reassessments. Gerbrands, cited above, believes that the highly stylised motifs which appear in Asmat carving—the centipede, praying mantis, black king cockatoo, crocodile, sea pelican and so on—constituted a symbolism so widely understood throughout the huge Asmat area as to represent the cultural evolutionary stage of pre-ideogrammatic language. If this is so, it is interesting to speculate what changes in the normal order of things were required to transform a non-literate society, its knowledge of history extending back no further than the oral traditions of perhaps five generations, into creating a written language.

Some of the most complex aspects of New Guinean society are the various ways of determining descent. Land rights are invested in kinship groups, individuals having well defined rights to harvest certain trees, to work the land and consume its produce, as in any human society, but possessing no title to it through single ownership. The means of determining group ownership, that is who should work and harvest the land, varies with the type of society. The means of determining descent are complicated and depend broadly on whether the society is a matriliny, in which descent and sometimes property, is reckoned through the female line, or a patriliny in which descent and property are determined through the male line. Thus in a patrilineage, men and women substantiate descent through a common known male ancestor.[10] In a matrilineage men and women substantiate descent through a common known female ancestor. In a patrician or matrician society, which can include patri- and matrilineages, descent from a common known male or female ancestor is claimed but *not* substantiated. Tribes comprise a number of patricians and are found in the Eastern Highlands. In the Western Highlands there are phraties which resemble tribes, but in which a further common male ancestor is claimed. Moieties are societies divided into halves to one of which each member clan must belong. They may be patrimoieties as in mainland New Guinea, or matrimoieties as existing on the outer islands. Another impor-

---

[10] As Professor Peter Lawrence points out in *New Guinea*, No. 1, 1967, patrilineal societies are inherently more stable under European administration than matrilineal societies, because European societies work on the basis of patriliny.

tant descent and property system in New Guinea is the cognatic group in which males and females claim membership in a number of groups through either the male or female line on both the father's and mother's side. Coastal and island societies may comprise thousands, but Highlands societies comprise tens of thousands where the tribe or phratry organisation can organise greater numbers of people giving them, potentially at least, greater social mobility. Each of these societies was and is accompanied, not only by differences in land tenure and property rights, but also by differences in the marriage, gift exchange and other important social customs.

## The intruders

The effect of the white man's intrusion on these New Guinea mini-cultures was therefore immediate and dramatic. The steel axe, chisel and saw were not only miracles of efficiency compared with implements of stone, wood and bone, but also changed the nature of the society itself, altering forever the ancient, delicate balance of traditional forces and creating new, previously unimaginable demands. The steel axe, making its way into remote areas sometimes well before the white man reached them, took only a quarter the time and exertion needed to cut down trees and undergrowth with a stone axe and produced paradoxical effects. There was suddenly more time for warfare and feasting than there had been, but there was less time for looking after the gardens or husbanding the pigs. But even if some went hungrier than before, the taste for new things was firmly planted, and as time went by other of the white man's possessions became desirable, for calico was preferable to plaited grass and tinned foods to sweet potato. Desire for the white man's matches and candles, kerosene lamps and packaged salt, his beads and trinkets, spread rapidly among a people who knew neither how they were made nor how they could be obtained. In the beginning the coastal native could barter his coconuts, the only cash crop he owned, with the European for goods in kind. Later, with the establishment of the copra

B

plantations he sought to offer the only thing of monetary value he possessed—his labour.

The introduction of indentured labour, almost invariably of single men, for the copra plantations of far distant places, sometimes for six months, sometimes for five years, further disrupted the traditional way of life not only in the area of recruitment, but far beyond as the 'talk' went out over the years. The indentured labour system was, in itself, frequently brutal and dehumanising despite attempts to police it. Flogging was legal, both in German and in Australian New Guinea, and although illegal in Papua, breaches were hard to detect. The chief hardship in the system was probably the incapacity of the recruit to know what he was signing on for. The wider effects of the system on traditional society were many and varied. Young men from the villages of New Ireland and the Sepik sent to work in faraway places could scarcely return untouched from a world of almost unimaginable strangeness where they had received wages, accommodation and food and had lived in better health and in greater security than they had ever known before. A proportion of their wages kept as deferred pay enabled them to take glittering, prestigious purchases back to their admiring villages, while those who returned with money as well introduced an entirely novel element into the traditional gift-exchange system creating in limited form the notion of 'payment', rather than goods in kind or services, in return for obligations incurred. Despite the long absences from home and the rigours of the system, many 'signed on' for further periods before returning to their villages with their comparative wealth and new sophistication.

But whatever their age upon returning, they had been permanently marked by the new world outside, for none could ever quite again look on village life or accept its traditional sanctions in the old way. To those who had been *bosbois*, or labour foremen, neither the big men nor elders could carry quite the same authority as before. Not quite, for while it was one thing to return sceptical of the old authority, it was entirely another to challenge it when it was entrenched in the sanctions of village life; after all, the bride price had still to be paid and the gift exchange manipulated. Nevertheless, new and bewildering conflicts intruded on all sides. For the villagers themselves many ceremonials became relatively meaningless because the young men essential to their occasion were absent. Some men never returned at all, preferring permanent exile in domestic service, in the police force, or in the job of *bosboi*. Village life ceased to have its ancient corporate character, for, wanting that which only money could buy required attitudes, as C. D. Rowley points out, 'diametrically opposed to the village *mores*, for to succeed one must save rather than share, invest in improvements to one's land rather than in the social insurance of the gift exchange . . .'.[11]

Lacking a unifying monoculture, the effects of the New Guinean's introduction to the cash economy were psychologically frustrating in effect rather than galvanic. The impact of European civilisation on Asia, for example, introduced new skills, techniques and appetites into advanced, competitive religious societies and city-states where the principle of investment and capital gain was already well understood. In New Guinea's self-contained, isolated societies there were not, as in Java for instance, either the relative skills, the competition or the crops themselves to make transition an easy matter. Where natives undertook cash cropping and failed, they mostly returned to full time subsistence gardening, thus justifying the time-worn European complaint of their lack of motivation.

The European brought other dangers. Not the least damaging of white activities in the Territory has been land alienation. The overall percentage of alienation has been low—private and Administration alienation amounting to less than three per cent of the total island area—but that of suitable land, as in German New Guinea, has been considerable, especially in some parts of New Britain, New Ireland and on the mainland near Madang. Compensation was negligible and in any case its principle mostly misunderstood. The land alienated was nearly always the best land where convenient access roads could be built to nearby ports. In many cases the land did not appear to belong to any-

[11] C. D. Rowley, *The New Guinea Villager*, Cheshire, Melbourne, 1965.

body, but there is usually a customary claim to nearly all land in New Guinea—even virgin forest. Alienation led directly to outbreaks of native violence in the years before World War I and to continuous anxiety and resentment ever since, which now finds its expression in sporadic native claims to ancestral land being brought before the courts. Even the alienation of scarcely used land containing sub-surface minerals has created strong resentment, as both the Administration and Conzinc Rio Tinto found over the copper deposits in Bougainville. Alienation of land for timber exploitation has fared better. The results of land alienation, even in its more enlightened forms in the Highlands in the 1950's and 1960's, first for coffee and later for tea, has often been to turn the native against the idea of further alienation to the point where requests for land urgently required by the Administration for urban development, schools, access roads and other facilities are frequently strongly resisted or refused outright. These problems, added to those of tenure conversion, make land and the uses to which it can be put, a major political problem in New Guinea's economic development. In no single area of his existence will the New Guinean be more acutely in a conflict situation than over the conversion of customary land tenure to that of single ownership.

Indeed, according to the Rowton-Simpson Report on Land Problems, delivered to the Government in August 1969, there have been only 252 native land tenure conversions to date and to none of these have certificates yet been issued. Reluctance to seek single tenure conversion is nevertheless not surprising. Land is usually claimed by villagers within a broad linguistic area. The land lying between villages, whether of the same linguistic group or a different one, is subject usually to unresolved claim by both sides and there is no issue on which villagers, whether of the same linguistic group or not, will more readily confront each other, regardless of whether one side has a land surplus or not. The position is additionally complicated by the fact that through inheritance, or perhaps through merely shifting the site of their village, individuals may have customary claim to use land or harvest trees far from the place in which they were born. It is both the complexity and intensity of group claims that make group or co-operative land use in cash cropping more likely to succeed than attempting to persuade obdurate, suspicious villagers to consider conversion to individual ownership. At the same time where there are land shortages combined with population pressure, as in the Chimbu District and in the Gazelle Peninsula, traditional forms of land usage are becoming increasingly incapable of supporting larger populations thus creating acute social and political tensions.

Nevertheless despite the New Guineans' deep social and spiritual attachment to their land, the source of existence, it is also a possession. Owned collectively it forms part of their wealth and consequently they are ever avid of more. New Guineans will lay claim to land as being held in their customary tenure since time immemorial when they have never cultivated it, never fired it for game and have scarcely set foot upon it. An extremely vigorous view of this problem was put to the 1968 UN Visiting Mission by a prominent Goroka planter, Mr P. W. Reilly, a former Administration agricultural officer. His statement, subsequently printed in the *New Guinea Highlands Bulletin*, April 1969, asked why the Administration should allow indigenous squatters to freeze vast unused tracts of land which in more cases than not are actually ownerless? The vast majority of New Guinea land is in true fact 'waste and vacant land' which should be vested in the State.

This assertion that most (but not all) New Guinea land does not belong to the current native squatters may come as a surprise to you. But it is a fact that is easily proved by historical record. It is not more widely proclaimed because most Europeans are comparatively newly arrived and political pressures and job security and conformity to pattern effectively smother the views of those Administration officers who are aware of the truth.

Take this Asaro Valley—where you are now—as an example. Over thirty years ago, when the first European explorers penetrated, this valley floor was a waste and vacant land with no native settlement, no gardens, no trees, no houses, no birds. A glance at the mountain ranges around you will show that the primeval forests were being cleared years ago almost to the ridges of mountain crests, and in some cases, completely. The existing native population was clawing higher for security and more easily defensible positions.

The valley floor was vacant grassland given over to burning grass to catch rats and lizards, and for fighting and pillaging. With the advent of Administration-imposed (I repeat 'imposed') law and order, peace, security and free medical services, the mountain dwellers flocked to the valley floor, laid claim to it and the population exploded. But there is a vast difference between 'laying claim to' land and developing it. Your own observations will quickly prove that these squatters have developed only the merest fraction of the land.

Therefore, the vast majority of areas in the valley floor do not belong to the present native squatters; nor do they really belong to anyone. They should be vested in the State as security for future generations and to allow their full potential to be unlocked.

While Mr Reilly's observations about indigenous alacrity in laying instant and immediate claim to any land which might be claimed by others is both amusing and accurate, it tends to overlook the fact that the New Guinean likes to look at all land as something not only to be acquired, but to be defended from acquisition by the intruder, whether brown or white, more especially the white whom he perceives as unfairly and incomparably privileged through possession of superior knowledge and resources.

In all of this, then, a major effect of white skills, goods and power on the New Guinean has been his feeling of uncertainty and deprivation which throughout the island has led to cargo cult in various forms at various times with varying intensity. The sense of deprivation has been accompanied by a sense of dependancy, expressing itself in an ambivalent need to retain the white man until the secrets of his power and his possessions have been revealed. In the non-literate micro-societies of

Melanesia, the superiority of white possessions and native incapacity to comprehend how they had been made or obtained, could lead the New Guinean to but one conclusion—he had been deprived of them, either through his own 'original sin', through accident, through white conspiracy or through a combination of all three. The desire of New Guineans for the skills, possessions and powers of the white accompanied by incomprehension of their real nature has created a painful conflict for eighty years. For the majority it is scarcely less a conflict today.[12]

For a very long time European observers regarded cargo cult as an occasional and temporary derangement and its manifestation, such as belief in the imminent cargo-bearing ship or in the efficacy of a painfully constructed airstrip, as typically Melanesian attempts to obtain the coveted cargo through the exercise of childish magic. It was not understood for a very long time, or only imperfectly, that there was an intellectual rationalisation behind the apparent foolishness, the disrupted village life and outbreaks of hysteria—the descriptive term 'Vailala Madness' is suggestive of European attitudes—that was neither unintelligent nor illogical when viewed within the framework of systematised, indigenous belief. The world of the New Guinea villager, as we have seen, contained both the living and the dead. As we have also seen the knowledge required to grow yams, build a *lakatoi* or weave a basket was not in itself of such great moment compared with the importance of properly observing the ritual without which the making of these things, indeed of all things, could not be successful. The deities had created the world and all that was in it including the white man whom the villager thought to be his ancestors' spirits. The deities had also obviously imparted to the white man the knowledge and ritual by which he had made or obtained the desirable objects he had brought with him.

The proper rituals by which the whites obtained their cargo frequently seemed of no great complexity. They included such things as all singing together at certain times on certain days

[12] For a brilliant fictionalised account of cargo cult see David Fenbury's short story, 'The White Cassowary,' *New Guinea*, No. 5, March-April 1969.

(church service) or pushing a writing stick across a sheet of paper to make strange patterns (making out an invoice). Why had the brown man been denied the secrets by which the white man obtained his knives, axes and matches? In some instances the creator deity had denied the knowledge to the brown man in the far distant, long ago in punishment for an offence or for mere stupidity. In other instances the deities had expressly sent the white men back to hand over the secrets to the brown men, but for one reason or another, through malice, greed or indifference, they had refused to do so. Whatever the reasons for the failure of brown men to possess the cargo there was a road to it, a way through proper ritual, if only it could be found.

In the area around Madang and along the Rai Coast, cargo cult has flourished endemically since the arrival of Baron Miklouho-Maclay, the Russian naval officer and explorer, in 1871. The arrival of the Germans, and the Christian Missions shortly afterwards, brought two different styles of behaviour, both of which implied different roads to the cargo.

Professor Peter Lawrence in his *Road Belong Cargo*,[13] traces five major cargo beliefs between the advent of Miklouho-Maclay and the rise and fall of Yali, an illiterate New Guinea peasant, after World War II. In each successive cargo expression the basic rationalisations of the Rai Coast people were expanded to accommodate new phenomena, or past disillusionments. In the First Cargo Belief, Miklouho-Maclay was simply regarded as the source of gifts and the repository of divine knowledge. In the Second Cargo Belief, coinciding with harsh treatment by the Germans, old beliefs were extended to accommodate the conclusion that the knowledge of the cargo had been offered to the people at the time of creation and they had stupidly refused it. With the establishment of the missions and the propagation of Christianity, it was believed that the missionaries would eventually reveal the secrets and thus 'all the main teachings of the new religion—The Creation, The Fall of Man, The Great Flood, and even the Resurrection and the

[13] P. Lawrence, *Road Belong Cargo*, Melbourne University Press, 1964.

Second Coming—were stripped of their spirituality and given a thoroughly pragmatic meaning. They became a new origin myth of the cargo, while Christian faith, worship and morality were understood as the effective means of obtaining it . . .' The Fourth Cargo Belief rationalised disappointment over the failure to obtain the secrets to the cargo by saying that one of the creator deities had been reborn as Jesus and would have delivered the cargo except for his untimely crucifixion.

The Fifth Cargo Belief brings us to more recent times with the strange story of Yali, a Ngaing villager who fought extremely well with the Australians and visited Brisbane with a wartime party, where he was told along with other natives that the government intended a new deal for them after the war with Japan was over. Yali was intelligent, but illiterate. He interpreted the promise of better things literally to mean every thing from electric light to motor cars—a firm conviction he took back with him to New Guinea. After the war he re-organised his village and those nearby in such exemplary fashion that the Administration put him on its pay roll. Alas, the exemplary villages and semi-military discipline he introduced did not bring the promised cargo, while his repudiation of multiple wives made as a concession to the missions had led to many of the women hanging themselves in shame for which the Administration then blamed him. Things went from bad to worse. He rejected Christian teaching in his own philosophy. The missions sought his public disgrace. The Administration realised belatedly that he was not leading a model reform movement, but was in fact leading a cargo movement. He was tried and received a harsh five years' imprisonment.

Yali's story, and especially Professor Lawrence's account of cargo cult in the Southern Madang district, raises important political and social questions. Chiliasm is certainly intense along the Rai Coast, but is sporadically persistent in other parts of New Guinea as the President Johnson cult of New Hanover, the Hahalis Welfare Society of Bougainville, and the New Britain Submarine cult indicate. It does not appear to be as prevalent in the Highlands as along the Papuan and New Guinean coasts. Even this may be illusory and the answers are not entirely satisfactory. Cargo cult certainly tends to flourish intermittently in areas of lengthy European contact and of low economic development. In the Highlands where contact has been relatively recent, more sensitively handled, and where, because of better climate and soils there has been more rapid native economic development, it seems to be less in evidence, possibly, too, because of a more 'secular' culture. It is nevertheless in existence there as everywhere else on the island. In that case, at what stage of indigenous development does cargo cease to have appeal?

The most hopeful answer is that it ceases to be an effective motivation at that stage of economic development when the New Guinean has access to goods through his own economic capacity and finally perceives the connection between the end product, whether a steel axe or a biro, and the processes by which it has been designed and made. For very large numbers of New Guineas, while there may be acquiescence in the fact of white skills and possessions, realisation of how they have been achieved is still distant. The villagers' assumptions about man, his environment and the cosmological order have remained curiously untouched over the years of contact and in very many places have remained fundamentally unchanged. As recently as 1961, a native catechist in an excommunicated Roman Catholic village near Madang, dramatically arranged for another to slit his throat in a desperate parody of the crucifixion, and as a way to the cargo, in the presence of a horrified Bishop. In the 1968 elections there were numerous cargo manifestations among candidates, ranging from comprehensive promises of pie in the sky to more specific proposals, such as that of a candidate who offered to have himself crucified on the steps of the Federal House in Canberra, and that of another who, in New Britain, hoped to find $30,000 to keep the whites in the area long enough for natives to learn the secrets to the cargo before they left.

It is undoubtedly true that a combination of economic development, education, communications, travel to distant unheard of parts of the island and the sheer impact of the great world outside the village is slowly eroding the basis of chiliasm, even if the realisation that it brings, namely that there are no short cuts to either knowledge or possessions, is probably as depressing as it is illuminating. Nevertheless the cultural mainsprings of cargoism are obdurate and pervasive, even if increasingly attenuated. It is not unreasonable to suppose that for a long time to come, for very many New Guineans, that numerous roads to the cargo, other than religion, will appear to be open including 'national' politics.

# 2 A Brief History

*The Queen looks upon you as her children, and will not allow anyone to harm you.*

Commodore J. E. Erskine, RN, Port Moresby, 6 November 1884

*. . . the abysmal difference between the Stone Age and the twentieth century forms a chasm which it is almost impossible to span. . . .*

Sir Hubert Murray, *Annual Report*, 1906–7

*. . . even though they are blacks, they are human beings.*

R. James, M.H.R., House of Representatives, 2 November 1932

## Papua

What is history in New Guinea? And whose is it? What we have is largely contained in written European accounts of exploration, contact, administration and legislation. The New Guineans had no recorded history of their own, only the oral traditions of perhaps a half-dozen generations. There is no linear B script to tell us, or themselves, what they once thought, how they once lived or how they reacted to the intruders who touched their island, in the west, longer ago than is generally thought. There are European accounts of New Guinea, and Malay records and some dubious Chinese ones. We probably never will know what New Guineans thought of the effect on their society of the newcomer—seen from the inside.

Thus, in 1916, an acting Resident Magistrate in Papua was reporting that the most noteworthy thing in his opinion about the dreadful Kukukukus (who wore girdles of human thigh bones and murdered their neighbours with more single-minded enjoyment than possibly any other people in New Guinea) was their tendency to faint in terrified groups at the sight of a white man. A little earlier, Bishop Newton, who had studied the Wedau people and language fairly intensively, was able to say wistfully of the exchange between native orators at a feast, 'If one only really knew the language, which no white man does, what an insight one would get to the thoughts and ideas of people at feasts.'[1] The great Murray in 1906 put it more negatively, '. . . the abysmal difference between the Stone Age and the twentieth century forms a chasm which it is almost impossible to span.'[2] Nor, thirty years later, had things changed much when F. E. Williams, the percipient government anthropologist, tartly observed that 'the present means of communication are Pidgin Motu, Pidgin English, telepathy and swearing.'[3]

In a particular sense, a New Guinea history must be guess work for it necessarily comprises the written records and speculations of the intruders only. Nevertheless, the micro-societies of New Guinea were obviously neither as restricted, except relatively, nor as circumscribed in communications, as we tend to think them. Quite obviously from the description of the kula trading ring in Chapter 1, and similarly with the hiri trading posts along the Papuan coast and the moka ceremonial exchange of the Western Highlands today, there were extensive, carefully regulated, traditional contacts, not only of great politico-religious importance, but of considerable geographic range. As we have seen, the shell that became so important to the people of the highlands made its long and arduous way, bartered for commodities or services, over the traditional trade routes. Meanwhile, in fleeting contacts over great periods of time, the coastal world of the New Guineans was visited by voyagers from the Pacific in the east and the Malay world to the west.

New Guinea was first sighted by Europeans in 1511, 277 years before the First Fleet sailed into Sydney, by the Portuguese, d'Abreu and Serrano. Twenty-five years later the Portuguese Governor-General of the Moluccas, the centre of the Spice Islands trade, was blown on to the Vogelkop. He liked

[1] As quoted by Hank Nelson in a discerning essay on early Australian attitudes in Papua, 'Papua is the Country!', *New Guinea*, No. 4, 1968-69. The nearest attempt I know of a description from the 'inside' is Albert Maori Kiki's autobiography, *10,000 Years in a Lifetime* (Cheshire, 1968), the first part of which describes very vividly both the traditional life and the impact of contact.

[2] Hubert Murray, *Annual Report*, 1906-7.

[3] S. W. Reed, *The Making of Modern New Guinea*, American Philosophical Society, Philadelphia, 1943.

neither the country nor its people and left as soon as possible after naming it *Ilhas dos Papuas,* a Portuguese rendition of *orang papuah,* a Malay term meaning frizzy haired man. Over the next two centuries there was a series of New Guinea sightings and landings by Spanish, Portuguese, Dutch and British navigators. A Spaniard, Ynigo Ortiz de Retes, called the island *Nueva Guinea,* because of the resemblance between Africans and Melanesians, a likeness which the President of Dahomey commented on more than 400 years later on a state visit to Dutch New Guinea.

In the early exploratory days most European contacts with New Guinea were characterised by bloodshed and inevitable retribution. Partly due to these brief, violent encounters, partly due to the very appearance of the great island with its forbidding shoreline and more forbidding mountain ranges, partly due to its remoteness from the known centres of civilisation, it began to capture the imagination of European explorers and mariners as a land of great wealth. This it never proved to be, but the legend was to persist well into this century with the Australian administration in Papua.

In the west of the island there were tenuous Asian links. The sultans of Ternate and Tidore, in the Halmaheras, claimed a vague suzerainty over the far western part of the Vogelkop around Maccluer Gulf and the Onin Peninsula, exacting reluctant acknowledgment from some coastal tribes, to whom they sent periodic *hongis,* or tribute fleets, to bring back slaves and bird of paradise feathers, both of which were greatly prized by the courts of the Malay world further west. This contact was in fact probably both localised and sporadic. The western Vogelkop was the easternmost point of contact and influence for South-East Asia's rice civilisations (rice growing reached its easternmost point in the Halmaheras), much as West Irian is the end of the line today in terms of Indonesian influence and administration. In pre-European times the entrepreneurs of the Arafura who bartered china, brassware, sarongs and knives for trepang, tortoise and pearl shell, aromatic barks and slaves, were centred on Ceram.

In fact the Ceramese had a corner on trade with West New

Guinea, especially in the south-west where the savage Asmat people met all foreigners with spears and arrows. Lieutenant D. H. Kolff who travelled the area in 1825-26 in the Dutch brig *Dourga*, reported the 'sinister dealings of the Ceramese who, to retain their exclusive trade with the coast, inspire them (Asmatters) with hatred and aversion to all foreigners but themselves.' But to anyone who has travelled that area, or along the northern coast of the Vogelkop, it is hard to believe that Indonesian culture was ever diffused among any but insignificant numbers of people through the means of precarious trading posts and periodic *hongis*. What this sort of activity did create was a Papuan distaste for the Indonesian intruders from the west which, despite large numbers of West New Guineans who were pro-Indonesian in the last years of the Netherlands-Indonesian dispute, has lasted to the present day. (See Chapter 6).

An indefatigable English traveller and translator of Dutch chronicles, George Windor Earle, in 1853 wrote a description, based on a Dutch narrative, of a village near Triton Bay where a Moslem missionary resided and Papuans wore sarong and kebaya. Bruijn Kops, a Dutch naval officer, wrote an account of the visit of the Dutch warship, *Circe*, to Dorei in 1850 to establish Netherlands claims of sovereignty over West New Guinea made formally two years earlier. The ship was accompanied by ships of the Sultan of Tidore and his representatives. At Dorei, Kops found Papuan men and women dressed in Malay style, using Malay titles and living in Malay style houses. The *hongi* continued, after the ceremonies were over, almost as far east as Humboldt Bay.[4]

Despite evidence of Malay influence in Western New Guinea, the Melanesians probably penetrated much further west than is generally believed. The languages of the southern Halmaheras are more strictly related to those of Melanesia than to the main

[4] C. D. Rowley, *The New Guinea Villager*, Cheshire, Melbourne, 1965. See also Gavin Souter, *New Guinea, The Last Unknown*, Angus and Robertson, Sydney, 1963. Souter's book is a well researched and beautifully written account, among other things, of the exploration of New Guinea, a subject outside the scope of my own study.

islands of Indonesia. Over the centuries, coastal west Papuans probably infiltrated the offshore islands of West New Guinea by diffusion as frequently as they reached that area through the slave trade. In the medley of archipelagic races to be found among students making their way to High School or the University, any morning in Djakarta, one is astonished by the unmistakably Papuan cast of features found among many Ambonese and Halmaherans. They come from what C. D. Rowley aptly calls the Arafura world, a mixture of Melanesian, Sulawesi, Ceramese, and Ambonese cultures; its peoples—largely animist and pagan—heavily influenced by a diffusion of political and cultural forces from the larger islands to the west, even though Islam only partly established itself throughout the area which accounted for the relative ease with which Christian missionaries under the Dutch flag were able to convert so many of the pagans of what is now *Indonesia Timur*.

The real impact of Indonesian, or more accurately, East Indies influence in West New Guinea, including the spread of what is now Bahasa Indonesia as a *lingua franca*, resulted from Dutch administrative influence from about 1850 until the transfer of sovereignty in 1962. The Dutch administration in West New Guinea used Ambonese, Ceramese and Makassarese soldiers, police, school teachers and low grade civil servants, while Dutch officials tended to use market Malay, their only *lingua franca* in the outlying islands. In their post-World War II administration in West New Guinea they adopted East Indies civil service hours and ate, as they had always done, East Indies food. Many of the lay preachers brought by the Christian missionaries to West Irian were of Indonesian ethnic origin. In many respects West Irian was more strongly subject to Malay world influence in a century of intermittent Dutch contact than in centuries of contact with the Arafura world. The failure of Islam, in the last seven years of Indonesian administration, to make any headway in what is nominally, especially in the coastal areas, a Christian country, suggests that the degree of Malay influence in pre-Dutch times was tenuous at best. Nevertheless, partly because of western New Guinea's shadowy but

relatively ancient links with the eastern islands of the Netherlands East Indies, the Dutch were the first to assert a claim over
any part of the island. The establishment of Netherlands
sovereignty in 1848, designed to secure the far eastern flank of
their Indies empire and their lucrative spice trade from foreign
encroachment, was based legally on a claim to West New Guinea
made as early as 1660 when the Dutch East India Company
established sovereignty over the possessions of the Sultan of
Ternate and Tidore in the Halmaheras. These included 'trading
posts' on New Guinea's west coast. In the event the Dutch
showed little interest in their easternmost possession. They were
far too busy pacifying, exploiting and settling, far to the west,
three of the richest islands in the world—Java, Sulawesi and
Sumatra. It took a very long time for the Dutch to pacify their
rich, island empire. The rebellious Achinese, of north Sumatra,
for example, were not finally defeated by the Dutch until 1909.

Dutch administrative settlement in New Guinea was therefore relatively late in coming. There was an abortive attempt
to set up a post on the Vogelkop in 1828 and another after the
formal declaration of sovereignty in 1850. It was not until
nearly fifty years later that an administrative centre was
established at Fak Fak on the west coast. Others followed at
Manokwari on the Bird's Head in 1898, at Merauke in the
south in 1902 and at Hollandia, now Djayapura, in 1910.
Except for a few extremely well organised military expeditions,
and some private ones, little if anything was done to exploit or
pacify West New Guinea until after World War II when it
formally became a Dutch crown territory and the subject of a
long and bitter political dispute with Indonesia, dealt with in
another chapter of this book.

As the seventeenth century drew to a close quite a large part
of New Guinea's coasts had been explored by Europeans;
Carstenz had glimpsed, far off, the permanent snowcaps of
West Irian's central massif, Tasman had sailed New Ireland's
coast and Dampier had discovered New Britain. The eighteenth
century reflected burgeoning British global power and naval
supremacy in the increasing number of British discoveries in the
islands—Carteret discovered the Duke of Yorks in 1767, Cook

rediscovered the Torres Straits in 1770, Maccluer in 1791 had found the large bay in West New Guinea that bears his name, and Bampton the Gulf of Papua in 1793. In the same year there was an unsuccessful British East India Company attempt to establish a settlement and nutmeg industry near Manokwari. Discovery, exploration and mapping of New Guinea's shores, and early settlement, were an almost entirely British affair in the nineteenth century. Response in Europe to these sightings prompted a considerable volume of speculative literature devoted to New Guinea's supposed wealth. The island's alleged riches notwithstanding, the British government repudiated two early attempts to claim eastern New Guinea as British territory; that of Lieutenant Yule to take possession of southern Papua in 1845 and that of Captain Moresby in 1873. The New Guinea Company, formed in 1867, to exploit New Guinea's natural resources, quickly collapsed mainly through lack of Colonial Office support.

Nevertheless, there were sporadic attempts to settle the inhospitable island. French Marists, driven out of the Solomons, settled in 1849 on Woodlark Island, where sickness and native animosity made their task almost impossible, and forced them to hand over the mission in 1852 to two Italian priests who worked on for another three years before giving up. At the same time the eastern islands of New Guinea were becoming well known to blackbirders, traders and whalers. In the 1860's for example, there were trading settlements on the Torres Straits Islands and traders and whalers were regularly calling at New Ireland, New Britain, New Hanover and the Loyalties which, together with the Solomons, were a prized source of blackbirded labour. In 1871 the firm of Johann Cesar Godeffroy und Sohn, based on Apia in Samoa, started trading throughout the Bismarck archipelago for copra, turtle shell and trochus and in 1873 established a shore base on the Gazelle Peninsula. Two years previously the Russian biologist Baron Nicolai Miklouho-Maclay, had landed with a small party on mainland New Guinea at Astrolabe Bay in the Madang area. Three years later the Rev. W. G. Lawes permanently settled in Port Moresby, and in 1877, three years after his arrival, there was a small gold-rush in the area behind Port Moresby. The country was in the process of initial settlement and the phase of imperial conquest was about to begin.

The Imperial government in London showed little interest in New Guinea. Such interest as there was lay in the Australian colonies where opinions were divided. New Guinea was optimistically believed to house untold riches, and there was a growing body of colonial belief that New Guinea was essential to Australia's continental defence—as seventy years later it so proved. The operations of Godeffroy und Sohn and other German companies in New Britain led to growing Australian fears about German encroachment in the Pacific which previously had fixated on the Russians, the French, and even the Japanese as a menace to Australian life and property. Colonial opinion on how to deal with this threat seemed divided between those favouring an Australian type, British-backed Monroe Doctrine for New Guinea and those propounding a nineteenth century version of Fortress Australia. An article in a German periodical in 1881, urging German annexation of northern New Guinea, helped to reconcile Australian annexationist and anti-interventionist opinion. The Rev. W. G. Lawes, for example, formerly strongly anti-annexationist, returned to Sydney from New Guinea a firm advocate of intervention as a means of preserving New Guineans from the depredations of the labour recruiter and the commercial trader. Annexationist sentiments began to gather momentum and as an anonymous Australian pamphleteer of the time observed: 'It might be presumed that the conservative press of the colonies, as elsewhere, would have been in favour of extending the territorial boundaries of the empire; but when we find the liberal journals of Australia following suit, and even exceeding them on the same side, a force of public opinion is represented which no prudent statesman can despise. . . .'

In 1883, in response to popular agitation over a German corvette clearing Sydney for the islands, the Queensland Premier, Sir Thomas McIlwraith, ordered the magistrate at Thursday Island, H. M. Chester, to claim southern New Guinea as a British crown possession. Chester claimed the area on 4

April of that year, but the Imperial Government in London later repudiated his action maintaining that 'exceptionally strong reasons' were needed to warrant annexation. One of London's reservations was quite plainly its suspicion that the Queensland government had an eye to yet another source of cheap, black labour. Following upon this rebuff, McIlwraith prevailed upon the NSW Premier, James Service, to organise an inter-colonial convention comprising the Australian colonies, New Zealand and Fiji, which met in Sydney in November and December of the same year. While the convention itself was primarily an expression of nascent pre-federation Australian nationalism, defence was a dominant theme and New Guinea, therefore, of specific interest even though some of the resolutions were concerned with the fact that there were no existing laws, because there was no existing authority through which to frame them, to govern the relations of outsiders with the indigenous inhabitants of New Guinea. But the principal concern remained defence as expressed in the first resolution: 'That further acquisition of dominion in the Pacific, south of the Equator, by any foreign power, would be highly detrimental to the safety and well-being of the British possessions in Australasia, and injurious to the interests of the Empire. . . .' Convention feeling became so strong on the need for annexation that the states resolved: '. . . to submit and recommend to their respective Legislatures measures of permanent appropriation for defraying, in proportion to population, such share of the cost incurred in giving effect to the foregoing resolutions as Her Majesty's Government . . . may deem fair and reasonable. . . .'[5]

Despite British promises promptly to consider the convention's proposals, the British Colonial Secretary of the day, Lord Derby, was in fact tardy and did not answer until May of the following year when he gave it as his opinion that 'no foreign power contemplated interference with New Guinea.' Soon afterwards Berlin announced the formation of the Neu Guinea Kompagnie specifically empowered to exploit New Guinea, followed by another announcement that the new company

[5] T. Richards, NSW Government Printer, Sydney, 1883.

had the support of the German government. While this forced London's hand, Britain was not able to claim as much of southern New Guinea as it intended and after negotiations with the German Government it was decided to claim that area constituting the present Territory of Papua. One of the British Deputy Commissioners for the Western Pacific, H. H. Romilly, proclaimed the protectorate and raised the flag at Port Moresby on 23 October 1884, apparently misreading his instructions. The claim had to be made again on 6 November, by Commodore J. E. Erskine, who arrived in HMS *Nelson* just three days after the cruiser *Elizabeth* had hoisted the German flag in New Britain.

British fears about Australian, specifically Queensland, intentions regarding Papuans were reflected in Erskine's speech to Port Moresby natives and local chiefs made through the Rev. Frank Chalmers, who spoke in Motuan. Today, some Papuans refer to the proclamation with a pointed jocularity:

Your lands will be assured to you, your wives and children will be protected. Should any injury be done to you, you will immediately inform Her Majesty's officers, who will reside amongst you, and they will hear your complaints and do justice. You will look upon all white persons whom the Queen permits to reside amongst you as your friends, and as Her Majesty's subjects.

The Queen will permit nobody to reside here who does you injury. You will under no circumstances inflict punishment upon any white person; but if such person has done you wrong, you will tell Her Majesty's officers of that wrong, in order that the case may be fairly inquired into. You must know that it is for your security, and to prevent bloodshed, that the Queen sends me to you, and will send her officers to live amongst you.

And now I hope that you clearly understand that we are here amongst you as friends; you will all keep peace amongst yourselves, and if you do have disputes with each other, you will bring them before the Queen's officers, who will settle them for you without bloodshed.

Should bad men come amongst you, bringing firearms and gunpowder and intoxicating liquors, you are not to buy them, and are to give notice at once to the Queen's officers, so that such men may be punished. Always keep in your minds that the Queen guards and watches over you, looks upon you as her children, and will not allow anyone to harm you, and will soon send her trusted officers to carry out her gracious intentions in the establishment of this Protectorate.[6]

Historians differ in their views on the administrative achievements of the Protectorate. Murray Groves argues that it was during the Protectorate that 'the outlines of Papua's subsequent constitution and administrative system were formulated'.[7] J. D. Legge describes the period simply as one of 'suspended animation'.[8] One is inclined to agree with Legge. After all, the Special Commissioners appointed to the Protectorate had neither powers nor a policy other than that of exploration and native protectionism. The first Special Commissioner, Sir Peter Scratchley, arrived in August 1885, bought 552 acres of land for a town site at Port Moresby, sailed his official yacht, the *Governor Blackall,* round the eastern coast as far as the border, walked over the Astrolabe ranges and died of malaria three months after assuming office. He was succeeded by two Commissioners, H. H. Romilly and John Douglas, who had to contend with the pressure of those, mainly in London, who insisted on a native protectionist policy and pressure from Australian interests which believed that as the new colony had untapped wealth it should be opened up to white settlement. Protectionism proved the stronger sentiment leading Romilly to complain that his chief duties lay 'in hoisting flags innumerable' and that the administration of the Protectorate was 'not a very weighty charge'.

Originally Queensland, NSW and Victoria had promised £5000 each towards the annual administrative costs of the Protectorate to which the United Kingdom contributed £3000

[6] Broadsheet, Government Printer, Sydney, 1884.
[7] Murray Groves.
[8] J. D. Legge, *Australian Colonial Policy*, Angus and Robertson, Sydney, 1956.

annually and donated the official yacht which was valued at £18,000. By the time John Douglas completed his two-year term in 1888, South Australia, followed by Western Australia, Tasmania and New Zealand had already ceased paying their administrative contributions, leaving the three major states and Great Britain to carry the burden. As Romilly sourly commented before his departure: 'We are getting tremendously abused for shutting up the country, but till we get a good working establishment there it would be absurd to allow a rush of white men, and begin our work with a lot of murders and other trouble on our hands . . .' It was to secure a basis of legality in administrative matters that Papua ceased to be a Protectorate in 1888 and became the crown colony of British New Guinea. Annexation coincided with the arrival of the redoubtable Dr (later Sir) William Macgregor, a decisive, energetic Scot and the only administrator in the history of either Papua or New Guinea with actual previous experience in colonial administration—in the Seychelles, Mauritius and Fiji. In his ten year term, Macgregor forcefully laid down both a policy and philosophy of administration which was peculiarly his own for he inherited very little from his predecessors other than the bare framework of government and four stations at Port Moresby, Samarai, Rigo and Motu Motu—the last three being in any case manned by private residents, such as the Burns Philp agent, rather than by full time government officers.

Through a clumsy administrative arrangement, Macgregor was responsible to the British Government through the Governor of Queensland—a post which he also held in later years, after becoming Governor of Lagos, and later of Newfoundland. He had a Legislative and Executive Council, but in name only. Asked on one occasion by one of its members what would happen if the Council had sought to do otherwise than Macgregor wished, he replied in braw Scots: 'Man, the result would be the same.'[9] He spent the first years of his office as Administrator—he was created Lieutenant-Governor in 1895—formulating legislation for the government of the colony, creating

[9] C. A. W. Monckton, *Some Experiences of a New Guinea Resident Magistrate*, John Lane, London, 1921.

a workable administration and laying down a programme of exploration and pacification with the aid of a tiny staff which never numbered more than twenty, whom he drove mercilessly, a scanty budget and a great deal of determination. He travelled indefatigably on his yacht *Merrie England* and, as indefatigably, he walked. The son of a Scots farmer who achieved his medical degree by means of bursaries, he was a quite extraordinary man. Authoritarian, terrible in rage, he wrote his diaries in French and German and read the New Testament in Greek. Exuding energy and confidence he brought his own ideas and initiatives to the Protectorate's administration.

In 1890 Macgregor created an indigenous police force, initially comprising twelve Solomon Islanders and two Fijians, divided British New Guinea into two, later three, divisions with Resident Magistrates and promulgated a series of 'regulations bearing upon or affecting the good government and well-being of the natives'. In a general way he was genuinely concerned with the well-being of the Papuan although the tone of his concern was essentially Victorian and uplifting, for Macgregor believed in the Papuan's eventual perfectability. But in the face of what he regarded as Papuan insolence, laziness, deception or treachery, perfectability could wait while the guilty were punished. Macgregor enthusiastically chased offending cannibal raiders up rivers and across swamps, relentlessly pursued murderers of prospectors and missionaries and laid waste to villages without compunction. When he was not doing these things, the ubiquitous Scot was exploring, harrying his subordinates, climbing Mt Victoria (13,363 feet), drafting his legislation or 'dropping in' to see what gold diggers were doing at Sudest Island.

Macgregor laboured under formidable handicaps. The colony's annual budget was now only £15,000. His field staff was negligible for the task of exploring and attempting to control so vast and savage a territory. His government was situated in the squalid little shanty town of Port Moresby, invaded from time to time by some of the most brutal Europeans in the Pacific, come to Papua in search of gold, and whose activities he had to try and control, as on the Yodda fields where they lived, fought, murdered and died under the most frightful conditions. On the whole he was a good deal more successful in controlling Papuans than Europeans. He was a good deal more successful in controlling both than in reconciling the continuing conflict of interests inherent in a native land protectionist policy devised in Britain and a white settler policy espoused in the Australian colonies which were footing half the administration bill and in which, now that fears of invasion had been allayed by annexation, interest in New Guinea, other than to exploit its mythical riches, was now rapidly dwindling. It was only in the last year of his governorship that he felt able to attempt framing a land policy which, while protectionist, might encourage responsible white settlement in long term agricultural industry.

Macgregor's going coincided with the end of the joint agreement between the United Kingdom and the Australian colonies on the government of British New Guinea. The British were anxious to be rid of the territory and in Australia, although the intention to take over Papua was there, federation was in the air overshadowing all else. As a result there was an eight years' scandalous interregnum in Port Moresby before Papua formally became an Australian Territory in 1906. 'The limitations of native administration in Papua,' says J. D. Legge, 'were the limitations of Australian and British policy. The virtues on the other hand were Macgregor's own . . .'[10] And yet, while experimentation in some directions was one of them, such as his appointment of native magistrates, Macgregor had been essentially assimilationist in his native administration philosophy. His successors were even more so. An integrationist approach by which native institutions might be modified to become part of the administrative process and function was never contemplated, then or later. This was perhaps not so surprising given the times and the confused conditions in which the colony had been reluctantly annexed. What is surprising is that political assimilationist policies should have persisted so long. They still persist in current Australian

[10] Legge, op. cit.

official insistence that a Westminster system is by definition best suited to New Guinea's needs. Even Macgregor's apparent belief in ultimate native perfectability underwent a slow modification under the long reign of Hubert Murray. Until the Australian Government became directly responsible for Papua it was possible legally, at all events, for a Papuan to become a magistrate, a provision which lapsed under Murray until the present decade. Moreover, while Macgregor's regulations may have been uplifting in moral tone, they were essentially destructive of Papuan society, and probably as demoralising, as any Murray later introduced.

Colonising powers have invariably sought to administer colonial dependencies through the political structures, mechanisms and social values of the home country. Confronted in Papua by tribalism, continuous small scale warfare, linguistic fragmentation and numerous, repugnant practices including cannibalism, the need to interfere quite arbitrarily with native social custom must have appeared overwhelming. It seemed a deceptively simple solution, for example, to replace traditional group decision-making processes—in so far as Europeans recognised them as such—by the appointment of village constables. The government in effect not only failed to recognise the mechanism by which group tensions were resolved, but in appointing its own individual village leaders (most unrecognised as such by the villagers) proceeded to strip them of all real power by telling them that they must report all disputes and breaches of the law—in themselves breaches conceived by an alien civilisation—to the Magistrate who became official arbitrator in all disputes brought before him. Government-appointed village officials were frequently neither more nor less than spies in many instances using their position to bully, receive bribes or extort. Often they were merely used by the villagers as front runners to frustrate or modify the bewildering, uncomprehended requirements of the government.

Government requirements must have seemed mysterious and frequently intolerable to a people devoted to socio-magic beliefs and divided by language and geography into small, mutually hostile, ethnic groups. The government not only banned villagers from warfare and payback killings, but also required them to plant coconuts in each village, to send their children to a mission school if one was nearby, and to bury their dead outside their villages. It also required them, on order, under threat of penalties if they disobeyed, to carry for the Magistrate and to work on the roads. There were also penalties for such things as spreading what the Magistrate might deem false rumours. At the same time the village constable, for example, while empowered to report breaches of any of these regulations to the Magistrate, was neither supposed nor encouraged to administer or help formulate them. The regulations promulgated in 1895 setting out penalties for 'persons who pretend that the Government has conferred on them' authority and for persons actually possessing authority who 'ill use and rob the people and, at the same time . . . tell the people that the Government approves of their bad behaviour' suggests that there must have been a great deal of native resentment as well as many indigenous individual and group attempts to assume local leadership. In short native society was neither as inchoate nor as incapable of seeking political participation as governing whites liked to believe. In fact European attempts to police 'secret' native activities, rationalised as part of the European civilising mission, were obviously reflected in the anti-sorcery regulation of 1893 which declared that 'White men know that sorcery is only deceit, but the lies of the sorcerer frighten many people. The deceit of the sorcerer should be stopped.' The regulation forbade sorcery and imposed a three month's gaol sentence with hard labour and no pay, on any natives found guilty of practising, pretending to practise or threatening to employ sorcery. The fear that secret, and therefore uncontrollable, native activities might become 'political' and organised has plagued every colonial administration in history, and Papua's no less so.[11]

Macgregor's departure was regarded by many as a disaster

[11] These fears arose in New Guinea from time to time, notably when tribes around Madang in 1904 and Kokopo in 1905 forgot their traditional differences and united to attack the Europeans. Even more foreboding, one assumes, was the Rabaul General Strike in 1929.

for the infant colony and in 1906 the Australian government actually approached him to return. Macgregor's successors were men of inferior calibre who faced even greater political uncertainty than himself over their authority and the colony's development. His immediate successor, Sir Francis Winter, administered the colony for only a very brief period. He was succeeded by Sir George Le Hunte who, by temperament, education and training, was a very different sort of person. For all Macgregor's unrelenting toughness, he was a very capable colonial administrator. He had a theory of colonial administration and a theory of native development. In declining the offer of promotion in the Ceylon colonial government in favour of becoming Administrator of British New Guinea, he had written to one of his admirers, Gordon, the former Governor of Fiji, thanking him for all that he had taught Macgregor, stating that in New Guinea he hoped to be able 'to put into practice many of the principles which I believe are founded on a high sense of justice, although in many quarters they are not appreciated, not fashionable'. Nor were they, and Sir George Le Hunte was less interested in Macgregor's experiments in native administration than in tightening up the administration. Macgregor said once that he spent no more than a sixth of his time in Government House. Le Hunte spent about that fraction of time inspecting his savage domain, although he could be quite as vengeful as Macgregor when occasion warranted it, as over the much publicised Goaribari massacres.

In April 1901 the Rev. James Chalmers, a colleague of the Rev. W. G. Lawes of the London Missionary Society, together with a young missionary, the Rev. Oliver Tomkins, visited Goaribari Island, which lies in the Gulf of Papua to the west of the Kikori River delta. Besieged by angry Goaribaris on arrival in the small mission schooner and well aware of their reputation for inviting enemies into their *dobus* or long houses, there beheading and ritually eating them, Chalmers, a missionary of great experience, nevertheless anchored overnight after promising to visit the island in the morning. The next day he was as good as his word and went ashore where he, Tomkins and ten native members of the party were clubbed in a *dobu*, beheaded, dismembered, cooked and eaten. When the news reached Port Moresby, Le Hunte mounted a massive punitive expedition which sailed to Goaribari and killed a probable 100 or more natives with concentrated rifle fire. Le Hunte was unhappy about his actions and there were some misgivings in Melbourne. However, the affair was settled, and peace made with the people after Chalmers' skull had been retrieved.

Le Hunte was succeeded in May, 1903, by Christopher Robinson, the chief judicial officer and a man temperamentally unfitted for his job. Robinson was determined to mete out more vengeance to the people of Goaribari Island, where he and a party sailed in the government yacht. They were received as friends, but on trying to arrest two Goaribaris they understandably met with arrows. Robinson ordered his police party to open fire on the massed canoes, killing and wounding some sixty Goaribaris. Back in Port Moresby, Robinson faced bitter criticism from missionaries and other elements in the colony. The Australian Government took alarm and recalled him to Melbourne for a judicial inquiry, appointing Captain F. R. Barton, the chief judicial officer, as acting administrator. Ashamed and overwrought, Robinson shot himself in the head early on the morning of 20 June 1904, near Government House flagstaff.

F. R. Barton, an amiable Englishman, was an officer of undistinguished record in a West Indian regiment, who had served in West Africa. He was essentially a weak man, tolerant of factionalism and incapable of resisting advice, whether good or bad, especially bad, from men intellectually and temperamentally more decisive than he. While administration policy was still based on native welfare and protection, it was really presiding over a slow and inexorable erosion of native society wherever there was prolonged contact and control. Thus, in 1902, it had become illegal for Papuans in controlled areas to leave their villages and settle on vacant land. Certainly the Administration gave no signs that it understood why this was happening. The reasons were probably that with warfare outlawed, there were more villagers with time on their hands and who were no longer frightened, if they moved into a new area, of sneak attack. But a deeper motive undoubtedly existed— fear of further alienation of lands to which there was traditional customary claim, even though the Government seeing un-occupied land might regard it as waste and vacant. The Government also took the view that scattered settlement would mean an increase in local animosities. In the same regulations the Administration was empowered, on a Magistrate's advice, to declare any village a 'forbidden settlement' on the grounds of health or for other reasons. Villagers could be, and were, ordered to rebuild their villages where and how a Magistrate might choose.

In 1905 Magistrates were further empowered to order the improvement and sanitation of villages as they saw fit. While for every one of these measures there were soundly conceived western reasons, they comprised an arbitrary right of interference with native life, while none had been framed with the notion that villagers might be included in the decision-making process. As inclusion in government deliberations could only have been meaningful to Papuans through traditional mechanisms such as group discussion, which Europeans neither understood nor approved, the Administration ruled by fiat insisting not only on social change as a desirable end in itself, but that it should be accomplished through regulation and inspection. The pres-sures on the Administration in turn were considerable. Primary policy remained native protectionist while white settlement was negligible and overall land alienation minimal. Papua was a frontier administration and its officers had to deal with intractable, warring savages 'without the law'. Nevertheless if the protection of indigenous society, and its eventual adaptation to western civilisation was the principal aim of the Adminis-tration, the techniques employed were counter-productive, becoming increasingly anti-integrationist after 1906 under the lieutenant-governorship of Sir Hubert Murray. In that year regulations were promulgated requiring native contract-labourers to remain in quarters after nine p.m. reflecting the prevalent belief that, left to their own devices, Papuans were irresponsible savages. The same labourers were also required to wear, publicly at least, a loin cloth on the grounds, apparently, that they might otherwise appear as the savages most people believed them fundamentally to be. The insidious doctrine that was to obtain until very recently in New Guinea was now fully launched—New Guineans were to be segregated, looked after, legislated for and against, missionised and exhorted, until in the fullness of time they should by some magical means become European in all but colour when they would, of course, be accepted as members of the community. But whose community?

Quite apart from its aims and policies the Administration was falling to pieces. Divided into Australian and Colonial Office cliques over policy, and into personal factions through Barton's incapacity to take a firm stand on any issue, Melbourne began to scent scandal. In March 1906, the Prime Minister, Deakin, wrote to Hubert Murray, then Chief Judicial Officer, for a confidential report on the Administration. Murray wrote a lengthy reply criticising the Administration in detail. As scandal mounted, Barton demanded a Royal Commission before which Murray gave evidence in November of the same year, forever destroying the reputation of Barton who was given a year's leave before resigning and taking up a minor post in Zanzibar. Murray, who in 1905 had vainly sought a transfer to the British Colonial Service, returned to Port Moresby as Acting Administrator with high hopes of the Governorship. In his evidence to the Royal Commission Murray unhesitatingly came down on the side of encouraging white settlement which he did not believe incompatible with native welfare. The natives, he said, had been treated too well and had been placed on a pedestal with absolutely no result.[12]

The scope of this chapter allows only a brief description of Murray, the man whom Sir Robert Menzies said on 29 February 1940, two days after his death, had become a legendary figure. And so, after thirty-six years in Papua, he had. Murray was brought up as an Irish-Australian gentleman. He won a double first at Oxford, won the amateur heavyweight championship of Great Britain, and won a DSO in the Boer War.

[12] See Francis West, *Hubert Murray: The Australian Pro-Consul*, Oxford University Press, 1969.

He was a very big man who, almost to the end of his life, could outwalk and outride men half his age. He widely and constantly read in the classics, and each year re-read, it is said, *Paradise Lost*, *Faust* and Pindar's *Epinicia*. In the provincial white society of Papua he was, as the *Papuan Times* claimed on his seventieth birthday, a 'Gulliver among the Lilliputians'. During his long thirty years reign as Governor of Papua he achieved a minor international reputation as colonial administrator and as critic and correspondent of functional anthropologists. He was an honoured guest of learned societies and hailed in some quarters as the symbol of enlightened and progressive theories of colonial development. He was also greatly admired by McGregor, who, in 1919, was to say of him that Papua could not be in better hands.

Murray was also many other things. He was the failed lawyer of forty-two, who, in sheer ennui and frustrated careerism, went to Papua as chief judicial officer, a position of no great prestige. He appears to have been a cold and forbidding man, unhappy equally in Australian and English society, a man in whom intellectual arrogance, social pride and despair seemed to war destructively. Murray was a cultivated Victorian of diverse talents and diffuse ambitions who, by accident, found in Papua that for which he was temperamentally best suited—the governance of a primitive society. From Olympian heights he could ordain and control the impact of an alien white society upon a fragmented and uncomprehending brown one. In this he was not alone. Francis West, in his biography of Murray, perceptively points out that the other great pro-consuls of empire, Lugard, Gordon and Cameron were men in whom talents were also at war with social temperament. Murray, no more than Lugard or Gordon, was suited to governing the Straits Settlements or Ceylon with their highly developed societies and religions and their complex indigenous political structures. For the exercise of his talents, Murray needed the brown and primitive man, for whom he felt a genuine, if remote, sympathy, but of whose social psychology he was never certain. Thus, in 1931, after twenty-five years experience in Papua, he could still ask the Government Anthropologist, F .E.

Williams, if Lugard's observations in Nigeria to the effect that
native society still secretly maintained its traditional customary
law, applied in Papua—and received the discomforting reply
that it did.

The most obvious difference in temperament and intellectual
outlook between Murray and outstanding British colonial
administrators was that of training and vocation; the latter
were professionals likely in most instances to be moved from post
to post, able in most instances to call upon the services of better
trained, professional subordinates than was Murray and, despite
their individuality of outlook, the tempered products of an
imperial discipline comprising the accumulated knowledge and
experience of the Colonial Office. Murray was a characteristically Australian product, a gifted amateur, who, for thirty-one
years, ruled a territory very different from the Gold Coast,
Nigeria or Tanganyika. Few, if any, British colonial administrators were able to preside over the destiny of dependent
countries from the stage of exploration and initial contact to
that of consolidated administrative control. One wonders how
they might have fared if they had.

In West's phrase, Murray was a 'social evolutionist' believing
that native society was valid for its own circumstances and
purposes. (Eccentrically, he also believed that Papuan society
was at a pre-despotic stage and that without the stimulus of
European contact it would, for a very long time, perhaps for
ever, amount to nothing.) This, as West also points out, was
neither more nor less than the intellectual coin of similar
Victorians and did not militate against Murray's beliefs in the
ultimate perfectability of the Papuan; in fact it was part of it.
But there was plainly something nasty as well as unyielding in
its uncompromising reflections of racial pride and superiority.
Thus Murray was impelled to observe in 1911 that there were
some Papuans who simply did not respond in acceptible ways,
physically or morally, to a term of indentured labour. 'One
occasionally finds a native', he wrote, 'who might have been a
decent enough fellow if he had remained in his village, but who
has had his head turned by association with Europeans and has

C

been spoiled for life.'[13] Not a hint here that Murray either perceived, or sympathised with, the reasons leading natives actively to seek acceptance within the great white world, whose 'industrial ideal' he hoped to substitute for traditional warfare and payback. To the contrary, if they were to seek it, then officers should treat them with 'a certain amount of aloofness' and should never in their behaviour bring themselves to 'the native level'.[14] And yet the same man had sufficient, contemptuous insight into his European contemporaries to say that if they stayed in Papua long enough they would attempt to make the Papuans slaves. He never really hoped and certainly never tried, like Gordon in Fiji, so to manage and guide native political institutions as to encourage '. . .the capacities of the people for the management of their own affairs.' Murray apparently did not believe it could be done.

While he did not subscribe to the cruder beliefs shared by most of the white population that Papuans were lazy, unregenerate, childish and even licentious, Murray did not believe them capable of much more than to him appeared evident. After all, Macgregor had tried a system of government appointed chiefs and native magistrates and had reluctantly discarded it. Murray was not an innovator and it is interesting to speculate, if Papua had remained a British Colony, what might have been attempted in the political development of native institutions by administrators to whom Papua would have been only part of a career rather than, as in Murray's case, almost the whole of one.

And yet Murray had a complex and idealistic side to him and considerable courage which those who opposed him in Melbourne, in Papua and in New Guinea preferred to describe as mere obstinacy when they did not call it worse. Thus, before and during the war years he collected a considerable amount of information on the technical and general education given native peoples in other parts of the world. He did not hesitate

[13] See Hank Nelson, 'Papua is the Country!', *New Guinea*, No. 4, 1968-69, from the 1911-12 *Annual Report*.
[14] J. H. P. Murray, *Papua or British New Guinea*, Fisher Unwin, London, 1912.

to write to Governor Hahl, in 1914, asking for details of the new native school established some years before near Rabaul. His own notion was to establish an 'Industrial School for Native Papuans', believing, he said in a letter to a friend, that Papuans should not be confined to 'drawing (water) and hewing wood for others'. Of his Native Taxation Bill of 1918, he wrote in the same year to the Australian military administrator in Rabaul, saying that it deliberately contained provisions by which the 'money raised for tax is to be devoted to certain purposes, one of which is the technical education of the native.' Murray aimed, he said, 'to assist in the education of the native, both technical and general, and by a system of "native plantations" we expect to be able to improve native agriculture and to increase the economic value of the Territory to the highest state of civilisation which they are capable of attaining.'[15] He did not think it to be a very high state, however, and one gets the impression that his low assessment of native capacities militated against implementing the high ideals of his civilising mission which he expressed to the 1919 Royal Commission on the future of German New Guinea (dealt with later), in saying that, 'The history of German colonisation shows that even the most enlightened Germans seem never to have regarded the native population as anything but an "asset" to be used in the exploitation of the country, whereas in British colonies the welfare of the native is regarded as being in itself of the first importance.' There is surely irony in the fact that the Australians in New Guinea enthusiastically carried on the German policy of regarding the New Guinean as little else but an 'asset' while the Germans, whom Murray severely criticised, had started a government school details of which Murray only got around to seeking seven years after its establishment. Was Murray, at the end of his long reign, able to look back and be satisfied that he had governed Papuans in accordance with his loftily stated notions?

One gets a glimpse of the isolated and olympian nature of the Murray administration in his attitudes towards his none too well

[15] Murray, *Review of the Australian Administration in Papua from 1907 to 1920*, Government Printer, Port Moresby.

educated staff. He thought them good officers on the whole, and they probably were for Murray's needs which he perhaps unconsciously illustrated, in 1926, in opposing a suggestion that service recruits undergo a special pre-service course at the University of Sydney under the newly-appointed Professor of Anthropology, Radcliffe-Brown. Murray said he preferred to recruit staff locally in Papua, and that patrol officers should undertake such a course after two years field experience and Resident Magistrates once in their careers. The scheme fell through for lack of funds, although New Guinea Administration officers undertook a short course in later years. One gets the impression that the last thing Murray wanted was young, educated, argumentative service recruits arriving in the Territory with possibly dogmatic notions.

On his appointment to the lieutenant-governorship in November 1908, Murray inherited a very ramshackle empire. There had been some pacification of the south coast and river areas, quite large areas had been explored, immense areas remained to be, but contact and control were minimal. Port Moresby was a depressing frontier town, enlivened mostly by the riotous behaviour of miners who came in from the bush to spend their money. The sandalwood, copra and gold export trade was worth only £60,000 annually. The administration was divided into opposing cliques; there were those more or less supporting Murray and those violently opposing him, especially the redoubtable M. Staniforth Smith, a former young West Australian senator who dreamed of a career as a colonial administrator—he was as good as promised the governorship on one occasion—who came to Papua as Director of Mines, Agricultural Lands and Survey in 1907 and retained throughout his long career the extraordinary title of Administrator. The two men stubbornly and skilfully demeaned each other in interminable private correspondence with Melbourne. Nevertheless by 1912, despite problems with subordinates in Papua and superiors in Melbourne the whole tone of the administration had greatly improved. The Federal Government increased the grant-in-aid by £10,000 and there was a limited growth in white settlement. The Land Ordinance of 1906, which more or

less stands today, had attempted without great success to overcome the twin problems which still face New Guinea—how to
ensure that native lands would not be indiscriminately alienated
while managing to attract responsible white exploitation. The
ordinance allowed the Crown to buy under utilised 'waste and
vacant' land and then lease it for long periods to white settlers.
It was not satisfactory. However modest the alienation of
unused land, there were always customary claims to it, and as
a result prospective white settlers were discouraged by the
native lands policy. In 1908, for example, only 10,000 acres of
350,000 acres resumed for settlement had been taken up, and
of these a large number were forfeit through failure to comply
with the five year development clause. Nevertheless in the first
five years of Murray's rule Papua was, in his own words, 'in a
fair way to boom'. There remained an optimistic belief in big
mineral and oil strikes while annual export income from copra
and sandalwood rose from £60,000 to £360,000, although this
was due in large measure to the planting and development
efforts of the earlier administration rather than to Murray
himself.

As a lawyer, and the colony's chief judicial officer, he was
hard working and conscientious, travelling Papua from end to
end under very trying conditions; he once sat on 200 cases in a
single tour. In the application of the law he was, once again,
assimilationist. He was in Papua primarily to administer British
law in the interests of the country and civilisation he represented. While he would temper justice with mercy in taking
into account the inscrutabilities of Papuan motive, there was
to be no temporising with possible adaptations of native
customary law into the corpus of British law, such as were being
mildly experimented with in other British colonies. Native
customary law, while a factor to be taken into account, was
incomprehensible. The expatriate view was commonly
expressed in the phrase: 'It is pure Papuan to punish a
murderer by hanging his cousin.'

Francis West retells the story of the murder of a European
market gardener, Weaver, who lived not far from Port Moresby.
In April 1906 he was killed by the Koetapu people who wanted

his blood to sprinkle on the door posts of a new house. Hariki, the chief murderer, was executed and his accomplices given sentences up to fourteen years. Murray reasoned that had the act been done by savages over whom there was no administrative control, then the sentence would have been imprisonment. Hariki, he felt, had been in contact for some period and should therefore have realised the nature of European justice, if not the reasons for prohibiting murder. The price of ultimate Papuan perfectability, if Murray really believed in it, therefore carried the death sentence, although Murray probably also had to consider the feelings of the European community. And yet he gives retrospectively the strong impression that he was basically unsympathetic to the governed, despite his association with anthropologists like Seligman and his own interests in native custom and society. He could recognise, for example, that the prohibition on warfare, headhunting and payback could 'knock the fun and life' out of a native, but could believe at the same time that if only sorcery could be eradicated then most serious crimes such as murder, rape and bodily assault would disappear. Murray maintained an unabating detestation of sorcery to the end of his days just as he did of any native customs that were secret and uncontrolled. Sorcery was not only irrational in itself, and frightening and unpredictable in its alleged effects, but comprised part of that secret life over which the European had no control or direction. He showed the same suspicious animosity towards a Kiwai attempt in 1913 to import a council organisation from the nearby Torres Straits islands, which had been under increasing Queensland government control since 1863, and towards the system of native assessors in courts of native matters. Natives had to be closely watched. Left to their own devices they might do anything. Or nothing, as frequently was the case with the village councillors appointed increasingly throughout Papua from about 1923 on, hopefully to advise administration officers of general trends and the reactions of the people to government activities. They apparently had little to say, either individually or collectively, as Murray noted. But this may have been because of central government's strict and therefore inhibiting control over their activities. In his essay, The Machinery of Indirect Rule in Papua,[16] Murray records Papuan reaction in Port Moresby to the proposal to set up a council as reluctant: ' "Why should we have Councillors?" they would ask. "It is the white man's business to carry out the government; we do not know anything about it, and do not want to. We are quite satisfied with things as they are." ' This must have seemed a peculiarly dismal reaction from people who had been in contact with Europeans for two generations, but it reflected more than the dispiritedness of lengthy contact. It was probably a refusal to perform according to European concepts. In European eyes, councillors were chosen to act and respond as leaders of their people, which occasionally they were. More often than not the real leaders—who, unlike African tribal leaders, achieved their position in concert with others by 'merit'—were in the background deciding the real political issues of village life.

Murray's general administrative problems were nevertheless considerable. He not only had to deal with Melbourne—and frequently with unsympathetic ministers and bureaucrats some of whom detested him—but with the actual problems of running Papua with inadequate staff and funds. It was not only difficult to recruit and pay suitable administration officers on a wretched budget without pension rewards, but also to recruit doctors, surveyors, engineers, accountants, shipwrights and others as well. They were hard to get and harder to keep and staff turnover was high. Not the least of his administrative headaches was managing both the expatriate community generally, and the missionaries. Murray, although born an Anglican, came from an old Irish Catholic family to whose religion he returned, probably the result of ancestral pride—he used to read Irish mythology—as much as that of intellectual or emotional conviction. Throughout his term of office he was plagued by allegations in Papua and Australia that he favoured Catholics to government appointments and favoured Catholic missionaries above others—the obvious opinion of his colleagues in the 1919 Royal Commission on the future of the New Guinea

[16] Murray, *Essays in Honor of Gilbert Murray*, London, 1936.

Mandate. He seemed rather to be impartial and take a purely
functional view of the value of missionaries whom he urged
to spread the gospel because he seemed to believe that
Christianity, like hard work, might replace something of the old
Papuan values which he knew were slowly being wrecked 'in
the sea of an alien civilisation'.[17] Towards the end of his life
a sense of personal despair seems to suggest the realisation that
he had been chief agent of the wrecking process.

In the inevitable destruction by government and Christian
missionaries of the old traditional values, the Papuan in established contact suffered like the New Guinean. He was under-
employed with no outlets for his energy. While the steel axe
gave him more leisure, the prohibition on headhunting, warfare and sorcery deprived him of sanctioned, traditional ways
in which to spend it. Thus, for the people of the Fly, who
believed that they acquired virtue by ritually eating the flesh of
enemies, the new dispensation substituted nothing meaningful
for their past activities and must have produced the most
anguishing conflicts. At first Murray seemed to believe that
the 'industrial ideal' of indentured labour would provide an
answer—Papuans were not lazy, he said, but lacking in 'determination and perseverance'—because unless the Papuan
worked he was 'doomed' and would 'go under'. He seemed to
believe that it was better that Papua remained a nation of land
owning peasants rather than the home of a dispossessed
proletariat, but the belief may have represented his rationalised
frustrations over a workable labour and land policy. Murray
tried to maintain as humane a labour policy as possible by the
standards of the times, but found it difficult. Native labourers
were recruited for three year contracts, paid ten shillings
monthly and forced to work at virtually meaningless tasks nine
hours daily for a maximum of fifty hours weekly, with Sundays
free. Employers were obliged to feed, clothe and medically care
for the men under their control. Employers argued against the
expensive necessity to feed their labourers on imported foods,
saying that native foods were nutritious and adequate. Murray

[17] Dyason Lectures, Australian Institute of International Affairs, Melbourne, 1967.

privately thought so too, but partly because of his fear of
mainland and mission criticism and partly because he was only
too well aware of the nature of most employers, he insisted on
the ordinance's provisions being observed. Some employers
were reasonably humane. Most were not and, despite Murray's
system of spot checks, they ruled their labour lines by beatings,
deprivation and intimidation.

Murray himself does not seem to have been very happy in
Papua or with his job. It was merely that he was happier in
that situation than in any he had experienced in the forty-two
years before he first went there. He disliked the provincial and
uneducated white society of Papua, he feared for his position,
he anguished over his enemies and he lusted for preferment
and recognition. In 1912 he unsuccessfully got his brother Gilbert (later Regius Professor of Greek at Oxford) and the Australian Prime Minister to sound out the possibilities of a British
colonial governorship and was uncompromisingly refused. He
toyed with the notion of a state governorship which would
never have been offered him. In the middle of World War I he
hoped that at the war's conclusion he might become governor
of a united Papua, New Guinea, British Solomons and Netherlands New Guinea, adding that the latter might be bought for
a 'fiver'.[18] He openly canvassed the governorship of a united
Papua and New Guinea and served as chairman of the Royal
Commission in 1919 which examined the proposition. He was
in a minority of one. His reasons for amalgamating the two
services were sound, certainly sounder than those of his two
fellow Royal Commissioners, Attlee Hunt, the former Secretary of External Affairs, and Walter Lucas of Burns Philp. But
the government's desires were manifest: New Guinea was more
advanced in business and production than Papua and should
remain, therefore, a separate administration. In short, while
everyone might pay lip service to Murray's protectionist policies
in Papua, no one wanted them in New Guinea where a combination of richer soils and more systematic German exploitation of a larger labour force had resulted in profitable estates

[18] West, op. cit.

which the Australian government was determined to expropriate and exploit.

And so Murray remained in Papua, growing old and despairing, worrying about his unsuccessful marriages and the possible impoverishment of his children—his salary was a munificent £1800 a year. Despite an intellectual capacity to entertain new ideas, he became more entrenched in his essential conservatism, preferring, he said, 'the native "conservative" . . . to the type of native who wears trousers, a bowler hat, smokes a clay pipe and affects to despise his fellow countrymen . . .' and believing that 'it would be unwise to give the Papuan a first class education unless we can also provide him with the opportunity to use it'.[19] Despite the care and concern for human life that he demanded his patrol officers exercise in the bush, in the end it is almost impossible to discern what the Murray policy was. At one and the same time it was humane and protectionist, despotic and reactionary. It was probably, in Lord Hailey's memorable words, one of 'benevolent police rule'. To the end of his days Murray seemed to remain far more interested in pacifying outlying savages according to the famous Murray method of peaceful penetration than in finding needed political initiatives for those Papuans, who, by then, had been in close contact around Port Moresby and other centres for more than fifty years. 'Radios come in shoals', he said contemptuously of Canberra. Everything seemed discordant.

Murray died at Samarai on 27 February 1940, just twelve days after he had written to his daughter that he felt 'inclined to curse God and die'. Murray never suggested any long range plans for Papua, other than vaguely assuming that in the fullness of time it would become a state of Australia and that New Guinea would have a different destiny, even though he had once sought amalgamation of the two. Nor did he have any plan for internal political development. 'We are not going to make the brown man white, but to make him a better brown man than before', he had said many years previously. But whose sort of better brown man?

[19] Murray, *Annual Report*, 1911-12.

## New Guinea

The exploration, pacification and settlement of German New Guinea closely followed the classical Leninist definition of nineteenth century imperialist exploitation. It was firstly annexed by Germany, purely as an exploitative colony and in the belief, prevalent in Berlin, that it was rich in resources and labour. As it happened, labour, although more abundant than in Papua, proved quite as hard to recruit as in the southern colony, and the territory itself not a very great deal richer. The Kompagnie was given a charter by Bismarck, who wished to avoid the imperial government being involved in the problems of day-to-day administration. The charter enabled the Kompagnie freely to acquire land, administer the law and recruit labour. The first settlement site, named after the German zoologist, Dr Otto Finsch, who had discovered the Sepik, was at Finschhafen and comprised, in Gavin Souter's bland words, 'a dreary little settlement spurred to unwilling action by voluminous correspondence from Berlin, stifled by a murderous climate, fevered by a particularly virulent strain of malaria, shaken from time to time by earth tremors, and consoled only by alcohol'.[20] The Kompagnie was maladministered, rapacious, brutal and above all totally inefficient in all its operations. Souter quotes Stefan von Kotze, a nephew of the great Chancellor and a man of pungent wit, who worked in the colony for some years as a surveyor, as writing in a subsequent book, 'I am one of the few to get out of that malaria-hole, Finschhafen, with a whole skin, because I treated the fever with alcohol instead of quinine, and the orders of the New Guinea Kompagnie similarly—with alcohol instead of respect.'

The Kompagnie began a ruthless policy of land alienation and as ruthlessly pursued a largely unsuccessful policy of labour impressment. The people around Finschhafen showed no enthusiasm for either the labour or the pay and the Kompagnie fared no better with recruited labour from other parts of the coast. To remedy the situation it brought in contract Chinese, Japanese and Javanese labourers, many of whom, after a degree

[20] Gavin Souter, *The Last Unknown*.

of familiarisation with the work and the settlement attempted escape and, on capture, showed a melancholy tendency to suicide. The Kompagnie eventually asked the government to take over its administrative duties temporarily, receiving them back at the end of four years, but even then it was still unable to manage its own affairs properly or to carry out the government's requirements for exploration and extended control. Nor did moves to Stephansort, (Bogadjim) in 1892, and, after a smallpox epidemic, to malaria-ridden Friedrich Wilhelmshafen (Madang) in 1897, improve affairs. In 1899 the Imperial Government was forced to move, cancelling the Kompagnie's charter, paying shareholders four million marks compensation, and making them liberal grants of land for individual plantation development.

The first Imperial Governor was Rudolf von Benningsen. A tough and energetic man, he capably set about cleaning up the Kompagnie's tattered affairs. The capital was moved to Kokopo (New Britain) in 1901 and settled in Rabaul in 1910. Not long after von Benningsen took over the administration, the colony's conditions improved. By 1914 nearly 630,000 acres of native land had been bought and nearly 90,000 were planted to coconuts. Copra exports, valued at £A300,000, were almost eight times the value of those of Papua. The rapidly increasing pace of economic development was due in part to the larger number of choice areas available for planting, but as much to the twin policies of continuing land alienation and impressment of native labour which was paid only half the Papuan rate, and in trade goods if the employer wished it, while the indentured labour period was for seven years instead of Papua's three.

Employers were permitted to fine and imprison, with or without chains, their labourers and, if they thought it necessary, to flog offenders. Not infrequently an employer was a magistrate who acted as policeman, prosecutor, jury and judge in actions against his own labourers. Many villagers, beyond the immediate reach of the *kiaps*, simply went bush or resisted the blandishments of the labour recruiter. Many of the longer established, bigger companies eventually became more reason-

able employers, simply because it was bad business to be otherwise—word got around. Employers who freely resorted to
imprisonment, flogging and fines, or those who forced a native
to break his contract near its termination to avoid paying him
his deferred pay, found it hard to get new labour. Brutal or
dishonest recruiters fared similarly. Even so there were many
loopholes in the law and brutal and dishonest practices
flourished. A particular problem weighing heavily with government was maintenance of the labour supply. There are records
of whole villages being practically denuded of the working male
population which left the old, the women and the very young in
a situation of considerable hardship to carry on the everyday
work of the village. The psychological effects of this deprivation
of ritual life must have been frequently crippling. In yet earlier
days there were records of young, able-bodied New Irelanders
actually wading through the surf in their eagerness to reach the
recruiting ships which were to take them to the wonderful,
exciting world of blackbirded, canefields labour in Queensland.
Nevertheless expatriate interests were not the only ones at work
in the labour trade, for village elders frequently urged able-
bodied young men to seek employment and to bring back, at the
end of their time, trade goods and, at a later stage, cash. For
these reasons the Government, in German and in Australian
times, well aware that the colony's most precious asset was
cheap labour, used to try and ensure that only a third of the
available male labour force was recruited from a village or area
at any one time. This allowed for natural replacement. Villages
were regarded as labour farms. Some areas had been so depleted
that the government closed them off to recruiting. In German
times, New Ireland was at one period closed for some years.
At the same time pressures from Berlin for profitability were
such that the colonial government sought ways and means of
forcing natives into the cash economy in order to increase
revenue. The governor not only imposed a head tax, as in
Papua, but on a sliding scale which made it a punitive weapon.
The only way to pay the tax was by increased productivity.
Thus, in New Britain he forbade, without much success, the
use by the Tolai of New Britain of traditional tambu shell

money in native or European business transactions. This had the effect of depressing native trade with Europeans rather than increasing it. The Tolai were less inclined to sell their labour or their copra for cash than before when the Germans had recognised tambu as legal currency.[21] Forced increases in native productivity was not without attendant problems, especially as Europeans did not seem to realise that tambu (coiled shell money), still used in all important ritual transactions today, was not merely a means of exchange like currency. It was also involved in prestige and he who could lend as many fathoms as were required by others placed them under great obligation. Nor was it understood that tambu was not something to be spent but to be saved.

Von Benningsen was replaced by Dr Albert Hahl, an enlightened administrator with a much more 'liberal' policy towards native administration. However, the sense of injustice and outrage accumulated over twenty years of brutal contact, punitive expeditions—seven were sent into the area around Kieta in Bougainville in one year—forced labour and land alienation, was scarcely to be dissipated through the efforts of one man, especially as German official policy still included instant retribution for any offences against German life or property. The German theory of direct rule, and direct consequences for native offences, cost dearly in terms of maintaining law and order. As Osmar White notes, out of a permanent white population of nearly 250, over a twenty year period from 1885, more than one-fifth died as victims of native reprisals.[22]

---

[21] See Scarlett Epstein, *Capitalism, Primitive and Modern: Some Aspects of Tolai Economic Growth*, Australian National University Press, Canberra, 1968—a fascinating account of the Tolai economy. Despite land alienation and repressive administration measures, the Tolai must have done well out of their introduction to the cash economy. Dr Epstein points out that in 1892 some Tolai were offering £480 for a European boat and many were able to afford imported tobacco, rice, tinned foods and spirits, let alone ammunition, rifles and, most important of all, steel tools including the axe. Because of inbuilt cultural traits and of rich soils, the Tolai were, as they are now, a special case.

[22] Osmar White, *Parliament of a Thousand Tribes*, Heinemann, Melbourne, 1965.

German rule in the villages was conducted through two officials, the *luluai* and *tultul*, and occasionally a third, the *heil tultul* or *doktaboi*, a native trained to impart basic knowledge of hygiene. The system was similar to the appointment of village constables in Papua, but native officials were conceded a greater degree of authority and *luluais* frequently held 'courts' and ordered floggings either on their own account or, not infrequently, at the instigation of the missionaries. In actual fact the system, maintained by the incoming Australians later, was inefficient, frequently brutal and more often than not was used, as discussed in a later chapter, by villagers to frustrate the demands of government.

Despite the colony's shaky start, between 1910 and 1914 it began to thrive economically. The need for cooking oil for the kitchens of Europe ensured that copra boomed. Native labour was available if reluctant, control over outlying areas beyond the main centres had been established with increasing effect, and there was a growing number of immigrants. Of 1,273 Europeans in German New Guinea in 1914, nearly 700 were on New Britain and more than 300 on the main island, while there were about 1800 Chinese and Japanese engaged in small trading, labour recruiting and copra buying. Of the German population, only 135 were engaged in administration while 400 were missionaries. In the same year annual internal revenue in the colony had exceeded for the first time the grant-in-aid from Berlin.

After the declaration of war, at London's request an Australian Naval and Military Expeditionary Force (ANMEF) occupied the area around Kokopo in New Britain in September 1914, suffering five deaths before they advanced upon and senselessly destroyed the Bitapaka wireless station. Immediately upon establishing an Australian military administration, it was business as usual. Germans owning or working copra plantations were allowed to remain and were exhorted to greater efforts. German civil law and native administration ordinances were retained, including head tax and the native labour regulations devised by Governor Hahl were incorporated in those issued by the Australian military administration in 1915. While they prohibited native floggings by employers, they allowed the latter to impose fines and prison sentences and reserved floggings for the courts to order, sometimes for minor offences. As Osmar White notes, Field Punishment No. 1, hanging by the wrists, was not withdrawn until 1922.[23] As C. D. Rowley points out, some witnesses before the 1939 Labour Commission advocated a return to flogging as a means of ensuring efficient labour.[24] ANMEF's administration must have been quite as brutal as the preceding German regime. Gavin Souter quotes the story of an Australian punitive expedition on Bougainville which shot and beheaded the two principal murderers of a European. 'I think that . . . the hanging up of their heads will do an immense amount of good in the district visited,' was the opinion of the Australian police-master in charge. The Administration could also conscript labour for such government projects as road building and force natives to work for four months a year on government plantations. The purpose of administration policy was to continue German economic development. With high wartime prices the economy boomed, even though the export tax on copra had risen from 10/- to 25/- a ton. Pre-war copra and rubber plantations came increasingly into bearing, and the Australians had at their disposal the undoubtedly efficient services of German plantation owners and managers who were living on borrowed time and destined to see their possessions expropriated within a few years. An indication of New Guinea's wartime prosperity is the fact that the number of indentured labourers increased from nearly 18,000 in 1914 to 31,000 at the end of the military administration period in 1921 while nearly 20,000 additional acres of native copra had been planted. New Guinean resentment over land alienation must have been acute. C. D. Rowley estimates that in 1914, 700,000 acres had been alienated throughout the 'old Protectorate'. While this represented only one per cent of the land surface, it was the best land in the best positions. On the Gazelle Peninsula the Tolai had lost thirty-nine per cent of their land; under the Australians they lost more.

[23] White, op. cit.
[24] Rowley, op. cit.

Australian attitudes to New Guinea, official or private, were never as ambivalent as those Papua had evoked. Throughout the war years there had been a growing assumption in Australia that somehow or other New Guinea would and should become Australian territory. New Guinea was believed to be necessary to Australian defence and as a bastion against Asian, that is Japanese, encroachment in the Pacific. With the successful conclusion of the German war Australian fears of invasion were once again fixating, with good cause, on the Japanese. In more simple terms New Guinea was regarded as spoils of war. In Paris, W. M. Hughes had sought outright annexation, but in Europe and the United States the spirit of the times worked against old style colonial expansion and the compromise was a C Class, or easy terms, mandate. At the same time the Australian Government sought to clarify the administrative and developmental problems of the new territory through the Royal Commission of 1919, chaired by Hubert Murray, who, as we have seen, was privately consumed with the idea of a joint administration for Papua and New Guinea—two for the price of one—headed by himself. He had other motives. He knew something of the Australian military administration record throughout the war, he knew a great deal more about the German administration; he liked neither. The Commission was to report what sort of government could be established for New Guinea under the terms of the mandate and to consider associated questions of cost, communications, trade, the future of German holdings and New Guinea's future relationship with Papua and the Solomons.

In the event, with Murray dissenting, the Commission recommended a separate New Guinea administration on several grounds, including one which must have sorely wounded Murray—that the Papuan government was not in all respects superior to that of New Guinea. Obviously the chief anti-amalgamation argument was that the advanced economic development of New Guinea—as contrasted with Murray's Papua where native protectionism and fewer exploitive opportunities had made the country economically unrewarding —required for its continued growth a separate administration.

The Commission noted somewhat significantly that while the welfare of the natives under the Mandate must be the administering authority's 'first consideration', it must be consistent with economic development for the 'benefit of all'. 'All' meant the white settlers on whose activities the Territory's capacity for self-support depended. With the Papuan experiment in mind, the Commissioners wanted, more than anything else, profitable enterprises in New Guinea with minimal subsidisation. While Lucas and Atlee Hunt did not rule out the possibility of future administrative merger with Papua, for the time being New Guinea was to have a separate administration. The first step coincidental with the Mandate's establishment was expropriation of all German estates and the deportation of most German settlers by the end of 1921. The plantations were taken over by the Public Solicitor and their management entrusted to the Expropriation Board—the means by which the spoils were scandalously shared, mostly among returned servicemen qualifying under repatriation provisions and frequently dummying for large companies. Inexperience, mismanagement and inadequate financing led to a high rate of financial failures. Falling post-war prices for coconut oil combined with the effects of the 1920 Navigation Act—requiring all Papua and New Guinea exports and imports to be routed an extra 2,000 miles through Australian ports—severely cut export profits and sharply increased import prices.

Relieved of the effects of the Navigation Act clauses in 1925, both Papua and New Guinea copra had scarcely recovered when the Depression arrived. In 1925 copra represented more than 90 per cent of New Guinea's exports by value. In 1932 copra comprised only 32 per cent of the value and when World War II arrived it was about 14 per cent. Although New Guinea copra production amounted to 700,000 tons annually between 1925 and 1941, prices remained low. In 1932, it was a fifth the pre-World War I price and it fluctuated between £5 and £14 a ton until World War II. While the decline in copra prices was a cruel blow to Papua, New Guinea boomed on gold production which by 1935 exceeded £2 million annually, whereas in Papua in the first two decades of exploitation it had yielded only £1,500,000 yearly until its decline. The result was a fairly buoyant economy in the Mandated Territory and a rapid growth in white settlement which fluctuated with the mining population of the gold strikes, which proved as bloody and uncontrolled as those of earlier decades in Papua. Only the advent of air services between Lae and Wau in the thirties brought law and order to the wild frontier.

New Guinea was a Mandate and as such the Australian government had internationally accepted obligations towards native welfare and development. Indeed Article 22 of the Versailles Treaty specifically described those obligations as 'a sacred trust to civilisation.' The Australian Government took no more notice of its sacred trust than it did of the major sentiment expressed by Hugh Mahon, External Affairs Minister and acting Attorney General in 1916 in refusing an ANMEF request to give German settlers in New Guinea freehold tenure. Referring to the Papuan practice of leasehold, Mahon added, significantly, that '. . . there is the further question, even more important, of the right of the native race to the soil.'[25] The view taken from Geneva of Australia's discharge of its Mandate is a fair indication of Australia's administration. The League's Permanent Mandates Commission (PMC) view of Australian activities was mostly sceptical and, on occasions, sharply critical. In 1921 the annual report to the PMC in Geneva itemised the expenditure of £12 on native education. Eighteen years later on the eve of war, expenditure on native education was only £8000 from an internal revenue of £400,000 of which more than £20,000 had been raised in native head tax. The only obligations Australia seriously undertook in New Guinea were those of native health and these to a substantial extent because of tacit recognition of the necessity to maintain a healthy labour force for the plantations. In 1939 the Territory Administration was spending £100,000 annually, or approximately 20 per cent of its internal revenue, on public health which should be evaluated against the 1941 figure of 40,000 native indentured labourers. Even allowing for the

[25] C. D. Rowley, *The Australians in German New Guinea*, Melbourne University Press, Melbourne, 1958.

general indifference of the period, the sharp criticisms of the
PMC were perhaps not so surprising considering that they
emanated from British representatives comprising, for the most
part, distinguished former colonial governors like Lugard, who
took the terms of the Mandate seriously. It was quite plain to
them, as James McAuley has noted in another context, that
Australia had 'no thought of promoting development by the
deliberate intervention of Commonwealth finance'.[26] But it was
not merely a matter of finance. Other than economically and
for the benefit of whites, there was simply no intention to
develop. The country was considered essential to Australia's
defence, it had fallen into Australian hands as spoils of war,
and as it had the potential to support itself on a restricted
budget there the matter ended. Colonel John Ainsworth, who
caused so much discomfort to the *kiaps* of New Guinea, like
George Townsend,[27] had reported in 1924 'an absence of any
constructive policy' for New Guinea and had noticed, like the
sharp-eyed critics in Geneva, that the administration of New
Guinea cost Australia virtually nothing.[28] For years, members
of the PMC asked the Australian representative for a formal
declaration of policy regarding the Mandate. For years they
received precisely nothing in the way of replies, beyond vague
assurances. As W. J. Hudson points out,[29] in 1932 the Australian
minister piloting through the House of Representatives a bill
providing for a New Guinea executive and legislative council
comprising nominees, mentioned as the 'main heads' of Australian policy in the Territory precisely the statements made by
Sir Joseph Cook years before to the PMC in Geneva. In 1925, in
Geneva, Lugard blandly pointed out that the development of
New Guinea, by which he meant native development, would
require more than an annual £10,000 subsidy. No answer. The
Commission heavily attacked Australia's education policy in

[26] A. H. McDonald (ed.), *Trusteeship in Practice*, Sydney, 1949.
[27] G. W. L. Townsend, *District Officer*, Pacific Publications, Sydney, 1968;
introduction by Judy Tudor.
[28] For an interesting description of Australia and Geneva, to which I am
indebted, see W. J. Hudson, *Australian Outlook*, no. 1, 1965, p. 35.
[29] Hudson, op. cit.

the Mandate and throughout the twenties and thirties PMC members frequently needled Australian representatives. In 1934 the PMC rejected an Australian suggestion that education be handed over to the missions unreservedly. In 1936 the PMC wondered if one per cent of the Territory's budget was sufficient for native education.

Australia fared scarcely any better over questions on native labour usage, although its representatives were much more reluctant to answer them. In 1936 the Australian representative pointedly refused to furnish figures to Lord Lugard who had asked for an indication of what percentage of village labour should be indentured in the Australian government's view. In succeeding meetings PMC representatives voiced dissatisfaction with tardy Australian replies to the same question. The proportion of indentured labour, it was pointed out, remained high in a country said to be 'one step from the stone age'. Over the years pessimistic Australian statements on the capacity of New Guineans to participate in administrative or political institutions occasionally elicited disbelieving replies. Australia nevertheless eventually reacted to PMC needling over education, and in 1939 told the PMC that the Administration would impose its own syllabus on mission schools, establish its own schools, and promote the teaching of English.

In Australia there was occasional official sensitivity about League of Nations 'meddling' in New Guinea, accompanied by a general determination to ignore its criticisms as ill founded. However, on some matters Australians could be disturbed, such as a 1923 League Council decision that the PMC could receive petitions from mandated territories provided they had first been submitted to the mandatory power for its criticisms. On the application of the White Australia policy to New Guinea, the Australian representatives were always suspicious and PMC representatives like Lugard, always critical. As for more general Australian political reaction at home, one can best quote W. J. Hudson, '. . . a perusal of *Hansard* for members' views on the natives gives the impression of an immensely assured and vaguely benign paternalism, finding ultimate expression in the words of R. James (one of the few members, mainly Labour, to express concern about the working conditions of natives) who said of the "poor unfortunate niggers" in New Guinea that "even though they are blacks, they are human beings".' That was in the House of Representatives on 2 November 1932.[30]

The three periods of European administration in New Guinea, those of the German colonial government, ANMEF and the Australian Mandate, comprised on the whole a fairly straight history of imperialist economic rapacity combined with a chilling indifference not only towards native welfare, in the widest sense, but towards native aspirations as well. While it is true that the New Guinean's aspirations were frequently diffuse they nevertheless existed and there must have been throughout areas of long contact, especially where there had been successful cash cropping, a festering sense of deprivation. The Gazelle Peninsula was an example. There, in German times, despite anger and resentment over land alienation, the Tolai were participating in the general prosperity of the area and earning cash incomes through the sale of market produce and, particularly, copra which in 1896 amounted to about 2,000 tons.[31] This was in marked contrast to the failure of the people to grow profitable excess garden produce for sale to Europeans in the Madang area[32] and is partly explained by an inbuilt Tolai capacity for marketing. A. L. Epstein[33] quotes J. Lyng's observation in 1914 of the Tolai that 'he likes his tobacco, he enjoys tin-meat, he glories in European clothes, puts a keen value on umbrellas, mouth-organs, lanterns and the hundred and one knick-knacks he sees the white man has.' Dr Epstein himself recalls elderly Tolai who had served on German vessels and travelled 'around the turn of the century to Australia, India, the Philippines, and even as far afield as America. Some of the sailors, on their return, had taken to wearing European-style suits and clothing.'

All of this, in addition to the fact that many Tolai were

[30] Hudson, op. cit.
[31] Scarlett Epstein, op. cit.
[32] See A. L. Epstein, *Matupit*, Australian National University Press, Canberra, 1969.
[33] A. L. Epstein, op. cit.

living in substantial European-type houses, eating European tinned foods and using kerosene lanterns, steel tools and drinking European spirits, suggests not only that the Tolai were cashing in—significantly they did not offer for plantation labour by choice—on new found prosperity, but were adapting their traditional society to a remarkable degree to new and different horizons. In addition, many were receiving an education. The German administration started a school at Namanula, overlooking Rabaul, in 1907, with twenty-seven pupils.

The following year forty pupils were being taught reading, writing, object lessons, arithmetic, singing, gymnastics, local geography. Local Kuanua was the language of instruction with the intention of replacing it with German in the third year. The Roman script was used. In 1909, third year technical students were providing skilled labour for the government printery while locksmithing, bookbinding and cabinet-making were also taught. In 1913 there were two European and two native teachers and ninety-two pupils from New Britain, New Ireland, New Hanover, The Solomons, the Admiralties, and Kaiser Wilhelmsland. The following year, the Administration had planned to establish within three years government schools at Friedrich Wilhelmshafen, Aitape, Kavieng and Kieta. It was also determined to continue teaching German for the desire to be rid of the barbarous Pidgin was then no less, among some, than it is today. The school never had any graduates and ceased operations with the Australian occupation. Neither the Australian Military nor Mandated Territory administrations were ever as liberal or progressive as the Germans had been and between wars education was largely left to the missions and in C. D. Rowley's words, 'was devoted to mission purposes . . . in vernacular only, and an introduction to the world of the mission rather than a link with the great world of Western materialism.'[34]

However, the effect of the Tolai's introduction to cash cropping, to a degree of education, to travel, to relatively high-priced western goods and, in some cases, to western style housing, even in the 1930's to the apparent practice of chartering

[34] A. L. Epstein, op. cit.

cars for joy rides,[35] must have aroused corresponding conflicts. While the mutually hostile system of isolated villages was being slowly replaced by a common sense of Tolai ethnicity—where was it all to lead? There were definite and palpable limits placed on Tolai social and political development. In 1936 the Administration attempted to establish a system of village councils in the Gazelle Peninsula but, like that established by Murray in Papua, it was under strict government supervision. In fact, J. K. McCarthy, an ADO in the area before the war pointedly records that he never received an official briefing as to what the village council functions were supposed to be.[36] It was quite possibly this sense of frustration, as much as the ostensible cause of wages, that had led to the Rabaul Strike seven years earlier when on a January morning the township's expatriates awoke to find that the entire native labour force, including Tolais, had decamped the night before—except for a handful of native police—and made their way to Malaguna Catholic Mission where they were eventually prevailed upon to return to their jobs. While the whole affair lasted only twenty-four hours, the Europeans of the area were outraged beyond measure, like the *Rabaul Times* editorialist who had earlier warned Europeans of the folly of allowing native 'boys' to ride on the running boards of European driven cars, thus inviting an insolent assumption of equality which would not have been tolerated for a moment under the old German regime. Underlying European fury must have been the same sort of chilling fear that beset the Germans in Madang in 1904, when three native tribes in the area, goaded beyond endurance by land alienation and the brutality of the labour recruiting system, buried their common differences to concert an ill-prepared attack on their common enemy, the Europeans. No one in Rabaul had ever given thought to the possibility that natives could either plan or deploy with such skill or restraint as the Rabaul episode evidenced. Nor, one suspects, in the

[35] A. L. Epstein, op. cit.
[36] J. K. McCarthy, *Patrol into Yesterday*, Angus and Robertson, Sydney, 1964.

years remaining before World War II, were Europeans ever quite to believe that it had happened.

In 1942 the Pacific War came to New Guinea, which had been allowed no fixed defences under the Mandate agreement. The Territory then had about 150 miles of roads, many of them German built, and most of them in New Britain and New Ireland. The Territory had more than 40,000 indentured native labourers and a handful of natives educated in trades, mostly by the missions. Just prior to the war the white population was about 4500 and the Territory's internal revenue exceeded £400,000. The effect of the war in New Guinea was incalculable. In Papua, more indirectly, hardly less so. In New Guinea thousands of natives were uprooted from villages and customary lands, while thousands saw the humiliating defeat of white masters by the Japanese, for whom they worked willingly enough until the Japanese became brutal and repressive in response to their own difficulties. Under ANGAU (Australian New Guinea Administrative Unit) many thousands of natives were recruited to carry and work for the Australians and Americans, to travel far beyond their homes, to eat better and more consistently than many had ever done, and to see Allied, particularly American, equipment and supplies in unbelievingly prodigal quantities. The whites of the returning armies treated them for the most part with a new egalitarianism, quite different from anything they had previously experienced. They saw negroes, black like themselves, in positions of relative power and affluence. J. K. McCarthy in his *Patrol Into Yesterday* observes that the war was 'a great destroyer and a great teacher', and that through the war 'the natives began to glimpse the future of their race'. Surely a very disparate glimpse of a very uncertain future.

# 3 The Economy

*Inspired by a strong sense of purpose to indigenise the economy,
Australia's task is to build on and modernise the indigenous
structure of society, not to attempt to impose an economic and
political structure in Australia's image.*

P. W. E. Curtin, *New Guinea*, No. 1, 1968

*This is a very critical stage of our development and I believe
that if we do not create a better political climate now, I am
afraid our effort in setting up elaborate programmes today will
be in vain tomorrow.*

John Kaputin, *New Guinea*, No. 1, 1969

*Official statements* (about indigenous participation in economic
development) *suggests sometimes that special parts get written
in later for indigenous extras in a play for expatriate actors.*

Marie Reay, *New Guinea*, No. 3, 1969

The current pattern of New Guinea's economic development
reflects the accumulative results of its colonial history, its geography, the traditional social attitudes of its people and the
gathering momentum of indigenous politics. While Australia
has spent very large sums of money on developing New Guinea
in the last ten years, for most of the period of its steward-
ship, Australia has been a neglectful colonial power and fifty
years or more of metropolitan indifference has resulted in a
very precarious basis for indigenous participation in the administration and economy of the country. There is still very
little in the way of an indigenous structure around which to
build the framework of a modern state. Other problems are
equally intractable. New Guinea has one of the world's most
difficult terrains comprising numerous high and frequently
inaccessible mountain ranges, vast areas of swamp, a large
number of meandrine rivers and many off shore islands making
for considerable difficulty in communications and economic
organisation. Social problems are also acute. While New
Guinea's 2.15 million people have ample land, except in a few
specific areas, for both subsistence living and cash cropping,
they are divided by tribalism, custom and 700 languages.

Communications in the sense of a modern state are still practically non-existent and the economic incentives required to
overcome traditional social attitudes are largely absent.

*Programmes and Policies*[1] (or the Five Year Plan, which
constitutes the Australian Government's blueprint for New
Guinea's economic development over the next five years)
mentions that in 1966 about 940,000, or 44 per cent, of the
indigenous population, was still *wholly* engaged in subsistence
activities, while of the remaining 1.21 million indigenes about
420,000 were wholly or mainly in cash cropping and about
790,000 were engaged in varying degrees in both the subsistence
and cash economy. The position had changed little by 1969. In
1966 about 30,000 New Guineans had received a primary
education, including those now in secondary and tertiary
institutions, about 14,000 had some secondary education and
33 had received tertiary education. As of July 1967, it was
estimated that about 123,000 New Guineans, other than those
in the armed forces, domestic service and seasonal work, were
in the 'wages' workforce. Of this number about 24 per cent
were in primary industry, 7.4 per cent in commerce, 6.3 per
cent in manufacturing, 5.5 per cent in building and construction and 12.8 per cent were employed in various categories by
the missions. Nearly two thirds of New Guinea's economic
activity is sustained by the annual Australian grant-in-aid and
Commonwealth departmental spending which together exceed
$100 million a year. The 1968–69 Australian grant was $86.5
million. There is a chronic, growing, unfavourable balance of
trade which rose from $19 million in 1961 to $75 million in
1967-68 and to $81 million in 1968-69. Predicted figures for
1969-70 comprised $96 million for the Australian grant-in-aid,
$66 million in internal revenue, $10.5 million raised by internal loan, $1.3 million by external loan. A further expenditure
of $22.6 million by Commonwealth departments in the Terri-
tory raised the total figure to $197 million. Imports principally

[1] Published by the Administration, 1968, embodying the 1964 World
Bank Report recommendations and subsequent Australian government
modifications.

comprise foodstuffs and, for productive purposes, metal, machinery and manufactures.[2]

The crucial political factor in this situation is the problem of reconciling rapid, indigenous political development with accompanying demands for participation at all levels, and the increasing concentration of economic power and resources in the expatriate section of the population.[3] Expatriates number about 34,000 of whom approximately 4000 are Asiatics, mainly Chinese, and the remaining 30,000 including Administration personnel, are overwhelmingly Australian and in whose hands are concentrated New Guinea's banking, insurance, commercial, retail and the greater part of the country's plantation interests, as well as construction, engineering, shipping, and airline interests. Indigenous commercial activity is restricted to New Guinea's co-operatives still relatively small at this stage, and to small trade stores and trucking businesses. An increasing political awareness, rising consumer expectations without corresponding economic motivation, and a more articulate and better educated, although still numerically small, élite are combining to create an increasingly general native recognition of the vast imbalance existing between expatriate and indigenous economic opportunity and expatriate and indigenous living standards. In its economic policies for New Guinea, the Australian government now faces a dilemma familiar to other de-colonising powers—whether, with a view to political problems, to maximise indigenous participation with its attendant penalties of slow economic development and inefficiency, or to seek, through large injections of private and government capital, maximum economic development which must inevitably place for a long time to come increasing economic power in the hands of a skilled, expatriate minority. In the Five Year Plan the Australian Government has opted for

[2] See Appendix A, Table I.
[3] For an earlier and prescient view of these problems see P. W. E. Curtin, *New Guinea*, No. 1, 1968, in which he said, 'It is one thing to seek as much indigenous political participation as possible within a programme of general development of the economy. It is quite another thing to make the development of the indigenous people the supreme aim of policy.'

maximum economic development and the establishment of a sound economic infrastructure as a basis for economic expansion in which, with rising levels of skills and increasing command of economic resources, it is hoped that New Guineans will gradually control their own economy. These assumptions involve inevitable political and social risks. In similar situations elsewhere, expatriates have tended to become resentfully entrenched in their economic interests and the indigenous inhabitants, frustrated by their apparent incapacity to obtain economic power in their own country, have sought to resolve the situation by political action. The programme outlined by the Five Year Plan does not make one feel confident that New Guinea will necessarily prove an exception.

Except for the huge low grade copper deposits on Bougainville—estimated at 750 million tons—which will be worked by Conzinc Rio Tinto (CRA) and which it is hoped will later add $100 million annually to New Guinea's export earnings,[4] and other potential mineral and oil finds, New Guinea's wealth is almost entirely agricultural. In the words of the Five Year Plan:

'. . . commercial agriculture in Papua and New Guinea has so far been restricted to tropical tree crops which have shown a marked regional pattern'. About half the total coconut acreage is concentrated in New Guinea, New Ireland and Bougainville, about 80 per cent of coffee is in the Eastern and Western Highlands, and about 80 per cent of rubber is grown in the south coast of Papua. This dependence on tropical tree crops *with uncertain world markets* makes realistic programming very difficult. Through the production of tea, palm oil and pyrethrum, however, the rural economy now shows promise of growth on a more diversified base than the Mission's programme provided. This is an important factor in the Territory which currently derives 94 per cent of its export earnings from primary industries of which coconut products, cocoa, coffee, rubber and timber contribute approximately 94 per cent. Nevertheless,

---

[4] The CRA venture has nevertheless drawn attention to perhaps the gravest and most intractable of New Guinea's problems in relation to a modern economy—land resumption and conversion to single ownership.

despite the heavy and continuing dependence on tree crops and on timber as major export earners, and on minor exports such as peanuts, passionfruit, crocodile skins, gold and other items, the industrial sector will grow rapidly over the next five years when large scale investment, primarily Australian, is expected to move to New Guinea into engineering, metal roofing, paint manufacture, soap, flour milling, glass, matches and other enterprises such as car and radio assembly and light industries. In manufacturing, the skills, resources and finance will be almost entirely expatriate although New Guineans will be employed at rising levels of skills if initially in unskilled and semi-skilled categories. This increasing expatriate domination of commerce and manufacturing is certain to create political and social tensions that are unlikely to be resolved by simply telling indigenes that they must wait until their level of skills and resources allow them to become economically significant in ownership and management of commercial or manufacturing enterprises. Nor, in political terms, is the position very much more reassuring in the agricultural sector.[5] It is true that at the end of the next five years indigenes will have more acres than expatriates planted to coconuts and rubber—the former being a subsistence food as well as cash crop, the latter comprising an export crop for which prices have dropped substantially in recent years—and already have in their hands 70 per cent of coffee production for which, because of uncertain Australian demand, there is no planned expansion. But in three big money earners, tea, cocoa and oil palm, expatriate plantings will remain substantially higher. Both the tea and oil palm ventures comprise nucleus estates and two different approaches to indigenous participation. Indigenous tea smallholdings will surround expatriate owned and operated tea factories which will determine the price offered for the leaf. While there are no grounds to suppose that the prices offered will not be fair, the system enables foreign owned factories to operate as monopolies whose decisions on price will be hard to appeal as there will be few factories. While factory management should

[5] See Appendix A, Table II.

be alert to the political implications of sustained indigenous dissatisfaction over price there is no guarantee that it will or can be when it is responsible to a board in Sydney or Melbourne. In this respect the oil palm venture has been better organised by the Administration's action in acquiring a substantial equity in the first estate and processing factory—an equity that becomes an asset of a self governing or independent New Guinea government.

The argument of maximum possible economic growth rate versus that of maximum indigenisation, more or less regardless of currently available skills, comprised a fascinating debate over two issues of *New Guinea*.[6] In the first mentioned of these two issues, Dr Ron Crocombe, then executive officer of the Australian National University Research Unit in Port Moresby, and an anthropologist by training, attacked the Five Year Plan for 'tokenism', saying that while the plan talked at great length of indigenous 'participation' it in effect arranged for increasing expatriate domination of the economy. 'One of the paradoxes of the plan is that during the period that Papua-New Guinea will probably cease to be a colony of the Australian Government, it could well become a colony of Australian business interests.' In the second mentioned issue Dr Crocombe was answered by three noted economists, Heinz Arndt, Ric Shand and E. K. Fisk.[7] While they undoubtedly won the case for proving that New Guinea's economy will eventually be substantially sounder and its people eventually economically substantially better off in absolute terms through a policy of maximum development they failed to solve the political dilemma which Dr Crocombe posed in pointing out that:

At the end of the Five Year Plan 52 per cent of all commercial agriculture will be in expatriate hands and even in the 1980's nearly half the value of rural production, and hence of rural income, will still be controlled by foreigners (p. 105 of the

---

[6] No. 4, 1968 and No. 2, 1969.

[7] Respectively Professor of Economics, Fellow in Economics and Professorial Fellow in Economics in the Australian National University's Research School of Pacific Studies.

Plan). No proportionate details are given for commerce and industry, yet it seems by the 1980's, if the plan is followed, at least 90 per cent of all business and industry, and probably over 95 per cent of all business profits, will be in the hands of foreigners. It this is so, the verbal reiteration of the paramountcy of indigenous interests acts, perhaps unconsciously, as a smoke-screen for the real consequences of the plan.

There is an implicit tendency to regard New Guineans and Australians as in some way equal in relation to New Guinea. The implication is that it is in some way equitable for the $98\frac{1}{2}$ per cent of the population which is New Guinean to get an eventual 50 per cent of the gross rural income while the other 50 per cent goes to the $1\frac{1}{2}$ per cent of foreigners. The inequity is even greater in relation to industry and commerce.

The plan claims that local people will slowly catch up with foreigners in entrepreneurial activity, but by the time they are in a position to, most of the highly profitable enterprises will be held by foreign interests. It is difficult to see the processes by which the indigenous people will catch up, for the plan makes no adequate provision to enable them to do so.

Dr Crocombe raised numerous objections to the Plan, some a good deal sounder than others, the more important of which are quoted below. This chapter cannot allow for detailed criticism of his points which I have quoted simply because they raise important political issues. In particular, Dr Crocombe queried:

☐ Half of New Guinea's 4500 trade stores being in European hands. He demanded that expatriates should be denied licences 'to trade or run trucks or other enterprises which New Guineans could operate'.

☐ The small loans made by expatriate owned banks and loan societies to indigenous borrowers to start their own businesses maintaining that probably only 'a tiny fraction' of the $11.5 million indigenous bank savings were lent back to indigenes. 'There is no point in telling local people to save their money in savings banks at three per cent which is then loaned to expatriates to invest at 25 to 40 per cent. This leaves the local people relatively poorer and the expatriates relatively richer, and leads to social and political crises.'

☐ The philosophy of nucleus estates. '. . . the tea estates in the highlands are highly capitalised, prosperous foreign cells surrounded by peasant farmers who will see themselves by comparison as poor and deprived, and whose livelihood is dependent on the factory they surround. . . . the number of indigenous workers on tea estates may rise to 14,000 (page 26 of the Plan). If they are to be paid $4 per month plus keep, or 60 cents a day without keep, it is a moot point whether the prospective figure of 14,000 is an encouraging or a frightening one.'

☐ The fact that at the end of the Five Year Plan New Guineans will own less than one quarter of the country's beef cattle and that expatriates will own more than three quarters. 'If indigenous beef production cannot possibly be increased at any faster rate, there may be a good case for not developing expatriate beef production as now proposed.'

☐ The failure of the Administration to plan for greater indigenous ownership of the increasingly important forestry industry. Cash royalties 'are largely dissipated' while 'savings bank interest' on money that *is* saved, 'hardly keeps up with the depreciation in value of the money' and 'the relative value of the resource diminishes all the time'.

☐ The failure of the Administration to plan for proper indigenous capital formation. Land sales, for example, are quite often at prices above current values but well below the long term value. 'The principle "involved" is a very clear one . . . it is not only that the living people have been deprived of a permanent asset, but that their descendants have been deprived of a permanent asset.' Dr Crocombe makes the same point about mining operations pointing out that while the returns in royalties to the government may be of a very large order, as is the case with the proposed CRA coffee venture, when the mining operation is finished the people have been deprived of an asset in their land. Such is not the case, for example, with

D

plantations which if bought out at later date by an indigenous people or government continue to be productive.

☐ While the Plan notes that indigenous people are being trained for management duties, '. . . the current degree of such training is not likely to lead to New Guineans holding the majority of management positions even within the next decade or so.'

☐ The failure of the Administration to seek maximum indigenisation of hotel, airline, shipping, immigration, customs and health staffs to the greatest degree within the shortest time possible. 'On a recent trip through most of the Pacific area, I was served by indigenous hostesses, stewards and ground staff as well as indigenous immigration, customs and health officers on almost every flight until we left Honiara (for New Guinea) and travelled with TAA.'

☐ The failure of the Administration (which is, of course, the Australian Government) to purchase equity capital on behalf of New Guineans in air and shipping lines and in hotels and other commercial enterprises with a view to giving New Guineans privileged access to these shares at later date.

☐ The Australian Government's application of the White Australia policy to New Guinea, manifest in its refusal to allow Asians, and even Pacific Islanders where relevant, to take government or other posts and who 'would be happy to work at local rates under local conditions, or much closer to them than Australians are'.

Dr Crocombe pointed out that External Territories had several years ago advertised in the United Kingdom for secondary teachers and that 'dozens of teachers were qualified in every way'—but were rejected because 'they were not white'. He makes the same point about 'large numbers of volunteers', most of them 'university graduates' prepared to work for two years at local pay rates and whom the Minister for External Territories, Mr C. E. Barnes, two years ago refused on the grounds presumably of colour, because Mr Barnes 'stated categorically that he would not then allow volunteers from countries other than Australia and the United Kingdom into

Australia'. At the time of writing there was no sign that the policy to which Dr Crocombe objected was likely to be changed.

The replies to Dr Crocombe's criticisms of the Plan by the three academics mentioned were frequently sharp, and even personal, but some of them illustrated very well the sort of dilemmas that even the most solicitous planners cannot hope to avoid once the political problems of modernising an under-developed economy are raised. Thus, Professor Arndt, in query-ing Dr Crocombe's assumptions about the growing imbalance of expatriate and indigenous economic power said that Dr Cro-combe was saying, that, 'In other words, any economic develop-ment in New Guinea is undesirable if it reduces the relative *share* of indigenes in enterprise and ownership, even if it raises the *absolute* level of living standards of the indigenous people or improves the prospects for a viable economy when indepen-dence comes.'[8] Regardless of what Dr Crocombe did or did not say the point is a difficult one to decide. It entirely depends upon the likely political climate, and what sort of risks the administering power is prepared to take. Dr Crocombe himself pointed out that while there were undoubted spill-over bene-fits to Cubans in the 1950's from increasing American economic activity, 'most of the benefits went to foreigners' and 'led to total rejection of American interests'. Thus, in taking Dr Cro-combe's point about the dangerous political nature of nucleus tea estates, Dr Shand observed that:

A policy of denying expatriates access to opportunities in commercial agriculture would, at this stage, be economically irrational. It would undoubtedly improve the future ratio of indigenous to total agricultural output, but would only do so by reducing the rate of expatriate output growth while scarcely effecting, and possibly, reducing, indigenous out-put. . . . The question of relative participation rates for expatriates and indigenes in agriculture is in my opinion an insignificant issue beside others facing the sector such as finding the export crops for the variety of physical conditions

[8] See Appendix A, Table III. For manpower projections and Depart-mental expenditures see Appendix A, Tables IV, V and VI.

in the Territory, raising food crop productivity, and most important, facilitating an increasing scale of cash crop output among individual smallholders.

Such a policy might be economically 'irrational' as Dr Shand maintains, but a more rigorous scrutiny of the alleged benefits of unfettered European economic activity might prove politically wise. Greater economic participation by indigenes, in the sense used by Dr Crocombe, will exact a particular price in terms of inefficiency, and a reduction in perceived expatriate opportunities and in absolute New Guinean living standards, but by the same token it might create a reasonably durable political climate in which Europeans can, if they wish, make both a national contribution and a living. There is surely something of the development economist's own special brand of irrationality in believing, as Dr Shand does, that in comparison with the problems he mentions above '. . . the question of relative participation rates for expatriates and indigenes in agriculture is in my opinion an insignificant issue.' It is certainly not an insignificant issue and politically may prove a crucial one. Relative 'participation rates for expatriates and indigenes', and the power, prestige and privilege that accrues to expatriates, are put into sharp focus in the 1968-69 estimates for expatriate and indigenous travel and allowances for two government departments.

| Department of Agriculture | Number | Amount |
|---|---|---|
| Expatriates | 539 | $3 million |
| Indigenes | 1747 | $1.3 million |

| Department of Education | | |
|---|---|---|
| Expatriates | 1641 | $8.4 million |
| Indigenes | 3000 | $3.4 million |

I am here not questioning the need for skilled overseas officers or the fact that they must qualify for higher rates or necessarily enjoy greater mobility at this stage. I am merely raising the question of the political consequences of perceived deprivation.

There is a point of time already approaching, at which New Guineans will become 'irrational' about the imbalance between their stake in the economy and that of the expatriates. Australian economic policy in the Territory has been aptly, if quite unintentionally, described by Clifford Geertz (in his book on Indonesia)[9] as that '. . . myopic, pragmatic optimism which allows short-run gains to obscure the general trends, which isolates purely technical improvements from the historically created cultural, social and psychological context in which they are set.' Geertz is not entirely irrelevant to New Guinea in maintaining that Indonesia's economic crises have had their roots in the colonial past which consisted '. . . amid all the fluctuations of policy, from the economic point of view, of one long attempt to bring Indonesia's crops into the modern world but not her people.'

The sort of policy described by Geertz leads to enduring resentments which over the tea estates are already being manifested among Western Highlanders. As the anthropologist, Dr Marie Reay points out: 'Resentment at the seemingly unearned affluence of expatriate planters including management personnel on tea estates is certainly widespread among the people who are only incidentally tea smallholders, for it seems to them that it is this affluence that makes it possible for the expatriates to enjoy many privileges in comparison with and at the expense of themselves. They rarely complain publicly, so resentment at expatriates' seeming immunity from the law and the high price of shoddy goods in plantation trade stores may go unnoticed by some observers, though planters themselves are well aware of it.'

Nor does Dr Reay exaggerate in saying of Dr Shand's judgment that, 'as independence approaches it is likely that the estates will view co-operation with smallholders as being in their own long term interest politically' is hopelessly naive considering that expatriates running estates and plantations have already discussed together the best means of the joint defence

[9] *Agricultural Involution, The Process of Ecological Change in Indonesia*, Berkely and Los Angeles, 1963.

of their persons and property in the event of takeover attempts.[10] Nevertheless very real problems exist in the way of seeking to hasten indigenous participation in the economy. While there have been successful indigenous business enterprises such as Namasu and the Chimbu Coffee Society, they are few. The former was instituted under Lutheran Mission auspices; half its Board members are New Guineans and fifty-three per cent of its share capital is indigenous. In 1965 it paid a ten per cent dividend. The Chimbu Coffee Society is another story. It has proved reasonably successful but has been white managed. There are few other stories like this in New Guinea. It is more usual to meet Highlands entrepreneurs in, say, a trucking business who cheerfully expect in the first year of their operations a dividend equal to their capitalisation or who take payment for services rendered in the form of enough petrol from 'clients' to travel between one village and the next. Most common of all are indigenous business enterprises whose capital is dissipated through the claims of kinship and obligation. But the greatest problem of all, even for these indigenous enterprises which, judged even by western criteria appear reasonable risks, is to obtain funds.

The Papua and New Guinea Development Bank was established in 1967 to help overcome this problem although it was specifically to lend to Europeans as well, as it had taken over not only the functions of the Native Loans Board but those of the Ex-Servicemen's Credit Board as well. The Bank's last published report[11] gives some idea of its lending policies:

| | Number | Amount |
|---|---|---|
| New Guineans | 125 | $122,914 |
| Mixed racial partnerships } Mixed race applicants | 12 | 615,481 |
| Expatriates or non-indigenes | 66 | 1,207,041 |

[10] *New Guinea*, No. 3, 1969—Dr Reay has some useful observations on how native business enterprises might be built on existing indigenous social structures such as the network of social exchange partnerships found in the Western Highlands for example.

[11] From P. W. E. Curtin, *New Guinea*, No. 4, 1969—a paper, entitled 'Money and The Plan: Localising the Financial System,' read to the Council on New Guinea Affairs Seminar on the Five Year Plan, held at Sydney, 20-21 September 1969.

A House of Assembly statement in June 1969, showed that from July 1967 to the end of May 1969, 870 indigenes had received loans totalling $1.3 million while 230 expatriates and non-indigenes (mixed race or Chinese) had received $8.6 million. Indigenous loan figures include a large number of loans made to New Britain's palm oil settlers. Expatriates quite obviously got the lion's share simply because they had the skills and capacities. Loans to New Guineans were mainly for beef cattle raising, commercial fishing and for plantation industries; for cocoa and coffee processing machinery, generators and baking machinery and for trucks and capital to finance trade stores. The foregoing is sufficient to illustrate that the Administration's approach to the problems of indigenous participation has been fundamentally to strengthen European economic supremacy. The Administration is, admittedly, on the horns of a dilemma—those of increasing local political pressure and a thoroughly Australian concept of 'development'. While it may want, and actively seeks, means by which New Guineans can participate in business enterprises and share profits, New Guineans themselves lack the skills and resources that enable them to share in ownership. There are various suggestions now being entertained, including an investment corporation, which would undertake investment in enterprises, to be held in trust for New Guineans, by purchasing selected shares. Another is the application of the unit trust principle on behalf of indigenous investors. This raises the problem as to whether units or shares should be available to all residents of New Guinea or only to New Guineans. Dr Curtin[12] rightly emphasises that any shares should be available to New Guineans *only* and suggests this principle should apply to shares in Bougainville Copper Company. He also suggests that there should be a 'national small business administration' devoted to the advancement in business of Papuans and New Guineans, but states that it would need 'considerable resources'. He also suggests as guide lines some points put forward by Paul Streeton, including joint ventures between expatriate and indigenous interests which may reduce

political tensions and remove fears of post-independence expropriation; joint private-government enterprises where private capital amounts to not more than 49 per cent; 'buying
out' options through which the government eventually buys
out the equity interests of foreign firms at the end of a fixed
period, say ten years.

There are undoubtedly remedies for the present situation
which is producing a great deal more political resentment
than is generally admitted, but they all involve the Australian
government in very considerable extra expenditures at a time
when it is plainly seeking to limit its subsidisation of New
Guinea—an important motive in the Five Year Plan. The
equity share in the New Britain palm oil venture, for example,
cost the Administration $1.3 million and its option on twenty
per cent of Bougainville Copper Company shares will cost it
$20 million. Equity shares in the tea factories and in the new
industrial enterprises taking shape would cost millions of dollars. But some large scale government scheme to secure the
interests of New Guineans in foreign owned or dominated
agricultural and industrial enterprises may be necessary unless
New Guineans are to be left increasingly behind in the developing economy of their own country. There are grave political risks in a situation in which while New Guineans may not
be growing poorer expatriates are all too obviously growing
richer and their economic power expanding rapidly.

The most frightening statistics in the Five Year Plan are those
comparing indigenous and expatriate population growths
bearing in mind the dominant economic position of the
expatriates. By 1976 the indigenous population will increase by
approximately one third to 2.8 million while the expatriate
population, which will be overwhelmingly Australian in composition, will on present trends nearly double to 64,500—a
sizeable foreign minority to be largely, in some instances
exclusively, controlling New Guinea's commercial, banking,
insurance, manufacturing, retailing, airline, shipping, and, to a
large extent, plantation interests. It seems unlikely that New
Guineans, despite their current economic and psychological
dependence on Australian skills and the continuing Australian

grant, will for long tolerate this situation even if it does mean cutting off their nose to spite their face. But the present course as outlined in the Five Year Plan is inviting trouble and as Heinz Arndt admits of Crocombe's prognosis, 'He may well be right. The history of the world in the past 20 years is full of examples—Indonesia is just one striking example of the tragic conflict between the forces of anti-colonialist nationalism and the economic interests of the ex-colonial people. The fact that an early victory of anti-colonialist nationalism, even when it is against the interests of the masses of the people, may be very much in the interests of the indigenous political élite for whom it means power and privilege does nothing to lessen the conflict and the tragedy.'

# 4 Assumptions

Caliban: . . . *and then, in dreaming,*
*The clouds me thought would open, and show riches*
*Ready to drop upon me; that when I wak'd,*
*I cried to dream again.*

*The Tempest*, Act III, Sc. III

The cemetery at Madang, that beautiful, sullen town washed by the Bismarck Sea, is neatly divided by hedges into three sections—European, Asian and native—symbolising a more innocent, unquestioning past when the three cultures hardly impinged on each other except at well defined official levels, a time when the points of contact while frequently more brutal were less equivocal, demanding and stressful.

It had to end, of course, because prolonged contact brings far reaching changes, some obvious and some of immense subtlety and complexity. Chief among them perhaps are the extensive and ramified interactions of two societies, of which one is all powerful and dominant in material resources. The points of contact between European and native are now many, varied and increasing and so is the friction that contact inevitably sponsors. This is the substance of race relations which seem to be deteriorating in the Territory and which may eventually prove as disheartening as those which have bedevilled other colonial situations. For Australians the most misleading element in them may prove to be the reluctance of Australians in New Guinea, and in Australia, to admit that they could be bad or deteriorate. In one sense Europeans never talk about the real point of race relations in New Guinea which is that much of what appears to be bad is quite as much the result of native attitudes, the envy of brown 'have nots' for white 'haves', as that of discriminatory European attitudes. Most New Guineans have the feeling that no matter how hard they try they cannot achieve European skills and affluence. To know that it is impossible to achieve the power, the prestige and possessions of the white community breeds native ambivalence and uncertainty even where there is genuine affection between blacks and whites.

Australian reluctance to acknowledge the realities of the race relations situation indicates a rather wistful desire for perfection. The Australian mythology of egalitarianism works against such an admission and many Australians in and out of the Territory tend to rationalise race relations out of existence. For some there is simply no such thing. Others, even while admitting race relations are bad, defensively assert them to be better than anywhere else in the world when, in fact, they may be neither better nor worse than anywhere else in the world. In fact relations between blacks and whites are a good deal better, on the whole, than relations between New Guineans of different ethnic origins in the urban centres and incomparably better than relations between New Guineans and *kongkongs* (Chinese) which are potentially explosive. For many Europeans bad race relations are largely the fabrications, even the contrived situations, of journalists, academics and missionaries. A good example of this kind of thinking was a touchy, defensive statement to this effect by the Territory's Secretary for Law, Mr W. Watkins, in the House of Assembly on 28 November 1966.

Another was the outraged reaction some years ago to Michael Charlton's famed *Four Corners* programme which featured Europeans at the Port Moresby RSL Club. His infuriated critics could not see that, one-sided and biased as that programme was, it nevertheless stunningly revealed attitudes the widespread existence of which they did not like to admit.

These attitudes have also been reinforced by a series of jingoist assumptions on the part of Australians on the mainland. After all, have we not been assured, despite evidence to the contrary in our treatment of the aborigines, that we have better racial attitudes than the British, the French, the Dutch or the Belgians, attitudes naturally and properly inherent in a people whose own past was 'anti-colonialist'? Along with these assumptions have gone others which in the national sense we have never really bothered to examine.

These include aspects of our colonial administration in Papua, and later in New Guinea, the enlightened influence of Murray and so on, in which we have always taken pride. The Australians have not plundered, or decimated, large numbers of the New Guinean peoples. They have brought law and order to

New Guinea, ended tribal fighting and made it possible for the indigenous women of large parts of New Guinea to walk unmolested about their village duties where once they went in fear. Nor have the Australians alienated land on a grand scale although it is well to heed C. D. Rowley's wry comment that, while the Administration has alienated only 2.08 per cent of all New Guinea land, nevertheless, on a basis that only a fifth of the country is actually arable, alienation adds up to 10 per cent of good lands, which is high.[1] However, our comparatively benign policies in New Guinea were, as much as anything, the results of particular historical accidents. Our primary interest in New Guinea began in Papua which we considered necessary to our defence. New Guinea's poor terrain offered relatively meagre resources for exploitation. Had it been a rich island with good communications our activities might have been as ruthless as those of other colonising powers which would, in any case, have settled nationals there long before us.

Australians have not been classic expatriate imperialists, forced to seek their fortunes in countries far away from their homeland. Australia itself was and remains a developing country needing all the capital, expertise and manpower it can get. Nevertheless our occupancy of New Guinea, sixty years in parts of Papua and fifty years in New Guinea, has led us to create a series of self-protective myths about our relations with New Guineans. One of them is still strong belief that a special relationship can be forged between Australian and New Guinean, both different from, and better than, that between Europeans and former colonial subjects elsewhere in the world.

The notion of a 'special relationship', with its sentimental overtones, hardly bears examining. It was certainly never based on the notion of equality. At best it was a paternalistic rationalisation of a continuing master–servant relationship, born of the obvious contradiction between democratic, egalitarian practices in Australia's white community and necessarily authoritarian practice in New Guinea. It was also an attempt to encompass

[1] See C. D. Rowley, *The New Guinea Villager*, Cheshire, 1965.

within a vaguely intellectualised framework the problems raised by the geographical proximity of the two countries.

In the Territory, its development until recently greatly hindered by soil, geography and lack of development capital, the special relationship after sixty years has so far brought astonishingly few New Guineans to positions of real responsibility. While Europeans in the Territory and on the mainland have frequently fostered the notion of a special relationship the hard fact is that for New Guineans it has abruptly ended in the realisation that they will not, and cannot, be subsidised to a mainland Australian standard of living.

The notion of a special relationship has lingered long in Australia. It has motivated those in the Territory and in Australia who dreamed of Australian statehood for New Guinea, a vision which has shattered rudely on the realities of the Australian immigration policy, on the enormous cultural gap between Australians and New Guineans and on the tremendous economic cost required to bridge the gap. For the educated Papuan, for example, the dream of a special relationship has long since dissipated in the realisation that although he was an Australian citizen, which the New Guinean was not, he would never have the rights of white Australian citizens, not even those ultimately of the Australian aboriginal or Torres Straits islander.[2] Closing the history books on Africa is also part of the special relationship dream. It is a tempting thing to do for large parts of Africa have been conditioned by events unknown to New Guinea—a long history of contact with European and Islamic societies at their most predatory, fierce punitive wars, unrelenting economic and human exploitation, ruthless alienation of native lands and the permanent settlement, in some parts, of large alien, white populations. Nevertheless, New Guinea and the African states do have some things in common precisely because they are emergent states populated by brown, backward peoples. In many New Guinean eyes, as in those of many Africans before home rule or independence, there has

[2] The Papuan has never been able to enter Australia except by special administrative arrangements, even though he is an Australian citizen.

been long contact with the European with little to show for it economically.[3]

The New Guinean has been subject to an enduring master–servant relationship and to an unbending paternalism, however wise or well-meaning in the eyes of the governing, which is only just beginning to show some signs of change. And while the grosser aspects of white supremacy familiar to Africa and to some parts of Asia have been absent in New Guinea—among other things our style is different, more egalitarian, matier; Australians in New Guinea dig their own ditches and drive their own trucks—the New Guinean has been subject to the inevitable snubs and slights that large sections of an unheeding European community offer a brown, subordinate one. Above all, the New Guinean lives in a world of brown 'have nots' through which white 'haves' walk with the seeming assurance of kings.

Race relations between natives and Europeans in the Territory—in so far as they involve actual feelings of prejudice, hatred or discrimination—vary widely according to locale, education, economic opportunity and length and nature of contact. There are subtle as well as obvious differences, for example, between the attitudes of coastal Papuans exposed to sixty years of purely Australian contact and those of coastal New Guineans who have known the Germans, the Australians, the Japanese briefly, and the returning Australians.

Native attitudes, like ours, are shot through with ambivalence so that there is nothing consistent about them. It is perfectly easy, and quite rational, for a native both to love and hate the European. The degree of ambivalence depends on education, contact and environment. Race relations are worse in the towns than in the coastal bush areas and are probably at their best in the Highlands where contact has been relatively recent, on the whole conscientiously benign and where a tough and intelligent indigenous people living at high altitudes on some of the best soils in the island have a greater economic opportunity,

[3] 'Whenever you have to see anybody about anything important, he is invariably a white Australian.' R. G. Crocombe in *New Guinea*, No. 6, 1966.

except for some of the outer islands, of successful cash cropping on a large scale.

Race relations are positively at their worst in Port Moresby which predictably concentrates all the dissident problems not only of urban but emergent New Guinea. At the 1966 census, Port Moresby had 42,000 people, some thousands more than anticipated, including large numbers of migrant native labour from all over the Territory. This urban proletariat, unskilled, living on the breadline in shanties erected in increasing numbers on the bare brown hills of that disagreeable town, is a polyglot force of men without jobs, women or land—the dispossessed of the new dispensation.

Additionally, there are the local natives of Port Moresby, like the Hanuabadans, living in a tin-roofed slum right next door to Government House and Administration Headquarters in Konedobu as well as the base-grade clerks and local officers of higher rank and skills, who live in the near slums of Hohola and Kaugere and on the edges of Boroko. It seems unreasonable to expect that most of these people would not have a continuing sense of resentment for the 'haves' even though the difficulties of obtaining suitable land from native land-holders contribute quite largely to the problem.

No matter how clear a Port Moresby native's intellectual grasp of the fact that the local economy will not, now or in the likely future, support a European standard of living, he resents the fact and resents the power, privileges and possessions of the Europeans. After all, discrepancies in living standards are both too obvious and too large for the native to accept with equanimity. While on his salary there is a real struggle to pay for rent, clothes, food, utilities and transport, he sees the Europeans occupy pleasant houses in pleasant suburbs, wear a variety of good clothes, run a car (sometimes two), eat good food, spend seemingly endless money on beer and cigarettes and belong to exclusive clubs. It is the Europeans who enjoy not only the secrets of a western, technological civilisation but the fruits as well. Power and privilege are perhaps the two white characteristics most wounding to brown sensitivities. While some members of an older generation of natives may tell scarifying stories of intimidation and humiliation at the hands of Europeans—even beatings—the younger generation is marked by different experiences which come with being on the threshold of a western society without quite being accepted into it.

It is undoubtedly a different story with the younger generation of Australians and the younger generation of natives—in the towns. Many of the former are decidedly more egalitarian, more relaxed and less influenced by the reservations of an older generation of whites. But more importantly the advent of the University, the Administrative College and other tertiary institutions in the Territory is producing an entirely different generation of natives expatriated from the influence of village and clan (like the younger Pacific Islands Regiment men) and who are more culturally approximate to their white contemporaries.[4] In short, for them the cultural gap is largely ceasing to exist. There are useful spin-offs from this. Sporting fixtures between football and cricket teams comprising browns and whites chosen strictly on merit are doing a great deal to remove some of the more blatant causes of racial tension, those of heedless discrimination. Drinking in the club or pub afterwards by all members of the team together does even more as does native acceptance in white homes and at white parties and the exchanges between the younger white and brown members of the general university and public service structure of Port Moresby.

While this is a welcome indication of change nevertheless, in terms of inter-racial exchange, it affects only a fraction of the white and brown populations. Although many of the friendships now being forged across the colour boundaries are both genuine and constructive, and perhaps enduring, they are conducted on the brown side from a position of economic inferiority and dependency. This is not the result either of white conspiracy or malevolence. The whites in the Territory are short term visitors living at mainland standards who, after a few years, are due to return south to Australia. The browns must remain to live in hopes of the future. They would be

---

[4] The same process has taken place in Australia with acceptance of the culturally approximate Asian student population.

inhuman if they did not at least envy, if not resent, the better fortunes of their white friends.

Although race relations are decidedly better in many aspects than they were ten years ago—when Europeans simply refused to believe that New Guineans would ever govern themselves—there is nevertheless a still detectable snarl of defeated lower middle class gentility which one hears from much of the island's white population. A great deal of the substance of better race relations is the result of increasing white acceptance of the inevitable. In turn, the removal of all discriminatory legislation has done a great deal to give New Guineans a new sense of security in their dealings with Europeans. Even so, actual examples of racial discrimination or of barely disguised European contempt are many more than most Europeans like to admit and which they rationalise by saying that they are infrequent or committed by a small percentage of the expatriate community. In fact, they happen quite frequently, and it takes a native of rare objectivity and forgiving temperament to distinguish continuously between good and bad Europeans. In the end the distinction becomes blurred and such acts are characterised as European even if only committed by a certain section of the expatriate community.

Many natives complain of the intolerable manner in which some Europeans speak to them, sometimes unconscious of the tone and manner they adopt. Many others complain of plain discrimination, of Europeans serving behind counters in shops who automatically serve Europeans before natives or who, in some instances, refuse by one stratagem or another, to serve natives at all. One remembers a soft-voiced young native Patrol Officer who relates that he was refused a bottle of soft drink in a New Guinea coastal town when it became apparent he intended drinking it on the spot. A European woman serving him said, 'We don't allow boys to drink in the shop.' He refused to leave, told the manager and the woman was reprimanded.

Mr Oala-Oala Rarua, member for Moresby Regional, and an Assistant Ministerial Member, recounts that it was not so long ago that he was told to wait in a butcher's shop until others (Europeans) had been served and was referred to in front of them as 'boy', that ubiquitous, unavoidable, loaded, New Guinea term used indiscriminately of bush natives and sophisticated New Guineans alike. In a hotel in a north coast New Guinea town a native Parliamentary Under-Secretary of the old House sitting with his European departmental director was referred to by a European receptionist in a question to the director in the phrase—'Is this boy with you?' A senior native medical officer told me he has heard Europeans, barely audible, refer to him as 'that native doctor boy'. There are other instances of discrimination in public transport and in aircraft. In December 1968, when in Port Moresby, I ordered a special air charter. I was asked by a white clerk if I wanted to reduce costs by sharing. When I agreed, the clerk asked 'Do you object to native or mixed race passengers?'

A native Patrol Officer of my acquaintance was working in a primitive area in which he was responsible for several thousand people. The only access from the coast was by air and two expatriate, Territory-based businessmen came to look at coffee interests in the area. The weather turned bad and both men were obliged to remain for two days. The Patrol Officer put them up in his own European style house and his boy cooked for them. 'Our relations were very good over the period and everything was normal. A fortnight later I had to go to town on business. I happened to meet both of them there and when I went to speak to them they could not be bothered answering.'

It is a dismal catalogue of real, exaggerated and frequently imaginary offences. However, offence is given and taken and causes greater psychological damage than the sympathetic and understanding attitudes of an undeniably large body of sensible expatriate men and women in the Territory can possibly repair, or the moving examples of many long established and genuine inter-racial friendships can ever hope to ameliorate, in a situation in which thousands of indigenes now have the education and the self-confidence to articulate their grievances. The long silence of the New Guinean on these matters, hitherto comfortably assumed by many Europeans in the past to be evidence of his acquiescence that he lived, for the most part in the best of all possible worlds, is coming to an end. This new literacy and articulation are having an extraordinary effect on some Australians in the Territory, who, made to look at the anger and resentment of the literate indigenes over European insensitivity, have reacted pragmatically by changing their manners if not their instincts.

After all, there is a point in the development of all colonialist societies, when the injustices and indignities of the past, real and imagined, big or small, commence to coalesce into active resentment; a point at which what has been hitherto perceived as an immutable order of things is no longer acceptable.

The town natives of the Territory, especially the Port Moresby natives, according to their social and educational status, resent many things. Some are important, some are not. Some natives complain of the absence of public seating at bus stops and the absence of footpaths in a hilly town where expatriates travel by car and the natives by bus or on foot. Others resent the use of dogs to guard expatriate unfenced houses from entry or theft by members of a shifting, migrant labour force in the town, especially dogs which attack and bite. Some resent the fact that the waiters in some of the Territory's hotels are still clothed without dignity in lap-laps on the excuse that such dress is traditional and cool. Others, in a day and age when English is more widely spoken, resent the continued use of numbered courses in urban hotel menus. Many resent the still disproportionate number of Europeans serving behind counters in milk bars, in shops and in offices and the fact that it seems to them that in most European homes the husband and wife each have a lucrative job. The expatriate wife with the second job, especially if she has no qualifications other than being white, is a primary and understandable target of resentment.[5] Many resent the fact that there are far too many European overseers in simple trades occupations and that there are still far too many European carpenters, electricians and bricklayers at work in the Territory in spite of the increasing number of New Guinean telephone operators, shop assistants, clerks, receptionists, typists and tradesmen.

[5] A criticism in the 1968 UN Visiting Mission Report.

Despite this sort of evidence of changing Australian attitudes native grievances remain far ranging. For most New Guineans of any education white clubs simply represent the citadels of European privilege and power. Relatively few white clubs want New Guineans as members, even those who are socially and educationally acceptable. Natives themselves say they could not in any case afford to join most white clubs, which is true, and would not want to join which is probably partly a rationalisation of their true feelings. Although they may not in fact have much interest in white clubs, whose members they frequently call 'white Kanakas', their very existence is a constant reminder of a world of affluence and power, and a particular ethnic camaraderie, from which they are excluded.[6]

In the towns educated natives complain that there is little mixing with Europeans. While increasingly less true of the younger generation on both sides it is certainly true of many of the older European generation which lives in segregated housing, seeks its own life in the pubs and clubs and mostly discourages contact with the native. The removal of discriminatory legislation has not brought corresponding social contact. How can it?

Another target for native resentment is the expatriate women of the Territory where once again the distinction between the 'good' and the 'bad' becomes blurred. If the old colonial cliche that all natives secretly wished sexually to possess a white woman has lost some of its currency and force it is nevertheless true that most Australian women in the Territory live in what they regard as an alien land. Their mores are those of Australia and in New Guinea they understandably recreate the ordinary suburban life of Australia. They have houses to run, children to look after and, more frequently than not, jobs to supplement the family income. They are the most conservative of the expatriate community and in recreating the security of mainland life their

---

[6] In 1965 a very influential and senior native politician wrote to me and said that efforts to obtain admission of several New Guinean ex-servicemen into the large RSL club of a large Territory town had resulted in a scurrilous campaign to vilify him as a 'Communist'. In 1969, despite similar letters, the club has not changed its policy.

attitude to the native is that he is not infrequently an intruder in his own country. As a result even those educated New Guineans who rationally appreciate the real or imagined need of many European women in coastal towns to arm themselves against possible night attack are often unreasonably the first to criticise them for doing so.

Despite the removal of all discriminatory legislation, despite the tremendous efforts of some of the missions (which generally seem to have better race relations than other sections of the community)[7] and despite considerable institutional efforts on the part of some clubs and organisations to mix Europeans and natives the fact remains that by his very economic superiority the European unavoidably remains an object of envy, something apart.

Many town natives observe with angry resentment the educated and well-dressed, attractive native girls who go out with Europeans and whose sexual availability is the price of western acceptance, just as they resent the Europeans who have the means to take them out. They also resent the fact that an increasing number of native families see economic salvation, if not for themselves, then for their daughters, by urging them to this course. It is impossible to call it prostitution for it has the sad, wistful quality pertaining to those who want to belong to the magic circle of the powerful and the assured.

The sum total of these factors affects natives in different ways. Some display open anger like Mr Albert Maori Kiki, Secretary of Pangu Pati,[8] who can say publicly: 'We have hatred

[7] The missions have been, in some cases, the catalyst of pro-nationalist 'anti-Australian' feelings on the part of their charges. The rather tough minded articles appearing in *Dialogue*, the journal of the native seminarians of the Holy Spirit Seminary (formerly in Madang, now in Port Moresby) are an example.

[8] See A. Maori Kiki, *New Guinea*, No. 6, 1966 and Maori Kiki's recently published autobiography *10,000 Years in a Lifetime*, which contains a dismal and authentic catalogue of gross racial insults he has suffered or witnessed throughout his adult life. Having witnessed the public humiliation of a native friend in a Port Moresby hotel some years ago, I don't think that Mr Maori Kiki is exaggerating, although on some occasions he may be provocative himself.

for the white man in our hearts.' Many hope for a 'change'. Others, like one man I know of, probably retire from an unequal contest. He was a native clerk living near Boroko in Port Moresby. He forbade his three children to go anywhere near the garden of his Australian neighbour. When he found his children playing with his Australian neighbour's children he tied them up to a garden fence and prepared to thrash them with a rope. On the Australians' shocked intervention he gave as his reason, 'Of course I don't want my children to play with yours. If anything is missing my children will be blamed. Nothing but trouble ever comes from knowing Europeans.' The absence of a palpable 'Go Home Australians' feeling is certainly an indication that race relations in New Guinea, for reasons, explained earlier, are different from those in large parts of Africa. But it is also due to continued dependency in part. As Mr Maori Kiki has explained, natives do not tell Europeans 'what is in their heart'. New Guineans are inherently polite.

Race attitudes on the part of the urban groups open up a probably unanswerable question as to at what point the resentments of the rapidly increasing educated groups link with those of the uneducated and semi-primitives. The results may be different from what one expects. The people of the Highlands, for example, who psychologically and economically depend on continuing white skills may well resist race doctrines espoused by city slickers—or at least for some time. Race relations are undoubtedly best in the areas of relatively recent contact which creates a situation in which there is sympathy and understanding on one side and acceptance and curiosity on the other. The two cultures remain intact, the native culture as yet only marginally touched by the conflicts which come with the breaking down of traditional values.

In the Highlands race relations are probably as good, by and large, as the European settler is always somewhat apprehensively asserting. There have been relatively so few whites, so little land alienation, and so much of that alienated has been reclaimed swamp land on the valley floors, that the points of friction have been minimal.

And yet, the seeds of conflict are undoubtedly there. In the

days of early contact much of the land was bought too cheaply
—today high prices are paid—and there is some resentment on
this score. There are now, in some parts, very definite projected
and present land and population pressures which may mean
that the day of the tea and coffee entrepreneur taking up large
tracts of land is just about over and that the future of European activity may be in cattle and meat by-product ventures,
in pyrethrum, in spice extraction and other semi-industrial
processes in which large numbers of natives can gain employment and profit although there seems little prospect in the near
future that they will be able to own their own enterprises in
significant numbers.

The process of increasingly sophisticated demands and lack
of economic capacity to satisfy them will bring its own racial
tensions which may have rather less to do with the methods and
manners of the Europeans than with the natives' increasing
awareness that the European remains a 'have' in a 'have not'
community. Except for the unknown possibilities of mineral
development, New Guinea is an agricultural country of
relatively poor soils and resources in which the majority of
people are subsistence culture peasants. By and large in the
past there has been enough land for customary usage and
enough food to go around. Economic motivation therefore, is
variable, although the demand for European goods and services
increases for a complex of reasons including prestige and other
considerations. Nevertheless the common European rationalisation of lack of native economic motivation as laziness is dangerous and misleading. The fact that a majority of natives
could earn something extra by greater effort but fail to do so
may be a sign of despair. If, after all, no matter how hard a
native cash cropper or urban wage earner works he can still
only aspire to a fraction of white affluence he will regard the
additional effort above that required to feed and clothe his
family as scarcely worthwhile. Nevertheless the absence of a
financial profit motive in traditional society remains a major
factor.

But in parts of coastal New Guinea where there has been a
combination of unhappy factors—early contact with a fre-

quently brutal and greedy European civilisation and land alienation together with an absence of native economic incentive in terms of profitable crops and markets—race relations are frequently strained, sometimes sullen. A friend of mine reports a statement made to him by a New Guinea villager living not very far from Lae that eloquently expresses two generations of frustration and resentment:

God sent the Germans to New Guinea and told them to help us. They were before my time but my father told me about them. Because they were bad and wicked God told the Australians to send them away. The Australians were not much better. They did not return our lands and they were sometimes cruel and beat us. God decided to punish the Australians and told the Japanese to come here. The Japanese were cruel and treated us badly and God decided to give the Australians another chance by sending the Americans, their clansmen, to help them beat the Japanese. After the war the Australians were much better and said they would help us and give us roads, hospitals, schools and things to grow. They have only done a little of this and now the Americans are coming here again to see whether the Australians are doing what they promised.

This is incipient cargo thinking and has all the anti-Australian, i.e. anti-white elements, that cargo possesses. The area around Madang, for instance, has been endemic with cargo cult since the arrival of the white man. It is also present in other parts of New Guinea, in the outer islands and to a lesser extent, in the Highlands where it has been assumed that better soils, greater productivity and new cash crops together with a more 'secular' culture would remove cargo's economic basis.[9] It does not seem altogether to have done so.

New Guinea's emerging élite—the Administration civil servants, school teachers, Suva and Port Moresby medical graduates, native patrol officers, clerks, agricultural officers and

[9] See Peter Lawrence, 'When God is Managing Director', *New Guinea*, No. 1, 1967.

university students—has remained bitter over the 1964 wages decision. Its resentment sprang from disappointed and often quite unrealistic hopes. However irrational it may seem in the Australian view, the New Guinean civil servants had always hoped for a standard of living commensurate with that of the expatriate Australian even though many local officers readily admit that this was an impossibility and that New Guinean salaries had to be geared to the country's capacity to pay. None had expected them to be geared quite so ruthlessly in the first instance. Most had expected that there would at least be a 'single line' salary structure with added incentives for expatriate officers without which, most New Guineans realised, it would be impossible to obtain, or retain adequate numbers of trained or skilled Australians.[10]

Even those who were reconciled to something a good deal less than Australian standards feel they were cheated by the long period of time when Australian government policy was implied as one of equal pay for equal work. It was then that many decided on government service as a career. Canberra's belated recognition of the hard economic facts of New Guinean economic capacity and the likely refusal of future Australian governments to pay out indefinitely ever larger annual sums for New Guinea's development led to the 1964 decision on differential pay rates for expatriate and local officers. Quite apart from the large discrepancy between European and native salaries for the same jobs there was also the Government's method of announcing the changes. The new salary levels were announced after the House of Assembly had adjourned, thus denying debate on the subject, followed by an Administration decision to increase rentals on Administration houses for which Europeans would receive an increased allowance denied to local officers.

Both acts were regarded widely as discriminatory and the situation has remained tense. Racial feelings have tended to find in the wages and housing issues a point of fusion which has hitherto been absent, although some of the heat generated

[10] See Chapter 5.

by earlier reactions dissipated in the long wait for the Arbitration's decision which came in 1967.

Even so, harmful effects flowed from the Arbitration's decision, which native civil servants thought anything but generous. Where there was a willingness on the part of natives to accept the fact that much higher overall salaries including incentive allowances must be paid to expatriate officers if they were to be induced to stay and work in the Territory, there is now a conviction that local officers have been badly treated and deliberately discriminated against.[11]

As a local officer put it: 'You Europeans have played a confidence trick on us. You told us that if we worked hard and learned your skills we could expect a similar pay and rewards. Then you told us that there would be two classifications of salary, yours and ours, which means two entirely different standards of living for every black and white doing the same job.'

The wages question should never have been allowed to become an arbitration issue because it was more than ordinarily bound up with a whole range of political problems including those of race relations.

Local officers' salaries would better have been settled at the political level. If substantial increases in local salaries meant future budget deficiencies, it is legitimate to wonder whether retarded development, fewer bridges, roads and schools in the rural areas, would have proved more serious in their political implications than the problems raised by working with a disheartened, resentful local civil service. While no one can minimise the problems attending a solution weighted one way or the other it does seem in retrospect that a political judgement would have proved more acceptable than an abdication of Government responsibility by recourse to an outside institution. Nor, of course, are wages the only grievance exercising local officers. There is also the vexed problem of housing. Again there are high expectations and it is absurd for the local officer community of New Guinea to expect either to step

[11] This feeling persists despite the introduction of single line salaries.

into every vacant European type house in the country or have them built to the same standards. But the fact remains that there is a considerable discrepancy between local officer and European housing. It is not merely that European housing is incomparably better, and cheaper because of his rental subsidy reflecting the skills, power and financial resources of an economically powerful expatriate civilisation, but that a very large part of local officer housing is in itself disgraceful as the concrete boxes of Hobola and the inadequate shacks of outlying centres reveal.

But while the wages and housing questions have given the educated natives of the Territory a focus for racial antipathy, its real causes lie deeper, comprising psychological tensions which are inevitable, the cure of which lies as much with increased native self-assurance as with Europeans. A greater part of the ambivalence in some native attitudes to Australians in the Territory springs not merely from European behaviour, or merely from the overwhelming evidence of European wealth and power, but from the natives' feelings of inferiority when confronted by white assurance and achievement.

Many natives are haunted by a forbidding sense of their own incapacity in a world not of their own making which over eighty years or more not even the Christian message of divine love and the equality of all men has contrived to overcome.

The first missionaries who came to New Guinea were members of the Society of Mary who settled on Woodlark Island in 1847 after a disastrous experience in the Solomons. They were brave, dedicated Christians who sought through the word of God to liberate the black pagan from his bonds of ignorance and savagery; to deliver him from ways repugnant to humanity and to bring him to the knowledge and love of Christ. For those who followed in the Fathers' footsteps in the ensuing years, many to face death, disease and sometimes martyrdom, the story has been largely the same. Nevertheless the degree of Melanesian understanding of the Christian faith has been open to question. In microcosmic societies comprising worlds inhabited alike by the spirits of the dead and the bodies of the living and for which time was telescoped into the oral traditions of perhaps a few generations, there were apt to be considerable differences in understanding between those who heard the Word and those who brought it. The notion of rewards in after life, for instance, became confused in the literal Melanesian mind with that of rewards in life here on earth. Nor were the Christian concepts of forgiveness, brotherly love and the equality of all men, in the eyes of God, regardless of colour, completely convincing. It was one thing to listen to the missionaries who were white and entirely another to observe the behaviour of nominal Christians like the planters and the Administration officers, who were also white. The Christian message was all too easily liable to misconstruction as was the purpose of Christian life. The subtlety and intellectual discipline of 1900 years were perforce missing from the Christian doctrine which was translated into Pidgin or *tokples*. The Christian message seemed to promise cargo and Christian ritual the road to it, a misconception compounded by the fact that the whites had the cargo and missionaries were white.

For the missionaries, as for planters and administrators, there was the repeatedly baffling experience of discovering that while they and the newly baptised might use the same words they were in fact talking about different things. For some the realisation scarcely, if ever, dawned.

Nor did the missionaries understand or, if they did, entirely approve, the spiritual basis of the culture of the people whom they sought to convert to Christianity. Masked dances, for example, were almost universally discouraged as libidinous or worse, when frequently they celebrated the communion between the living and the dead, ironically confirming that white Christian and Melanesian villager were at one in recognising a supernatural order to the universe. The missionaries who disapproved so strongly of plural marriages failed to perceive that the motives that lay behind them were not those of unrestrained sexual licence but those of prestige and the procurement of additional labour. Equally they failed to perceive that the bride price involved the principle of compensation rather than an act of purchase. Nor did missionaries understand the nature of the dilemmas they were creating which have lasted until the present day or that sullen acquiescence following upon an initial period of enthusiastic conversion frequently hid boiling tensions of almost unresolvable conflict.

Nevertheless it was frequently the missionaries who defended the New Guinean from the harsh exploitation of the planter and the often callous demands of the government. The missionary at least tended to think of his converts as the children of God rather than as names in a village book or as units of labour. Some of the early missionaries in German New Guinea purchased land and introduced natives to cash cropping not merely as a source of mission income but as a means whereby they might escape the claims of the labour recruiter. It was not infrequently the missionary who tried to resolve the conflict between native and administration and who sought to save him from administrative injustice and abuse. Above all, it was the missionary who, in translating the word of God into a hundred vernaculars, first taught the New Guinean to read and write. It was the missionary more than any other representative of the great world beyond the village who gave the New Guinean some sense of belonging to a universal brotherhood of man through the immediacy of his Christian experience. 'Those New Guineans who have conscientiously tried to live Christian lives have something of that simplicity one senses in early Christians,' writes C. D. Rowley, '. . . for what the missionary has taught, the stories of the creation, the crucifixion, the events of the early Church, will be accepted as literal truth by minds without historical perspective . . . thus Jesus and his apostles are not remote figures dimmed by the centuries, for people whose own creation myths generally go back only five generations or so the great events of the Christian myth might have happened yesterday.'[12] It was perhaps the New Guinean's immediate and literal response to the Christian message that gave so sharp an edge to the competition between the Christian missions for his conversion to belief in the one, true God. But which was the one true God? Among so many competing,

[12] Rowley, op. cit. See particularly his illuminating chapter on 'The Impact of the Christian Missions'.

even opposing, sects and creeds of the Christian faith, God must have appeared disconcertingly divisible.

Today there are twenty-two churches in the Territory controlling the activities of some fifty or more missions the loyalty of whose adherents testify as much to the enduring force of traditional motives of prestige and ethnic rivalry as to the strength of their religious convictions. In these circumstances Christian doctrine does not remain untouched for when it is transplanted to a different world of obdurate and enduring traditional values it inevitably undergoes a 'sea change' transmuting it, after a period of time, into something rather different from the original. As in Africa and in parts of Asia the Christian missions will probably leave a number of indigenous churches espousing doctrines that in time will be seen as passing strange in distant Rome, Lambeth or Los Angeles. A hint of how strange appeared in an article in *Dialogue*, the journal of the Holy Spirit Seminary, Port Moresby, contributed by the Reverend Camilo Teke, who warned:

> Unlike the western concept of the universe, as a closed system, the Melanesian view of the universe is not a systematic one, but freely admits features which seem to be contradictory . . . this is why our people find it easy to adopt the Christian God without any sense of incongruity with their basic religion. By adopting the external forms of Christianity and by transferring to the Christian saints the attributes of their deities, they continue to worship the latter under the guise of venerating the saints . . . the Christian practice of erecting churches and shrines on the old, sacred, pagan grounds did not succeed in leading to Christianity in any total sense, but actually facilitated the worship of pagan gods under Christian form.

In the end, however, the development of the indigenous church (one thinks for example of Papua Ekalesia) in which Christian faith grafted upon Melanesian beliefs, modifying and modified by them, may well give its New Guinea communicants a greater sense of their own moral and spiritual resources than the efforts of Caesar.

Nevertheless, the road to the European's apparent sense of assurance, as perceived by the native, let alone the road to anything approaching white affluence, seems long and hard. The educated New Guinean has not only to contend with the disabilities of his own culture but the intricacies and subtleties of a western one to master as far as possible. Early conditioning like one's first visit to the dentist shapes instinctive attitudes to the future. Mr John Guise once told me that he has never forgotten his childhood terror each time he heard that the 'government was coming', that is, a routine inspection by the patrol officer was imminent. He was not recalling cruelty or unpleasantness or implying it, merely the terrifying aura of white power that a village 'lining' evoked. Many Australians in the Territory consistently underestimate how frequently white skills arouse feelings of native inadequacy. A Suva graduate who grew up in the post-war period told me that when he heard that the *kiap* was coming he would try and hide. In later years, at school, these feelings took a different form when he and his classmates were convinced that white men were 'gods who knew everything' and the native schoolchildren were only 'bush kanakas' for whom it was 'useless' even to try. 'We used to attempt to hide these feelings,' he added.

The fact that many thousands of New Guineans manage to overcome these feelings which must be widespread, although probably not so pervasive as some years ago, is a tribute to Melanesian good humour and persistence as well as to Australian sympathy and effort. But one should not underestimate the slowness of acculturation or the price which is paid for it including that of detribalisation. While in one quite directly brutal sense the New Guinean has nothing to lose by detribalisation but his subsistence chains of illiteracy and savagery he does lose something—the security of being anchored in a culture whose traditional values give him sustenance and support.[13] Educated natives in government service and in business speak

[13] Mohammed Sjahrir in *Out of Exile* makes a relevant point about the values of western education for Indonesians whose culture, he felt, was rooted in the retarding influence of Javanese mysticism and Islamic obscurantism.

and write fluent English. Many of them have travelled to Australia and abroad or have an increasing knowledge of the great world beyond the village from which they came.

But for many this has brought a sense of loneliness and cultural displacement arising from alienation from the traditional village culture on the one hand and being merely on the threshold of a western expatriate culture on the other.[14] New Guineans of this younger group show in numerous activities and personal relations that they are extremely torn by the conflict of being between two different worlds. Many avoid going on home leave to their villages or at best look forward to it with ambivalent feelings despite strong ties of affection with their families and a sense of familial duty. As one of them said to me, 'What is there to talk about? I am both bored and ashamed. Bored because village life no longer interests me. Ashamed because I love my family and have nothing to say to them.' The situation will slowly change as a detribalised society of educated natives grows up in the towns in which its members can make friends across the traditional claims of tribalism, custom and *wontoks*. Many are intermarrying and in the houses of many the children speak Pidgin and English but not the language or place talk of the father or mother. But these changes are slow and the feelings of disorientation for many, especially for the local officer out in the bush, are very strong.

Nor can the corporate life of the educated local officers, Suva graduates and so on be organised institutionally in the same way as that of the Pacific Islands Regiment (or Police) where one effect of a deliberate and relatively successful policy of detribalisation has been the replacement among younger, better educated recruits, of traditional tribal animosities and suspicions

[14] Or merely being exposed to its demands. 'Poems to a Kazaruku Man', *New Guinea*, No. 3, 1968, by a Solomon Islander, Garumu Hite, expresses this conflict with a wistful precision.

> *And yet, my mother said, you were smiling when you died—*
> *What did you know that I do not?*
> *How could you live, not knowing my new knowledge?*
> *No Rome—or Wesley—Eto—Sevenday*
> *To bring you everlasting joy and gladness,*
> *How could you smile? . . .*

by a focus of common loyalties on the regiment itself. The PIR may in fact be in the process of becoming another tribe as Major Bell suggests in a fascinating article on Army integration.[15]

What is in fact happening with the creation of educated New Guinean groups is the appearance for the first time of a class increasingly divorced from its cultural origins. The effects of this are unpredictable. The class struggle has yet to come in New Guinea, if it ever comes. It could nevertheless manifest itself in various ways, perhaps through cargoism for example. It is the earnest hope of administrators, and apparently the belief of some anthropologists, that chiliasm in the cruder forms which it takes in New Guinea will be entirely susceptible to eventual economic change. That seems to be implicit in the statement made by Dr John Gunther, former Assistant Administrator (services) and now Vice-Chancellor of the Papua and New Guinea University, to a seminar held in Sydney, in 1966:[16] 'I believe it is fair to say that all these (millenial) movements exist in the face of actual or perceived deprivation, not necessarily absolute but relative, and discrimination is often an activator. I would dismiss the cargo cult and many millenarian movements as having any lasting influence on Territory constitutional development.' A very great deal depends upon how ingrained the fundamental belief in chiliastic remedies for actual or perceived deprivation really is and just how far Christian belief has made inroads on it. But even in an area with a long history of mission contact the capacity for constant adjustment of cargo belief to new phenomena seems indestructible. Around Madang two years ago I was shown several villages where, in specially built houses, 44 gallon drums had

[15] *New Guinea*, No. 2, 1967.
[16] Council on New Guinea Affairs Constitutional Future Seminar, Sydney, 23-24 April, see *New Guinea* No. 6, 1966. I quote Dr Gunther not only because he has a profoundly important point to make, with which on the whole I tend to disagree because of the reasons given, but because his views are to be respected coming from a former senior Administration officer who as an administrator, and particularly as a Government Leader in the House of Assembly, displayed great political insight and capacity.

E

been placed. Villagers were asked to deposit one or two dollars
in the drum, leave it there for a period of up to eight years,
when it would double in value. The analogy with money
deposited in a bank and earning interest was unmistakeable.
Quite possibly now the cult no longer exists having broken up
in disillusionment and frustration.

There seems the possibility that for a very long time to
come various aspects of development including education and
politics, may be perceived in chiliast terms. After all New Guinea
is a poor country and there is simply going to be continued
actual and perceived deprivation in various forms and at
various levels for which, presumably, there must be, as in the
past, explanations and chiliast solutions. It may in any case be
a mistake to think of cargo as applying only to situations of
primarily economic or social deprivation just as it may be a
mistake to believe that the fundamental religious or intellectual
beliefs of New Guineans about the nature of the world in which
they live, its creation and their relation to it will change all
that soon or all that much. G. C. O'Donnell, a former
Administration officer, at the same seminar, made the
point that in his belief and experience 'cargo cults . . . are the
seeds behind a very great deal of the political thought and
political ideas that will come up through some of the élite.'
He also described them as 'revolutionary'.

Millenarianism is by no means confined to New Guinea. In
refined forms it is very much part of Javanese life. The Indonesian scholar, Soedjatmoko, makes two points about the
traditional base of Javanese politics which are worth considering in relation to New Guinea.

The first is that one of the results of the Javanese traditional
view of life has led in a modern state to '. . . the tendency
towards paternalistic authoritarianism, the inclination to seek
employment in the civil service, the preoccupation with prestige
and status rather than function and performance, the unquestioning obedience to authority, the almost exclusive concentration of politics in the capital and the emphasis on
strengthening the national will through indoctrination and

revolutionary fervour rather than the solving of practical problems.'[17]

The second, complementary point Soedjatmoko makes is that of the continuing force of traditional chiliast beliefs in the Javanese tradition including the fact that 'the perfect state and the perfect society—a constant theme in traditional culture as well as in modern political thought in Indonesia—is not therefore a goal to be achieved through hard work and rational planning but . . . through the application of a key, a *kuntji*, the magically loaded formula. The door needs only to be unlocked by the strength of a nation's inner purpose and the application of the key formula or slogan.' Soedjatmoko also mentions another very strong chiliast belief that recurs constantly in Javanese history which is the expectation that the *Ratu Adil* (the Just King) will, with Divine Sanction, deliver the people from injustice and evil and establish 'the rule of peace, justice and prosperity.' Soedjatmoko remarks that '. . . millenarian movements of this sort, because of their total rejection of the present, are not reformist, but essentially revolutionary'.

It would be stretching it to suggest that the chiliast beliefs of Java and New Guinea are strictly comparable for both countries exist at vastly different stages of civilisation. Nevertheless points of comparison exist. There are signs that New Guineans in the modern state may very well fit a good deal of Soedjatmoko's description of Javanese predilection for paternalistic authoritarianism and there may well be an accurate description of New Guinea's future politics in his description of millenarianism as revolutionary, rather than reformist, a point of view which Mr G. C. O'Donnell and others seem to share.[18] There are also other points of comparison.

Despite a high literacy rate in their own language and in Indonesian, and despite the impact of Islam and at least 200

[17] Soedjatmoko, Australian Institute of International Affairs, Dyason Lecture, 1967. Dr Soedjatmoko is Indonesian Ambassador to the United States.

[18]

years of semi-continuous western contact, through Dutch colonialism, the East and Central Javanese have stubbornly clung, in their millions, to chiliast explanations and hopes. In so far as the alleged economic base of chiliasm is concerned it is worth noting that the East and Central Javanese are extremely poor and deprived and likely to remain so even on the basis of the most optimistic expectations. The same can be asserted about the mass of New Guineans who, for the most part, live in a poor, tropical country and who are going to remain mixed subsistence-cash crop peasants. Their economic situation will not improve greatly relative to that of the emerging élites unless Australia is prepared to undertake massive, indefinite subsidisation of New Guinea, which hardly seems likely. It is in this continuing combination of poor peasant farming and actual and perceived deprivation, to use Dr Gunther's term, that New Guinea's peasant farmers may very well transfer their puzzled resentment, in cargo terms, over the phenomenon of the white 'haves' to that of the new classes of brown 'haves'. This may prove the beginning of an eventual class struggle in New Guinea unless 'unquestioning obedience to authority' remains a primary Melanesian political characteristic as it has remained a characteristic of the Javanese. It is far too early to say and there remains the hope that economic improvement may yet remove the base of cargo thinking. If it does not, then for the mass of the people the politics of the future may very well be those of constant 'revolution', in Soedjatmoko's sense, and national politics may ultimately result in being in the Sukarnoist sense the élitist manipulation of irrational mass hopes and expectations.

There are also other comparisons to be made between transitional New Guineans and other South-East Asians, particularly those of the Malay world. One such is the misuse of public moneys in many of the co-operatives in village funds and allegedly the funds used by some local government councils. For instance, Dr Ted Schwartz, the anthropologist, recalls during his long stay in Manus that 'in some villages in which I have lived, virtually every such fund has been "spoiled" (*oli bagarapim mani*) or dispersed.'[19] He recalls that the money in such instances is placed in the hands of the most respected community persons including elders and young leaders. 'Each person is tried in turn . . . and eventually tried again as there is no one else and it is believed that it would be the same.' While he hastens to point out that corruption in New Guinea is not institutionalised as it is in Latin America (or anything like as institutionalised, he might have added, as it is in Thailand or to a lesser degree, Indonesia) he does beg the question as to whether corruption will not mark New Guinea as it has other newly developing countries. He also points out that the conditions for generalised corruption exist in the continuing disparity between indigenous earnings and the expatriate standard of living.

Schwartz may be near to predicting the emergence of corrupt practices in New Guinea when he refers to conditions for generalised corruption involving 'the village-linked person [in] the occasional bursts of wealth which prestige, self-esteem and the demands of kinship require.'

I remember a local officer in a certain small New Guinea town who was dismissed for stealing a hundred or so pounds of public funds. The reason for the theft was because he wanted the money as the price for a local bride and the girl's parents were pressing him hard to find the sum. The pressures of the demands of kinship and prestige and the continuing force of the gift exchange which adapts itself to changing circumstances, may make it very difficult in the future for all but the best paid civil servants to resist what are considered by westerners corrupt practices. It will be even more difficult for the civil servant in the bush situation anxious to be accepted and able to escape the detection of his urban based headquarters. Corruption can in any case be very easily rationalised by all parties.

Professor Lawrence takes a hypothetical case of a young educated clerk in a co-operative or private business venture who is approached by an important kinsman and asked for a cash or tobacco handout. 'What is the clerk to do: be a good

[19] 'The Co-operatives (Oli Bagarapim Mani)', *New Guinea*, No. 8, 1966-67.

citizen in our sense, save the business, and win a reputation for meanness among his kinsmen: or be a good kinsman, toss citizenship over the side, ruin the business' finances, but save his reputation for generosity among his kinsmen? The problem is so acute in the Port Moresby area, I believe, that many indigenous businessmen try to place their affairs in the hands of European accountants on the grounds that Europeans are known to have no sense of moral obligation—that is, are kinship proof.'[20]

Schwartz, for example, points out that on Manus the person who 'spoils' public funds is never said to steal them, a term confined mainly to breaking and entering, but is merely 'borrowing'. The loss is called a *dinau* or loan. He also points out that there are very rarely prosecutions and that very rarely is the money made good. In fact the very people who should prosecute, those of the village or the co-operative, and whose money collectively it is, are in any case compromised one way or another. The tendency, as in South-East Asian societies, is tolerantly to forget the whole affair and start again. In strict fairness to Dr Schwartz he does not suggest that corruption will establish itself in New Guinea and he sets out a complex series of reforms in respect of co-operatives to try and prevent its spread. But there remains a world of difference between Australian and New Guinean assumptions. Schwartz points out that the religious sanctions which in pre-contact or traditional society operated against corruption have been removed by Christianity and that the Manus, and one would presume most other New Guineans, now tend to leave 'the discipline to God who seems more concerned about adultery than such secular matters as public funds'. Of even greater significance, not only in relation to corruption in a modern state, is 'the complex involving the kinship network, ceremonial exchange and the prestige economy. All the speeches of disapproval of the last twenty years have not led to the eliminations of ceremonial exchanges (at marriages, birth, death and so on) which, under attack, take on modified forms and new rationalisations.'

[20] 'When God is Managing Director', *New Guinea*, No. 8, 1966-67.

As with cargo cult so with possible forms of corruption; we may have looked far too long at Africa for comparisons with New Guinea when many have existed much closer, in South-East Asia. Some comparisons between New Guinea and South-East Asian countries, particularly Indonesia, are compelling. Corruption in Indonesia, for example, and in Thailand, frequently involves 'kinship obligations' which are extensive and well established. The widespread Indonesian practice of *tau sama tau* (knowing together) through which the guilty person shares his guilt with friends, relatives or others by sharing the proceeds, or some of them, to ensure their silence seems little different from the practices of villages or co-operatives where a decisive number are involved in the corrupt act of an individual, share the benefits and become complicit and silent.

In any case traditional responses and assumptions as outlined above are not by any means the only forces at work to produce corruption in newly independent, underdeveloped states. As Herbert Feith points out:

One common feature of the political scene in the countries of South-east Asia has been the rapid expansion of government activities since the achievement of independence. New governments, faced by publics with very high expectations, have tended to respond by saying, 'We will establish a new agency to do that.' Thus various new departments, boards and institutes were formed, to do better the things the colonial regimes had done and also to do other things which had not been seen as part of the task of government in the colonial period. But government revenues did not rise, or at least not in the same proportion, and so the common experience has been that the real incomes of civil servants have fallen. In some countries they have fallen very dramatically. This has tended to produce corruption. It has tended to produce over-regulation, because whenever there is a new regulation, an additional channel to be gone through, it becomes possible for the poorly paid civil servant to get a new increment to his income. In many cases it has led to a more or less regularized pattern of petty extortion. All of us are aware that these consequences are likely to follow when you cannot pay civil servants adequate salaries, adequate by the standards to which they have been accustomed. The problem is not at all easy to solve because one cannot raise the salaries of civil servants without large inflationary consequences. This pattern of vicious circles is fairly familiar.[21]

The areas in which Australian and New Guinean assumptions radically differ are many and varied. It remains to mention one in particular, the creation of a native bar and judiciary, a matter of concern to Australian academic jurists. Indigenes are training as lawyers both in Australia and at the University of Papua and New Guinea. Steps are in process to procure a native magistracy. Ultimately it is hoped that New Guineans will practise and interpret the law in New Guinea courts just as a New Guinean constabulary will enforce it.

There is a considerable problem in obtaining native lawyers with practical experience over the next decade not only to practise, but to act as legal technicians concerned with constitutional problems such as whether a bill of rights should be written into the constitution, how to guarantee freedom of the judiciary from political pressure, the protection of individuals against abuse of power by government and so on.

A much greater problem concerns indigenous understanding of legal functions and processes. This involves not only the complexities of customary law but indigenous assumptions about the rule of law. The great mass of New Guineans do not comprehend the notion of abstract, impartial justice. They do not understand the rules of evidence or how it is that the all powerful *gavman* can litigate in courts and yet accept an adverse decision handed down by what are, after all, *men bilong gavman*. It was this simple fact that rendered irrelevant a large part of deliberations of the International Commission of Jurists' seminar on 'The Rule of Law in a Developing Country,' held in Port Moresby in September 1965. While the seminar was valuable as the first, and so far the only, public

[21] From a lecture given at the Young Asian Leaders Seminar, Tugu, Indonesia, 28 September 1968.

debate by practising and academic Australian lawyers on the general problems of framing a New Guinea constitution and on those pertaining to the Rule of Law generally, the fifth of its conclusions on constitutional questions, if taken at face value, comes perilously close to windy rhetoric: 'The form of government appropriate for Papua and New Guinea is a matter for decision by its people. *The Conference affirms its confidence that the institutions as developed will express the values of a democratic society imbued with respect for the Rule of Law,*[22] and draws attention to the papers and discussions at this Conference as indicating some of the problems and further detail as to the available methods for dealing with them. In this last statement the Conference is unanimous.'

Many lawyers at the conference had evidently done little homework on the real nature of New Guinea society or on the real nature of New Guinea assumptions. E. P. Wolfers, now a Fellow of the Institute of Current World Affairs, working in New Guinea, said in an article entitled 'On Framing Answers', 'In a sense . . . the white man's legal system seems to act at one remove from village life. If the court finds a man guilty, then why all the fuss? Everyone knew he was guilty anyway. If he is let off, then the court may as well not have sat, as either it was misled or merely reflecting the irrational behaviour of the person who carried out the arrest. The problem is not one of legal draughtsmanship in framing laws, but of jurisprudence. If the village is happy with the present system, might it not be better merely to institutionalise the present village legal systems within the general legal system, but to provide a right of appeal, especially for more Westernised New Guineans, into the general, Western-type legal system for those who feel unhappy with the decisions of the native courts?' But even this suggestion begs the question of who recognises which conventions. (*New Guinea*, No. 4, 1965-66.)

In any case this integrationist approach had been firmly knocked on the head by Mr Hasluck, the responsible Minister, four years earlier, when in the House of Representatives, he

---

[22] *New Guinea*, No. 3, 1969 (my italics).

referred to the Derham Report,[23] saying: 'A particular problem is the one of finding some means of associating the people of the Territory with the administration of justice. A firm policy decision was made in 1955 against any development in the Territory of a system of customary native courts outside the regular judicial system. Professor Derham, after reviewing the decision leading to that decision, commended it as sound. He recommended that participation by the native people in the processes of justice should be a part of the regular judicial system of the Territory.'

In a discerning article, 'Kot Bilong Gavman',[24] David Fenbury says that he will believe that the rule of law will have taken root in New Guinea when in a bitterly contested election the electors abide by the results; when a Hanuabadan magistrate can pass out a stiff sentence on a Kerema and subsequently sit unmolested among a crowd of Keremas at a football match and when an unescorted surveyor can measure up land compulsorily acquired for public purposes without being interfered with by disgruntled villagers. Mr Fenbury was writing as recently as 1965 when he said in the same article that 'it is a disquietening fact that New Guinea's indigenous community has for many years been operating a widespread, completely unsupervised and technically illicit system which has no contact with the Territory legal system. This development has dangerously reinforced the concept of legal separatism in indigenous thinking, which can be briefly illustrated by two common Melanesian Pidgin expressions: the Territory courts are *kot bilong gavman* (government courts); the unofficial village tribunals are *kot bilong mipela* (our courts).'

In a world not of his own making, the New Guinean is in a transitional stage of the island's history, caught between his fears of Australian 'desertion' in the future and his resentment at his own necessary dependence on continuing Australian aid and skills. Aware both of future hopes and present displace-

[23] Then Professor of Jurisprudence in the University of Melbourne (and now its Vice-Chancellor), Professor Derham delivered a report on the Territory's administration of justice to Mr Hasluck in December 1960.

[24] D. Fenbury, 'Kot Bilong Gavman', *New Guinea*, No. 4, 1965.

ment the educated native above all wants to be 'accepted' within the European community, desiring not only to share in its productivity and knowledge but to become an integral part of it; a member of the club in good standing.

It is difficult for him to do so. The larger part of Australian attitudes to the New Guinean, and his corresponding reactions, has been the result of a long, slow exposure. The Australians who went to the Territory in earlier years took with them the emotional and intellectual furniture of their homeland, the familiar bits and pieces with which they had grown up, to reassemble it as best they could in a radically different environment. C. D. Rowley also suggests that Australian experience with the aborigine, whom the Australians shot out and ultimately dispossessed, ill-equipped Australians to deal with New Guinea's small, settled, autonomous village cultures.[25]

As time went by the Europeans introduced into the alien land, which few regarded as home, the manners and attitudes as well as the possessions and techniques, of the civilisation from which they had come. For whoever went there, whether in search of adventure or to save souls or to administer government, New Guinea created special problems. It was not small and compact like most of the islands of the Pacific nor was it Java or mainland Asia, richly endowed with the attractions and charms of old and subtle civilisations. It was New Guinea—difficult in terrain, poor in soils and without communications; its people seeming intractably barbarous and perpetually disappointing.

The rewards of the planter were won against loneliness, isolation and disease. To the government field officer operating on parsimonious budgets and preoccupied with pacification and contact, with administering scarcely understood law and order and introducing elementary hygiene to a people speaking a multiplicity of languages, the job must frequently have seemed both endless and largely fruitless. To the missionary, no matter how understanding or sympathetic, there was the problem of communication and above all of understanding. How

[25] C. D. Rowley, 'The Villager and the Nomad', *New Guinea*, No. 1, 1967.

many of his converts really understood the implications of baptism? How many do now? How many of the Territory's educated natives still believe in sorcery? Government assumptions about indigenous understanding, like those about indigenous acquiescence in the role of the administration in the villages, were apt to be misplaced.

The Germans in New Guinea appointed part time village officials to maintain administrative contact, to act as legates of power at the centre. These were usually men of prestige in their own villages and were called *luluais* (in Papua they were called village constables). As assistants, the German administration appointed *tul tuls* who were men who had usually some experience, if only fleeting, of administrative ways and frequently spoke Pidgin. Both the *luluai* (authority) and the *tul tul* (representative) had a hard row to hoe. They were responsible to the government for collecting taxes and finding the labour for the roads, for example. They were equally responsible to the villagers to find ways of avoiding these requirements. Conflict was considerable. Frequently *luluais* who appeared to have village prestige and authority were in reality front runners for those with real power who used them to circumvent, so far as possible, the desires of the government. In other instances the villagers played off *luluai* and *tul tul* against each other as a means of nullifying administrative requirements. The New Guinea village culture is nothing if not resistant to change.

The Australians of the Territory were, therefore, intensely conscious of the immense cultural gap between them and the indigenes. This re-enforced the natural tendency of Australians, already conditioned by their fatal contact with the aborigine, towards creating an exclusive, white society with its dominant master-servant relationship with the natives. Despite the fact that the Territory has undergone tremendous economic and social changes in the last ten years many of these attitudes still obtain.

In a perceptive article on race relations,[26] Professor Ken Inglis, traces the changes that took place in race relations in

[26] K. Inglis, 'Myth and Reality, 1939-45', *New Guinea*, No. 3, 1968.

New Guinea during the war with the arrival of Allied troops, although he deals only with the Australians. He is concerned to show pre-war attitudes as expressed in contemporary journals and documents, the desertion of natives by civil authorities at the time of the invasion and the entirely different attitudes of incoming Australian troops with their egalitarian use of the word 'sport', their willingness to share a slit trench during an air raid and the sentimentalisation of the native in song and verse by some of their number. As Professor Inglis demonstrates, race relations did take a new turn during the war in which, for the first time, most of the Australians who came into contact with the native looked at him through eyes entirely different from those of the pre-war 'English' finding him 'dirty and cruel and loyal and brave'[27]—but at least looking at him as a man. Professor Inglis asks: 'Looking back from 1968 one may be struck more by what did not change after the war than by what did change . . . were wartime observers inclined to exaggerate the elements of dislocation and underestimate the continuity of control?'

One would have to say, yes, simply because the fragmented nature of New Guinea society, non-literate and rooted in village life and culture, made it inevitable that a colonial administration and society could return. It was not, as Professor Inglis implies, the Netherlands East Indies with its traditional, developed civilisation, with a high degree of literacy in a nationalistic *lingua franca* and with an extensive history of nationalist movements. The nationalistic use of the word Indonesia became popular during the nineteenth century while the majority of New Guineans do not know even today where or what New Guinea is. However, as Professor Inglis suggests, the change in white racial attitudes as expressed during the war in New Guinea was a brief one. New Guinea's returning colonial society took a very long time to learn that things had changed. In fact many of its older members have not realised it yet.

Today, race relations are marked on the expatriate side not so much by impatient, arrogant or contemptuous European

[27] T. A. G. Hungerford, *The Bridge and the River*, Pacific Books, Sydney, 1966.

attitudes but by European indifference. As a personal impression one feels that New Guinea's Europeans are divided into three classes—a minority of active ill will, whether covert or not, towards the native, a larger minority of active good-will, and a large majority which is mostly indifferent to him. However, while this latter class of Australian may unintentionally do more harm than those few who are actively ill disposed it is by the same token the class perhaps most susceptible to a change in outlook. It can, if nothing else, be pressured into changed attitudes.

For the most part it comprises Australians who are not basic-ally ill disposed to anybody and who are, as many of them say, in the Territory 'to do a job' even though it might as well in their own view be a job in Sydney or Cairns. Its members are characterised by an almost complete lack of real interest in the native personally, in his ambitions, hopes or in his culture. To them the cultural gap is not only unbridgeable, as it was to an earlier generation, but is hardly worth thinking about even in its political implications. It is sufficient that the gap exists and they are on the safe, white side of it. For most of them the native is an extra in a film of exotic background scenery. Many of them are in the Territory for short terms, or trying their luck, and many of them, as the natives complain, are those who have lost out in the more competitive society of Australia.[28] In a country perennially short of skills there is room for even the most mediocre, for the failed salesman and the dissatisfied boarding house keeper.

What these Australians, of whom there are fewer in the Administration than in private enterprise, seek, is both the Territorian microcosm of Australia with its club chatter about football, beer and parties and the advantages of New Guinea's tropical, provincial society which offers them that which is denied them at home, the prestige of relatively high incomes, club life and servants. They are intensely aware of the material superiority of their western, industrial society and are convinced of the need to keep it hygienically insulated from the con-

[28] See Oala-Oala Rarua, 'Wage Cuts and Race Discrimination', *New Guinea*, No. 1, 1965.

taminating thought that the native has an increasing place in New Guinea's society. They are not, for the most part, consciously bad mannered towards the native but deep down, unaggressively, they are practising white supremacists who must believe that New Guineans are at best backward children. Except where the New Guinean impinges on their jobs, their security or prestige they are not particularly concerned what happens to him for deeper intuitions as to his society, his hopes and struggles are almost completely absent. Deeper intuitions are, in any case, not easily arrived at and are apt to get mixed up with western judgements of the native in terms of performance and capacity. This uncertainty tends to reinforce a cautious paternalism which while genuine in many, more frequently in others rationalises basic attitudes of distrust or dislike. Thus, many Australians in the Territory will give you a dismal recital of all the failures in native training they have come across. While they may accurately catalogue native incapacities their tone contains that racially threatened note which one detects so frequently among a certain regrettably widespread class of Australians in the Territory. Often, this attitude is accompanied by another, a sense of grievance that natives almost wilfully fail to respond in European ways to European expectations. Natives are frequently failed Europeans. A common criticism among older whites is that the natives collaborated with the Japanese during the war. In a chapter entitled 'The Martyrs',[29] the authors describe the shocked disbelief of Fr Holland, a pre-war Anglican missionary in Northern Papua, who, in 1942, while trying to escape the invading Japanese, found that natives had suddenly ceased to be friendly. '. . . Father Holland asked the men of the village if some of them would help carry packages but received no response. Instead, the men told him that the day of Europeans in Papua was over, that the spirits of their dead relations and friends were returning dressed as soldiers and that soon ships and planes would come bearing great quantities of valuable cargo. Father Holland was surprised and shocked and told the

[29] Dorothea Tomkins and Brian Hughes, *The Road From Gona*, Angus and Robertson, Sydney, 1969.

people they were foolish to believe such rubbish. One of the men became so angry that he struck Father Holland on the face, knocking him to the ground.' Disenchanted with the alien white, New Guineans naturally turned in chiliast hopes to yet another intruder, the Japanese. It would have been extraordinary if they had not. Except where personal loyalties were concerned the natives owed nothing to the white man who, in fact, appeared to desert him at the time of the Japanese invasion. He had no loyalty to abstractions like King and country. How could he? In fact his collaboration with the Japanese was like his allegiance to the pre-war 'English' (Australians)—it was conditional. Kind or sympathetic Japanese, like those who occupied South Bougainville, the native served well. He turned against them only when they became brutal in their demands towards the end of the New Guinea campaigns.

Yet another element in many white attitudes comes from neither basic dislike of the New Guinean nor from indifference to him but from the anger of frustration. It is more marked in the older Territorians whether missionaries, administration officers or planters who for more than thirty years in many instances have worked to try to make some impression on an apparently unmotivated, highly conservative, peasant people. It is an entirely understandable form of anger deriving from unrewarded effort and often resolves itself in a despairing animosity towards both the natives ('lazy bastards') and towards the Europeans ('white bludgers') accompanied by the desire to crawl into a hole and pull the lid down.

In all of this it would be manifestly unfair to fail to pay tribute to the many Australians of at least two generations, who, to the limits of great capacities in some instances, have worked selflessly and hard for the betterment of the New Guinean and equally unfair to dismiss the genuine respect and affection in which many Australians and New Guineans hold each other. The closest and most enduring of these friendships have frequently been those forged across the barriers of cultural conditioning between frustrated tutelary *kiap* and baffled apprentice New Guinean, whether police, disgruntled villager or shy primitive. One has only to read Jim Sinclair's *Behind the*

*Ranges*[30] an honest and sympathetic account not only of retrospectively mostly relished dangers and hardships, but of a conscientious sense of mission. It is all there—sense, sensitivity and wistful, ineluctable romanticism: 'in any case most of the exploring is done and little restricted territory remains. There are still mist-shrouded ranges where patrol officers doggedly push their way on foot; people still live in deep mountain valleys, almost untouched, pursuing their traditional ways; but there are few of them. The old New Guinea is gone, we know what lies behind the ranges.' Where we may have made our major mistake as colonists was not in our failure to feel—we have in many ways shown a great generosity of spirit—but in our continued failure to understand. 'Perhaps our basic error all along,' says the Yale historian, Harry Benda, in another context, 'has been to examine Indonesia with Western eyes; or, to be more precise and more generous, with eyes that, though increasingly trained to see things Indonesian, have continued to look at them selectively, in accordance with preconceived western models . . .'[31] In our unflagging belief that New Guineans would eventually conform to Australian preconceptions, and in our frequently mindless self-congratulation that what we have transplanted to New Guinea by way of Australian institutions and practices was invariably suited to its people, we have done them and ourselves a disservice.

[30] J. P. Sinclair, *Behind The Ranges*, Melbourne University Press, Melbourne, 1966.
[31] 'Democracy in Indonesia', *Journal of Asian Studies*, 23, No. 3, May 1964, as quoted by Herbert Feith in his paper, 'The Study of Indonesian Politics: A Survey and an Apologia', delivered to the ASPA Conference, Sydney, August, 1969.

# 5 Political Development

*'I never knew before that Port Moresby was on the mainland of New Guinea and I thought that Port Moresby was beyond on another island.'*

Koitaga Mano, Member for Ialibu Open,
House of Assembly, 1964

*The House should 'decide whether we are a mere rubber stamp for propositions in which we are not consulted . . .'*

John Guise, Member for Milne Bay Open,
House of Assembly, 1966

*'. . . we members must forget about unimportant feuding—friction between one district and another, Papua versus New Guinea, white versus black, Highlands against coast—this could destroy us.'*

Tei Abal, Member for Wabag Open,
House of Assembly, 1968

## Education

The rate of indigenous political advancement in the Territory from the end of World War II until very recently has been extraordinarily slow. Successive Ministers for Territories and governments generally have been at great pains to stress the need for carefully supervised and spontaneous political growth in New Guinea. The absence of native political parties in the Territory, until latterly, and the absence of informed native political opinion, combined with the Government's failure to introduce a system of political education has meant that past Australian governments have never been obliged to defend their political policies either in the Territory where they have been supported on most issues by the majority of New Guinea's white settler population, or in Australia where they mostly had the support of the official opposition in Parliament. In addition, for the most part, these policies were a matter of indifference to the Australian electorate even if abroad they have been the subject of increasing attack.

In the United Nations, Australia, which has been able to point to a remarkable material effort in New Guinea, has for

long evaded its critics on political development by stating that
New Guineans are being developed for self-determination with
the addition that Australia will not pre-determine what form
self-determination will take. In defence of its gradualist political
policies in the Territory, the Government has always been at
pains to point to widespread indigenous fears of any talk of
self-government or independence. These fears have frequently
been very real in a linguistically and socially fragmented
country in which there are such marked disparities in the rate
of indigenous emergence ranging from the urban coastal people
with 80 years of contact to very large Southern Highlands
populations discovered less than twenty years ago. Notwithstanding the economic and psychological dependence of the
more backward New Guinea populations on continued Australian aid and skills, the Government's insistence on gradualism for these reasons alone is just about played out. The real
causes for the non-emergence of early native political
institutions, and the continuing absence of any signs of New
Guinean nationalism, lie to a great extent in the Government's
failure to initiate as soon as practicable after the war's end an
energetic education programme aimed at securing a large
number of secondary and tertiary students at the earliest
possible date. This in turn has reflected a confused paternalistic
reluctance to move swiftly.

In the post-war years Australian governments and Territories
Ministers tended, with occasional shifts in emphasis, to reject
the notion that the rapid changes taking place in Asia and
more particularly in Africa would affect the political demands
of New Guineans. For this reason they felt it unnecessary and
unwise to seek the early creation of a well-trained and educated
native élite for the tasks of government in the event of 'premature' independence. While the Government was shrewder
than many of its critics in its estimate of the effects of distant
African nationalism on Melanesian political development it
failed to exploit the time at its disposal.

Certainly the idea of élites was anathema to government
thinking and Mr Paul Hasluck occasionally said so throughout
his long period of office as Minister for Territories from 1951

to 1964. He innately distrusted the idea of training small numbers of specially qualified natives for the task of administering and governing the country. He preferred 'uniform development'—a long period of universal education and the emergence of grass roots politicians who would represent the 'real' feelings of the electorate. His policy seemed to imply a belief in 'perfectability' even though it meant that coastal New Guineans despite their long period of contact and relative sophistication in political and economic matters, would have to wait while the more primitive and vastly more numerous Highlands populations slowly caught up. Mr Hasluck felt that the results of this policy would be justified in the end by the growth of stable and representative political institutions. He preferred a 'broad primary school base so that the development of the country rests upon a wide distribution of education. This will permit a broad stream to enter secondary and tertiary education thus obviating the creation of a narrow, educated élite.' In a speech delivered to the Australian Institute of Political Science in January 1958, Mr Hasluck, apart from making it clear that he believed that 'It would be quite safe to predict that for the next thirty years at the very least a large part of the task of the Administration of the Territory will still be the establishment and maintenance of law and order among the people, whose habits or whose memories are still closely tied to primitive savagery', also made it clear that he believed there was no room for élites. 'Already,' he said, 'we face a situation where a small minority of the people might be regarded as advanced while the majority are still living in a primitive state. This situation is one which gives unusual and dangerous opportunities for the native demagogue who claims on behalf of himself or of a minority rights and powers which should belong to the whole of the people. It is also one that requires us to call on the advanced people to accept with patience and moderation a wider good for the whole of the people rather than the early serving of their own sectional advantage.' Having thus called on New Guinea's advanced people to demonstrate a patience that is beyond average human capacity, he delivered the *coup de grâce*. 'We sometimes talk of an élite and our special responsibility to it. They need to earn that title by the standards they set themselves.' Mr Hasluck was perfectly correct in implying that 'uniform development' was undoubtedly more likely to produce enduring results than a crash programme policy of producing instant élites.

However, the success of 'uniform development' depended on a far longer time period than Australia was likely to get, at least thirty years without undue external pressures, and a much more permissive attitude among the Afro-Asian and Communist states in the United Nations. It also assumed that New Guineans themselves would remain quiescent and unaffected by the winds of change, even the mild zephyrs blowing next door in West New Guinea, where a Dutch crash programme in the 1950's produced in an astonishingly short space of time a number of relatively well educated and politically sophisticated 'Papuans' in the face of considerable difficulties and with scarcer resources than were available to the Australians. At the time of the Dutch handover to Indonesia in 1963 there were two Papuan graduates of Dutch universities and more on the way. By contrast, no Australian New Guinean attended an Australian university before 1960 and the first graduate, in agricultural science, obtained a degree at Sydney University in 1964. Even now there are only four indigenous graduates of Australian universities in the Territory although it is hoped that fifteen graduates, (a third in science) of the University of Papua and New Guinea will be available by the end of 1970.

Education was literally non-existent in pre-war New Guinea outside the limited facilities and aims of the Missions without whose efforts against great odds there would have been no education at all. The Administration did not become concerned with 'national' education until late in the 1940's. Tardiness was excused on the grounds of the difficulties of the post-war period and the first secondary high school was started in 1957 following on from a seven year primary cycle which was started in 1952.

Remaining difficulties have been in the system of education itself with its misplaced emphasis on quantity and the Australian-oriented nature of the syllabus which has been singularly unattuned to native needs in the Territory and is only just now acknowledging the necessity to educate the New Guinean as a future citizen of his own country. A major result of Australia's late start on a secondary Territory education programme is that there are very few New Guineans of requisite skills and experience to fit into the current stage of economic and political development. In a few years time there may be too many. Present problems include a shortage of expatriate teachers and the general inadequacy of most indigenous ones, some of whom have to be retrained. Currently, about 40 per cent of indigenous children between six and fifteen years are at school and about 50 per cent of children now reaching school age will actually attend school. This may very well prove the maximum (and desirable?) number given the current level of expenditure, the availability of teachers and other priorities. In 1967–68 Administration spending on education was $21 million; in 1968-69 it was $25 million or about 16 per cent of total Administration expenditure and in 1969-70 will be $28.7 million. These figures include the costs of the University. Post-secondary education is centred primarily on the University of Papua and New Guinea, and on the Papuan Medical College, Dental College, Administrative Staff College, Vudal Agricultural College, Institute of Higher Technical Education, Goroka Teachers Training College and other institutions. The University offers bachelors' degrees in Law, Arts and Science.

The University, which might better have been the responsibility of the Australian Universities Commission, or some similar body, is in fact a Territory institution dependent for its financing on the Territory budget and is subject to the priorities accorded it by the Department of Territories through the Administration. For the 1968–69 financial year the amount it required by way of capital and recurrent expenditures was reduced from $4.5 million to $3.7 million, obliging the University to borrow some $200,000. In the 1969-70 academic year the University budgeted for expenditures of just on $4 million, but again had to resort to borrowing $200,000. An indication of the University's alarm over effects on its efficiency as a teaching institution was the publication of a Staff Association (academic) letter pointing out that if neither money nor facilities were available, standards would fall and academic staff seek employment elsewhere.[1] The cuts resulted in turning away thirty academically qualified students from admission to the 1968 Preliminary Year through lack of finance. The original estimate of 830 students by 1970 was optimistic and 500 may be nearer the mark. Just as optimistic was the original estimate of twenty-five graduates, a third in science, by the end of 1970; fifteen may prove nearer the mark. Required graduate output of the University is 200 a year by 1976 or as near to that date as possible. This will require a student body of between 1,200 and 1,500 undergraduates, allowing for normal wastage. The University will need a substantially higher budget for these requirements than it appears likely to get on present indications. The need for graduates in all disciplines is urgent and nowhere more so than in the field of law. One of the most important requirements in any country heading for independence is for lawyers, if only to handle the technicalities of government, legislation and constitution. It is hoped to have four graduates in law by the end of 1971.

## Political development

Against this background, political development has been correspondingly belated. Apart from cargo cults, a few with vague, semi-political overtones, indigenous political organisations simply did not exist until relatively recent times when two Papuan welfare societies were started up in the late 1950's, with Mission backing, by capable New Guineans like Mr Lepani Watson (Member for Kula Open), and Mr Albert Maori Kiki (Secretary of Pangu Pati), while Dr Reuben Taureka (Assistant Director for Public Health) and Mr Oala-Oala Rarua (now Assistant Ministerial Member for the Treasury) and other New Guineans were responsible for the inauguration of the Papua and New Guinea Workers' Association—New

[1] See Professor K. Inglis in *New Guinea*, No. 2, 1968, and the exchange of letters between the Minister (Mr C. E. Barnes) and the Vice-Chancellor (Dr J. T. Gunther) in *New Guinea*, No. 3, 1968.

Guinea's first trade union. While European companies and plantations professed to welcome this latter initiative they never greatly encouraged its activities which visibly suffered from lack of funds and personnel capable of devising and prosecuting vigorous trade union policies. Trade unionism in New Guinea is largely tokenism. The reason for the long absence of study, discussion and workers' clubs and similar political organisations lies partly in the lack of education of the older New Guinean élite. Partly, like everything else, the problem has resulted from a tacit European conspiracy to prevent the emergence of political parties and institutions, not invariably from an undemocratic dislike of them as such but from an innate fortified conviction that it has always been 'too early'. The workers' 'study clubs' of the early 1960's in Dutch New Guinea had no counterpart on the Australian side. Mr Hasluck, in a statement to the House of Representatives, 15 August 1961, had considerable reservations about the introduction of trade unions including the fact that they would have to be a function of the newly formed Department of Labour. 'I admit to having had some hesitation about committing this function to a government department. It will be difficult in practice for a conscientious officer to distinguish between the moment when he is assisting workers to form a union and when he is telling them what to do; between the moment when he is guiding and informing them and the moment when he is deciding what should be done . . . at present some groupings of workers . . . are tribal rather than occupational . . . there is a risk of unions being formed by native leaders who could act as "stand-over" men and manipulate unions for their own purposes. There is the risk of the promotion of unions primarily to serve the ends of political subversion. There is a risk of what I believe is called the "tame-cat" union . . .' After warning of these risks, Mr Hasluck observed: 'We have to keep enough flexibility in our own minds to recognise that their organisations may be different from our own.' In retrospect, one wonders whether Mr Hasluck meant in this, and in other things, not only the flexibility to accept but also to allow organisations 'different from our own', or merely the flexibility to perceive that they would be different—and to resist them.

The Administration, and certainly the Government in Canberra, has nevertheless placed great hopes in the development of native Local Government Councils from which, subsequently, the word 'native' was dropped. These were started in the early 1950's, as grass roots institutions to overcome traditional New Guinean fragmentation and as a means of imparting political education through the formation of a broad base of local government on which the eventual pyramid of a national government structure might be erected.

The first Council, at Hanuabada, was established in 1950. In 1968 there were 142 Councils controlling 8,000 villages representing 1.82 million people. The councils were originally established through groups of villages, sometimes between twenty and forty villages constituting a council. Their powers included passing and enforcing local rules of land clearance, care and maintenance of cash crops, instituting market facilities, the establishment and administration of co-operative enterprises, maintenance of local roads, water supplies, erection of medical aid posts, schools, teachers' houses and so on. Council revenue comes from grants, taxes levied on area inhabitants, charges for services and from other fees. In many instances there have been considerable achievements on the part of some councils not only in bridge and road construction and so on, but also in corporate enterprises involving the purchase of trucks and tractors for plantation use, the employment of skilled workers and the marketing of cash crops. However, there has been an enduring tendency in the Administration to regard Local Government Councils as administrative units carrying out instructions from the centre rather than as autonomous decision making institutions—although there is some evidence of change. Even so, the majority of councils seldom reach decisions without the help of Administration advisers. The failure of the councils to become local, autonomous decision making bodies partly explains the inability of most indigenous members of the 1964–68 House to 'understand politics', as 43 per cent of the native members were former councillors. In addition there have been other problems. Many of the early attempts to set up councils, as in the Gazelle Peninsula, were both resented and resisted by the local native population which feared that the Council might usurp the functions of the traditional leaders. Attempts to circumvent or defeat Administration purposes have been many and successful.

Under the amended ordinance which came into effect in 1965, provision was made for Councils to become multi-racial if they desired. In short, missions, some towns and plantations could have representatives elected to the council. Of the 142 councils now in existence, eighty-seven are multi-racial and eleven include urban areas. The new powers are considerable and include authority to maintain peace, order and good government within council bounds, organise, finance or engage in any business, carry out works for the benefit of the community and provide, or help provide, any public or social service. And yet the same criticism remains. Despite the implications of these new powers the councils have not been used as political catalysts of indigenous conflicts and problems but as agents for administering political decisions at the centre. In E. P. Wolfers' phrase they are legates of power.[2] While multiracial councils are of obvious importance in promoting greater racial accord they too frequently appear to the New Guinean as yet another institution in which Europeans display once again their unmatchable expatriate skills. In the greater number of issues, preponderant native membership has not meant the exercise of native 'control' any more than it has in the House of Assembly.

Similar problems arising from indigenous failure to understand properly the purpose and function of institutions have plagued many of the Territory's 303 co-operative societies. Despite the relative success of some (combined turnover is about $5.5 million annually), like those of Kundiawa (coffee), Moveave (timber), and Kairuku (crayfishing)[3] nearly all have been dependent on expatriate skills for their operations while

[2] E. P. Wolfers, *New Guinea*, No. 4, 1968.
[3] See *New Guinea Research Bulletin*, No. 25, for an account of the problems of New Guinea's indigenous industries.

the majority of their members have never understood the necessity or the nature of bookkeeping methods and accounts. A major problem of New Guinean understanding has been the utterly foreign and seemingly irrelevant nature of administrative organisation. This has never been better expressed than in the House of Assembly by the Member for Mendi Open, Momei Pangial, when he said that he used to think that 'government just happened' and that 'village people still think this'. Pangial before his election had been nothing less than President of the Upper Mendi Local Government Council.

In view of the slow manner in which political organisations have arrived in the Territory, and the realities lying behind the façade in each instance, the very late appearance of political parties causes no more surprise than Canberra's immediate displeasure and opposition.

The earliest parties—in the 1950's—were abortive, European-led organisations which quickly faded. The first indigenous-led party was the New Guinea United National Party formed in September 1965 principally by Oala-Oala Rarua, now Member for Central Regional, with full panoply of constitution and party platform. In general its aims were modest—a 100 seat House, ministerial government, with emphasis on control at the centre, by the end of 1968, expanded secondary education, expanded indigenous participation in business, technical and entrepreneurial enterprises, security for Australian investment and continuing close relations between Papua-New Guinea and Australia. The Party never even got off the ground. There was little indigenous support for it and European reaction both outside and inside the House (an expatriate Member referred to Party members as 'Communists' and 'homosexuals') was unrelentingly hostile. At its first public meeting three Special Branch officers took extensive and obvious notes of the proceedings. The Police Commissioner, Mr R. R. Cole, rationalised this objectionable procedure, closely identified by natives at the meeting and by many who stayed away, with deliberate Administration intimidation, by saying that there were in fact only two officers present and in a 'private capacity' at that. The Party folded through lack of support.

It was therefore an interesting indication of suppressed feelings among indigenes that less than a year later twelve native Public Servants and one Territory born Australian could sign so radical a document as their submission to the Select Committee on Constitutional Development and follow it up ten months later by forming, in conjunction with others, a party of relatively extensive links with parliamentary members and likeminded native trade union members, civil servants and native citizens elsewhere in the country. The Committee of Thirteen comprised Albert Maori Kiki (Patrol Officer), Reuben Taureka (Assistant Director of Public Health and Suva medical graduate), Oala-Oala Rarua (formerly an Administration officer and Trade Union leader), eight other native civil servants and one Territory born Australian, Cecil Abel (now member for Milne Bay Regional), of the famed Kwato Mission family. The preponderance of Papuans neatly symbolised the frustrations and resentments of the old Papuan civil service élite resulting from longer European contact and better education.

The same élite had bitter memories of the 1964 wages decision. In Mr Hasluck's early days the whole tenor of approach, representing an impulsive Australian egalitarianism, was that the principle of equal pay for equal work would eventually apply to indigenous and non-indigenous public servants alike. A hasty calculation in the early 1960's of the eventual costs of an indigenised public service, subsidised at mainland rates, revealed them to be progressively enormous. In 1964 the Administration fixed native public servants' salaries at 40 per cent of those of expatriate officers while increasing housing rentals. In some cases the new rates incurred real hardships. In all cases it provoked genuine anger, a sense of being racially discriminated against and a possibly lasting sense of betrayal. A fifteen months arbitration hearing ending in 1967 increased the basic rates, substantially increased the top ranges —at present applying to only one eligible native public servant —and awarded mean and paltry increases to the most important group among local officers—the middle range. Part of the sense of betrayal was the realisation that Australia by setting two different rates was, in effect, 'casting New Guinea adrift'. What alternative there could have been to making New Guineans begin to live within the country's capacity to pay has never been satisfactorily answered.

Currently the urban cash wage for an Administration base grade local employee is $338 p.a. in Port Moresby and $364 in Rabaul. The rural minimum wage is $225 p.a. made up of $30 for accommodation, $52 in cash and $173 "in kind." A middle grade Administration local employee receives an annual salary range of $1830 to $2100. In Rabaul, Moresby or Lae a first class sergeant of Police has a salary range of between $1830 and $1890. At the higher levels an indigenous Regional Medical Officer receives between $5675 and $6075. A European occupying the same position receives the same base salary under the single line salary structure but as much again, bringing total emoluments to $11590, in overseas allowances. Wage scales paid by private business vary enormously but are generally higher, and getting higher still, than those paid by the Administration, especially for indigenes with qualifications. But to return to the Committee of Thirteen.

The submission was in two parts. One comprised a stinging attack on Australian Government policies in New Guinea accusing Canberra of being 'autocratic, unrealistic and inflexible' and the other a detailed submission calling for Home Rule by 1968 as a transitional step towards full 'self government'.

The submission called principally for a House of Assembly elected on universal suffrage and for a 'cabinet' elected or appointed after the 1968 elections by the whole House of Assembly, responsible to the House for a four year term but *not* dependent on the confidence of the House for survival during that term and to consist of a Chief Minister and seven other Ministers to replace the current departmental directors. It also called for rapid localisation of the public service.

The submission also requested that after inaugurating the ministerial system the new government should deal only with the Department of External Affairs on the grounds that as 'defence and foreign relations will be two of the very last functions to be relinquished by Australia, it is logical and proper that External Affairs should, from now onwards, be in a position to lay the groundwork for future co-operation and association under whatever agreements or treaties will be mutually acceptable to both countries.' In short the country was to be all but independent, although Australia would control its external and defence policies.

The submission predictably shocked many blacks and whites alike and it was followed by another, no less contentious but more thoughtful, drawn up by Messrs Voutas and Holloway, then members for Kaindi and Kainantu Opens. This document called for a radical shift in political direction in the Territory away from the Westminster stereotype towards a Presidential system perhaps of the type existing in Tanzania. The particular significance of this statement was its timing in following so shortly after that of the Committee of Thirteen which, up until the Select Committee Report was tabled in June of 1967, had been extremely careful not to call itself a party (even though it had the appearance of one), possibly because it remembered the fate of Oala's New Guinea National United Party and possibly because its members needed time to obtain supporters and organise a party apparatus.

Nevertheless the Committee of Thirteen was one of the principal progenitors of Pangu Pati, which announced on its formation that it had nine members in the House of Assembly including Messrs Voutas and Holloway as well as unnamed indigenous members and the support, and possible membership, of John Guise, while it had self-allegedly established links throughout the country. The Party was milder in tone than the Committee had been. The emphasis seemed now to be less on Australian sins in the Territory and more on learning the difficult art of government while Australian advisers were still available. But as the rapid assumption of political power by New Guineans was inevitable it was time for New Guineans to start learning the art of government even if they made mistakes. The Party's platform says it believes in 'home rule' leading to 'ultimate independence', Pidgin as 'the principal common language', localisation of the Public Service, a road from New

Guinea to Papua, participation in all economic development schemes and, above all, 'one name, one country, one people'.

At all events it was obvious that both European and indigenous conservative pressure were sufficient to oblige the Party into quieter, more persuasive tactics. To this extent it reflected the Select Committee's shrewd insight into currently conservative attitudes on the part of most native electors. But the fact that the Party was as 'radical' as it was and had a base in the House, however slender, was also indication of the Select Committee's failure to recognise the changing mood of the growing urban *évolués*, especially in Port Moresby. The interesting question to resolve was whose assumptions would be the more correct for the 1968–72 period—that of the Select Committee's that the urban groups could be ignored because they would not, and could not, for an appreciable time, influence the mass of the rural population or the Pangu Pati's assumption that where its members went all others would in time surely follow. The latter seems inevitable.

In the closing sessions of the first House of Assembly there were signs that Pangu might become a political force but its election campaign did not give that impression. While it claimed that it had thirty candidates in the field it was difficult to find them. Those of its candidates who were openly known as Pangu candidates, e.g. Mr Anthony Voutas ('Tony') [who won Morobe Regional from the Speaker of the last House and a former District Commissioner of Morobe, Mr H. L. R. Niall ('Masta Nil')] and young Michael Somare, an Administration employee who won East Sepik Regional (against a daunting background of alleged native conservatism, and the unrelenting hostility and suspicion of the area's white settlers) were modest and careful in their campaign statements and promises. Other Pangu Members were just as careful and many were simply anonymous. The time for open organised Party campaigning has not yet arrived.

In fact with the exception of Pangu, the Territory's parties have been paper organisations, most members of which in the election campaigns were none too anxious to appear formally identified with any particular party believing themselves more secure, as they often were, in seeking election as individuals even if their policies in some cases were more or less those of the Party to which they nominally belonged. Frequently their election campaigns had little if anything to do with their alleged Party platforms.[4] Somewhere between twenty-five and fifty-two alleged Pangu sympathisers stood for the elections and twelve reputed Pangu candidates were returned to the House where the Party hopes to attract other elected members of like interests or even some with no specific allegiances but looking for a 'cause'. In all probability Pangu will eventually be able to do this but it will have to continue to modify its initial radicalism if it is to retain confidence or unless it can find 'national' grievances to exploit. Even so, opposition to it is considerable. Many members instinctively vote against it out of suspicion and the numerically large Independent Members' Group was formed almost entirely to oppose it and presumably any other party. The Group is a party, in effect, but is not established as one. It is subject to intense manipulation by European members.

The only other political party of numerical consequence is the United Christian Democratic Party—from which the word Christian has been dropped—which allegedly has 18,000 members. It seldom seems to meet, its political aims are confused and it is not politically effective. One of its principal founders is Simogen Pita, BEM, a greatly respected old time policeman who was one of the members of the old 1951–1960 Legislative Council, and member for Wewak-Aitape in the first House of Assembly. The party is backed by the Roman Catholic Sepik missions. An older 'wing' is still hopefully seventh state in outlook while a younger 'wing' holds much the same opinions as Pangu members. It is difficult to gauge the relevant strengths of the two opposed political wings of the Party but in view of Mr Barnes' assurance to Party members in 1967 that while a seventh state was 'out for the present' it might be possible after 'self-determination', it is probable that the older members will

[4] For what follows on political parties I am largely indebted to E. P. Wolfers. See Parts I and II of 'The Elections', *New Guinea*, Nos. 3 and 4, 1968-69.

continue to work among older, more conservative Sepiks for some close association with Australia after self-determination.

Four other parties comprise the political spectrum. At this stage none can be taken seriously. They are the All Peoples' Party (APP) Territory Country Party (TCP), National Progress Party (NAPRO), and the Agricultural Reform Party (ARP).

The APP, Eurocentric, its leaders comprising mainly Sepik based white traders and others, is anti-Pangu and indeed is anti-party. Predictably its two members in the House named themselves the 'All Peoples' Group'. NAPRO is Papua-oriented, believes in low cost self-help housing schemes and other good works. Badly organised, it failed at the elections. The ARP failed at the elections and was in any case devised as an answer to the activities of the secessionist Rabaul group called the Melanesian Independence Front. The Territory Country Party, founded by an expatriate, is conservative in tone and rural based. It seems to have all but faded away.

In short, with the exception of Pangu which is experiencing difficult times, parties are scarcely relevant to New Guinea politics at this stage. They did not get anyone elected and when openly affiliated party members were elected it was probably because they were individually attractive or prestigious and not because they belonged to a particular party. New Guinea's political parties have sprung up largely in prestigious imitation of, and fearful counterbalance to, one another. As with secessionism one should not underestimate the political striving that parties represent which is none the less real because it has not yet fastened on exploitable 'national' issues. Party politics are formless and vague because of the atomised nature of New Guinean society with all its divisive linguistic and tribal characteristics. This will change slowly and it may be that Pangu, representing the ambitions and aspirations of the évolués, will show the way.

## The House

The first essay in representative government was the Territory's Legislative Council which functioned between 1951-1961

F

comprising the Administrator, sixteen official members (Departmental heads), six expatriates appointed from business, planting and mission interests as non-official members, three elected Europeans and three natives appointed as non-official members.

Legco, as it was known, while scarcely a Territory wide representative institution, at least gave the expatriate non-official members a chance to have a say in those Territory policies which concerned them and to influence distant, unsympathetic Canberra. For its three native members, it was largely a matter of listening and as a result native contributions to discussions were notably few and uninspired. In 1961 the Council was reformed and enlarged to comprise the Administrator, fourteen official members, ten non-official appointed members of whom at least half had to be New Guineans, six non-indigenous elected members and six New Guineans chosen through an electoral college whose members in turn had been elected through the Native Local Government Councils or community groups in those areas lacking councils. While Europeans outnumbered natives twenty-six to eleven in the new Legislative Council, for the first time in Territory history non-official members predominated in the legislature. The new Legislative Council was intended to have a life of five years or so before review, but events overtook it in the form of the UN Visiting Mission of 1962 headed by Sir Hugh Foot[5] (now Lord Caradon) a retired senior British colonial civil servant of great experience and former Governor of Jamaica and of Cyprus.

The Foot Report, as it became known, was acidly but expertly critical of Australian Government policies in New Guinea which it regarded as being far too paternalistic in approach to the urgent requirements of education, political development and representative government. The report made it perfectly clear that mission members thought that the Australian Government was hopelessly out of touch with the realities of Afro-Asian anti-colonialist views and had miscalculated their probable effects on the rapidly dwindling number of remaining

[5] Now Permanent Head, United Kingdom Mission to the United Nations. See his *A Start in Freedom*, Hodder and Stoughton, London, 1964.

colonial dependencies. Most of the members of the mission, like Foot himself, were men who recognised, if they had not seen, the quickening political pace of colonial Africa, believing that it would inevitably follow in New Guinea and that the only way to prepare for it was by crash programmes in education, by rapid indigenisation of the public service and by an equally rapid extension of indigenous political responsibility. Neither Foot nor most of his colleagues were under any illusions that this was an ideal way to prepare so backward and fragmented a people as the New Guineans for responsible government but they clearly shared the notion that time was running out, even for New Guinea. This approach was scarcely popular in Canberra and an indication of the raging differences between the responsible Australian Minister and the Former British colonial governor is contained in Lord Caradon's description of Mr Hasluck and the Mission's description of its subsequent meeting with the Minister. Of Mr Hasluck, Lord Caradon, with telling insight, unmatched by a corresponding appreciation of the Minister's intellectual capacities, said:

> He is the District Officer of New Guinea. I at once recognised in him the characteristics which I knew so well in District Officers elsewhere, a passionate devotion to the well being of the people under his charge, a dedicated determination to serve them well—and an intense suspicion of interference from any outside authority. We were specially grateful to him for the special effort of patience and forebearance which he made in dealing with us.

Of Mr Hasluck the Mission noted:

> The Minister explained the attitude of his Government which was based upon the principle that the wishes of the people should predominate. He emphasised that the people must have the right to choose, and he referred to frequent direct discussions with representatives of the people in New Guinea with the object of ascertaining their wishes and their ideas on the next steps in political advancement. He said that these discussions had not indicated a desire for imme-

diate further advance following the establishment of the present Legislative Council last year, and the view of the Administering Authority was that decisions on future political advance should take place in consultation with the Legislative Council after the next elections, due to take place in about two years time.

Mr Hasluck was right, of course, in saying that Territory discussions 'had not indicated a desire for further immediate political advance' simply because there was no cohesive political institutions in the Territory, through which such a desire, had it existed, could be expressed. And when every allowance for the cumulative problems of history and geography was made—whose fault was that? A primary aim of Australian policy in New Guinea had been to prevent the emergence of that desire; and to prevent it for the very best of gradualist reasons even if they should ultimately prove the most misplaced. Mr Hasluck was not merely concerned with gradualism for its own sake over the development of a dependent and primitive part of the world for which Australia bore special responsibilities, but that change when it came would reflect the political and social values of New Guinea's Australian mentors, even though in his 1956 Roy Milne lecture, he had himself warned that Papuans could never become 'wholly European'.[6] In the same address he gave full vent to his doubts about the early establishment of universally representative institutions in New Guinea. 'There is not at present,' he said, 'and cannot be for many years to come any possibility for a Territory wide franchise for the native people. They are separated into so many

[6] Of the 'blending of cultures' in New Guinea Hasluck had asked, 'what do these phrases mean? If we adopt the idea of "blending of cultures", then we try to work out an education system which will draw on the best elements in the native life as well as on selected elements in western civilisation. To reach an opinion on this we have to form a judgement on whether we want to make the Papuan people into "coloured Europeans" or whether we want to make them into Papuans with their own distinctive culture (including a distinct language, laws, arts, social habit and custom, and institutions). We shall probably turn away from both of those paths. . . because . . . the native can never become wholly European or remain wholly Papuan.'

different language groups; they are at so many different stages of progress towards civilisation; and there are so many who are still unaware or only partly aware of what a legislative council is, that any attempt to form an electoral roll would be a travesty of any democratic principle and would only have the effect of allowing a very small minority of people in a few regions to assume the representation of the interests of tens of thousands of people about whom they know less than do the officers of the administration.'

This was an intelligent conservative's appraisal of the chances of Australian style political institutions taking root. But what alternatives did he ever entertain? Westminster, if one understood him correctly, was to take many years, perhaps generations. And anything less than Westminster, 'allowing a very small minority of people in a very few regions to assume the representation of the interest of tens of thousands of people' was inadmissible. He expressed with beautiful clarity his doubts about the obvious political changes taking place in New Guinea when he opened the Legislative Council buildings in October 1960, only two years before the Foot Mission arrived: 'Let me use a simple illustration. More of the people today are riding bicycles. Do they ride them on the same errands they used to do on foot or are they riding them on new errands? The true nature of change is not revealed by counting the number of bicycles but by asking how the owners use them.' This was a perfectly legitimate question but one is left with the feeling that Mr Hasluck was not asking whether the people were riding bicycles on new errands but whether those errands conformed to Australian pre-conceptions. His statement revealed not only an understandable preoccupation with the true nature of change, but a lively apprehension as to the unpredictable and discomforting directions it might take.

This fear was scarcely rationalised by the statement of the Government in Canberra, following the Visiting Mission's departure, that it had in any case already been considering the idea of extending the native franchise, quite apart from the Foot Mission Report and that it proposed to establish a sixty-four seat House of Assembly which excluded the Administrator and comprised ten official seats, ten special electorates for which only Europeans could stand on a common roll and forty-four open electorates in which candidates could stand for election by preference vote on a common roll. In view of the racial and tribal peculiarities of the country, the Foot Report had suggested that a hundred electorates would better serve the interests of minority peoples and prove more convenient in size.

One of the peculiarities of the proposed House was that it assured the election of at least ten expatriates while it did not guarantee the election of a single native in the open electorates. Natives however wanted some whites at least guaranteed a seat in the House. In point of fact natives did comprise the majority of those elected from the open electorates while only six out of ten European candidates were elected. The result was that the New House had ten official members (all expatriate heads of Departments), ten expatriate members from special electorates and six expatriates from open electorates, a total of twenty-six Europeans and thirty-eight native members.[7] Under the Papua and New Guinea Act, the House of Assembly has the power to make ordinances for the Territory's 'peace, order and good government' but the power of veto over Territory legislation remains with the Government. All ordinances must have the Administrator's assent, some must have that of the Governor-General who may, in any case, disallow an ordinance within six months of the Administrator's assent. All this means in fact is that the Minister for Territories has the power of veto either through an instruction to the Administrator or upon advice to the Governor-General. While in practice, so far, the Government has generally sought to obtain the consent of the House's native majority to policies the power of veto remains. In fact, in May 1968, the Governor-General's powers were enlarged to give him the right to exercise, on advice, the power of partial as well as total veto. This coupled with the fact that the 'govern-

[7] Of the fifty-four elective seats in the first House of Assembly (ten reserved for Europeans) about one third went to Europeans. In the second House about one quarter of the elective seats (fifteen requiring educational qualifications) went to Europeans.

ment' in New Guinea is the Administration, irremovable by legislation and subject to daily instruction from Canberra, means that the House is in effect tightly controlled through the Administration, which in turn is minutely instructed by Canberra.[8] In the lifetime of the 1964-68 House, the Administrator's Council had been changed to include the Administrator, three official members (expatriates) and seven elected members of whom five were natives. What did not change was the role of the Council which remained merely advisory at best.

Problems affecting the new House both in the complexities of compiling the electoral roll and in those of native assumptions about the nature of politics were considerable to say the least. As village books were all but useless and the only roll in existence contained the names of 6000 or more Europeans registered for the 1961 elections, *kiaps* (patrol officers) were despatched throughout the country to register the names of all those whom they considered to be over twenty-one. Difficulties proliferated on the problems of names alone. The Mekeo of Papua, for instance, considered it to be laying oneself open to sorcery to have one's name called aloud. An additional problem was that as they share only a small number of names large numbers tend to share the same name. How could one be sure of whom one was registering? Other practices were even more confusing as in Western Papua where people change their names at different periods of their lives. Political education for the elections was minimal. There were some quick, sharp visits to Australia of selected parties whose members presumably were supposed to understand everything on their return. There were pamphlets and innumerable pep talks by the *kiaps* who explained that Parliament belonged to all the people who should therefore vote for it. They also had to explain more mundane matters such as why there were electoral boundaries, where they were and why the people lived within them. Many indigenes remained unconvinced that a parliament could do much for them or even that it was a good idea for them, or

[8] For an excellent short summary of the problems of two Territory Administrations see Robert Parker, 'The Centre and the Perimeter', *New Guinea*, No. 2, 1967.

their representatives, to run New Guinea rather than the whites and many were fearful that if they did learn, Australians would walk out lock, stock and barrel taking the precious 'cargo' with them.

On the whole, most New Guineans were interested in the idea of a national assembly even if they hadn't much idea of what it was about or what it would do. Candidates stood for a variety of reasons; because they were 'bigmen' in their own area, because they promised the sky in traditional cargo terms and had cargo cult organisations behind them, because of linguistic ties and kinship claims, because of intense prestige rivalry, because they were popular with Europeans in the area or simply because, in a great number of instances, the *kiaps* were accommodating in telling people for whom they should vote. The ostensible substance of campaigning was, not surprisingly, that of more bridges, roads and schools. Those elected were not typical villagers but, as E. P. Wolfers describes them, 'members of what may be termed the local, non-traditional élite . . . men with some sort of favourable association with the post-contact forces of change'.[9] All but one of them were adherents of one or other of the Christian Missions, although the degree of their Christian understanding was questionable, and all but one, who had only his own *tokples,* spoke either Pidgin, English or Motu or sometimes all three. This picture did not substantially change in the 1968 elections although there were a number of younger, better educated, more atypical New Guineans standing.

In the newly assembled House in 1964 collective and individual understanding of national politics, government and the traditional forms of Westminster was generally and understandably low as the statement of the former Member for Ialibu quoted at the beginning of this chapter implies. While Australian Government propaganda was single mindedly directed to telling the Australian public and the world what a splendid representative institution it had created in New Guinea, the political reality behind the transplanted Westminster mystique of

[9] See E. P. Wolfers, *New Guinea,* No. 4, 1968.

mace, wig, Mr Speaker, standing orders and notice papers was sometimes alarming if not comic. Frequently it was both. The new members proved insatiably eager to speak; indeed, prestige depended upon it and so speak they did interminably about roads, bridges, local government and 'economic' development. They generally agreed in sententious terms that it was a good thing that they had all come together from all over the Territory as if this, in some magical way, either disposed of the Territory's multitudinous problems or showed that they knew what the Territory was—or where. They behaved in fact as they might at a picture show or a public lecture waiting to be entertained or instructed as the case might be. Some in their enthusiasm spoke on the wrong subject. All demonstrated that few in Government or Administration had given real thought to any detailed political instruction or education. It was painfully apparent that a few hastily prepared pamphlets and some tours 'down south' for selected indigenes were simply insufficient.

Some members quite obviously thought that the House itself was some super source of cargo which might provide their districts with money, picks, shovels and technical know-how. The failure to prepare politically for the institution of a Westminster parliamentary system—indeed, the failure of a Westminster transplant itself—became increasingly obvious as time went by. The creation of an elected members' caucus with John Guise as Leader of Elected Members was a case in point. The caucus was supposed to channel political demands into articulate form, to act in united members' collective interests and provide some unity of approach on at least major issues. In fact, it clearly revealed the deep divisions of the native members on nearly all the major issues before it ranging from the UN Visiting Missions to the constitutional future of the Territory. Eventually, the caucus could scarcely agree to meet and consult on proposed ordinances and Mr Guise and his Deputy Leader, Mr Matthias To Liman, in effect resigned to allow the offices to be abolished.

In a curious way the demise of the caucus gave individual members the appearance of being freer to express their own views and to express personal idiosyncrasy. The notion of a united elected members' voice on all matters disappeared. It is true that elected members opposed the administration in greater or lesser degree on aspects of the annual Appropriations Bill, but how much the majority of indigenous members have ever understood its provisions or to what extent they regarded them as formally confirming their suspicions that their own electorates would not get any greater share of the spoils is hard to say. Occasionally there was near native unanimity on some issues such as the Income Tax Bill and Mr Paul Lapun's amendment to the Mining Bill. In the income tax measure most natives supported the bill just possibly because they realised the money didn't grow on trees and had to be obtained by some means. More than likely near unanimity resulted from prestige rivalry. No indigenous member would admit that his con-stituents couldn't afford to pay taxes with the best of them. Even more probably their opposition, channelled by European politicians, expressed their desire to be effective despite accumulated frustrations deriving from their inability to under-stand or influence the proceedings of the House. In the case of the Mining Bill, which arose out of the Government's wilful and clumsy handling of the Bougainville copper affair[10] the basic issue was the universally explosive one of land tenure and rights. The amendment was supported by the Highlands bloc as much as by any other group of indigenous members.

The most resistant elements in the House to innovation or threatened change—a state of affairs not unpleasing to, or un-assisted by, some official members—are the attitudes of the Highlands members. Representing the greatest concentration of New Guinea peoples and the most recently contacted, High-lands members are avid of progress which they see almost entirely in terms of roads, schools and bridges. They are deter-mined that Australia shall not leave the Territory until progress has been achieved in these and similar terms.

The progressive reactions of many native members to parlia-mentary politics over four years were very instructive. While the excitement felt by most indigenous members in the early

[10] See Secessionism, end of this chapter.

days of the House had to dissipate, there were other and more significant reactions. Some members became visibly bored by what they could not understand.[11] Others became openly resentful over what they regarded as the 'rubbishing' attitude of the Official Members, yet others were fearful of not being able to take 'something' back to their electorates with them even if it was only an inadequate comprehension of what the whole thing was about. Some showed fear of sorcery in their electorates. Some thought their duty was to 'help' the *gavman*. Most mournfully concluded that what they felt or said made no difference whatsoever to the processes of government—something completely beyond the comprehension of most and certainly beyond the influence of all. Many indigenous members just forgot about their electorates and paid the penalty in 1968 by failing to obtain nomination. Very few actually nursed their electorates as did the ubiquitous, experienced and determined Mr John Guise or Mr Tei Abal.

Similar emotions of frustration must have been felt by the ten Under Secretaries who were appointed from native members of the House. The general notion was they would be understudy 'ministers' in training for the future, probably for the enlarged 1968 House of Assembly. With some of their number fluent and literate in English they were to represent departments not already represented in the House, have access to departmental files, have the right to ask questions and the right to criticise government policies as private members provided they warned the Administration beforehand and did not divulge 'government information'. They were also to be consulted by the Administration on all official policy affecting their departments and in turn would report 'public reactions' to policy to the Administration. There turned out to be very little reality in all of this elaborate parade of Westminster practice. All, at one time or another, complained privately, and some publicly, that they were treated as a nuisance and, that while files were made available on request nobody had the time or interest to 'teach' them what the files were all about. Some complained

[11] See E. P. Wolfers, 'Voting in the House', *New Guinea*, No. 1, 1968.

that when they did offer criticisms they were brushed aside. In addition, most felt that other elected native members never really understood what their delicate position entailed any more than their electorates understood the reasons for their prolonged absences in Port Moresby. The Administration in turn made it clear privately that the job was beyond most of them, that few read the files or tried to understand the complexities of government administration. Some support for this view came from Zure Zurecnuoc, the Member for Finschhafen and Under-Secretary for the Treasury, who said simply that he could never be Treasurer as he simply could not 'comprehend the job'. Mr Simogen Pita, Under-Secretary for Police, told the House on one occasion, 'The Government has made me an Under-Secretary, but I do not know what I am supposed to do and my Department has not shown me . . .' Anxious to progress from the present system, the House voted overwhelmingly to adopt recommendations of the Select Committee on Constitutional Development for an enlarged House of Assembly with sixty-nine open seats, fifteen regional seats (replacing the former specials) and ten official seats. Boredom, disillusionment and, sometimes, resentment—despite all in all some surprising achievements—might have been expected to reveal a different attitude. However they did not.

Partly it was the indigenous members' sense of belonging to an institution larger in horizons than their districts or their villages, partly it was the pleasant thought that they stood a good chance of being returned to an enlarged House—in fact, only nineteen were returned—to receive a salary and living and travelling expenses for another four years.[12] Partly it may have been in some, at least, the embryonic stirrings of a sense of scarcely comprehended nationalism.

Given all the divisions of race and language that stand in the way of the growth of nationalism, which the Australian Government has in many ways striven to maintain, it is scarcely remarkable that nationalist sentiments have not been evident in

[12] Private members receive $3,000 annually, Assistant Ministerial Members $3,500 and Ministerial Members $5,000 and in addition the exclusive use of a chauffeured car.

the House. Nevertheless there are signs that embryonic nationalism is present. One is the increasing use of Pidgin in House of Assembly debates in preference to English or, on the Papuan side, Motu. There is a strong proto-nationalist element in the increasing insistence on its use by New Guineas notwithstanding that its use in the House has been partly a matter of convenience. Most Highlanders and many coastal New Guineans either do not speak English or speak it inadequately. Many Europeans began to use Pidgin in latter sessions simply because they could not get their meaning across otherwise. New Guineans nevertheless did not promote its use entirely as a matter of convenience any more than Papuans retreated on the use of Motu because they wanted to. Political motives were involved.

The increasing use of Pidgin throughout the island, let alone the House, anguishes many academics and many in the Administration on two grounds. In the first place they regard neo-Melanesian as a barbarous language, or scarcely a language at all, and they fear that its increasing spread as a *lingua franca* will have the effect of cutting off large numbers of New Guineans in the future from English—a global language of civilised discourse, technical instruction and the communication of ideas. This is certainly a very serious disqualification to the use of Pidgin but the question remains as to whether English can be successfully substituted in its place. English will undoubtedly be the language of the future educated classes but if the mass of the New Guineans seeking to communicate with each other across the barriers of 700 vernaculars choose Pidgin who is to stop them and, more importantly, could they be stopped?[13] The argument is raised that if New Guineans choose

[13] 'Teach them English, English and more English . . . I would condemn those who do not use English in every teaching technique. There is a crying need for mass education and those who persist in using Pidgin English or "police Motu" are thoughtless or are conceited in thinking they are bilingual—or there may be some wicked enough to wish to slow down the development of the people . . .' (Dr J. T. Gunther, 'The People', a paper delivered to the Australian Institute of Political Science Summer School, January, 1958, published in *New Guinea and Australia*). And yet it was

Pidgin, future New Guinea governments will not only have to deal with a people largely cut off from English but face the cost of translating innumerable technical and other texts into a language allegedly incapable of adequately expressing technical and abstract terms. The same was said of Indonesian at one time but it proved admirably flexible in this regard. English is taught throughout Territory schools and increasing numbers speak it well but one's impression is that Pidgin is going to be the *lingua franca* whether we like it or not, especially if its use has increasing nationalist implications.

The Australian Government has always taken a negative attitude towards the promotion of nationalism in New Guinea. It has never helped to promote, or even impose if necessary, a national flag, anthem, coat of arms and motto as symbols of national unity. It is true that these questions have been the prerogative of the House Select Committee on Constitutional

---

neither thoughtlessness nor conceit that led Mr D. O. Hay, the Administrator eight years later, to use Pidgin in his public addresses in the Territory, but the need to communicate in the one language understood by a large number of people.

The arguments for and against Pidgin continue with unabated fervour although there seems to be a general consensus that Pidgin is slowly winning the battle of becoming New Guinea's only, if territorially still relatively limited, *lingua franca*. Those interested can do no better than refer to the four papers on the subject read at the Council on New Guinea Affairs Pidgin Seminar (Port Moresby, 7-9 March, 1969), by Drs Wurm and Laycock, linguistic specialists in the Australian National University, Mr Geoffrey Smith of the Education Department of the University of Papua and New Guinea and Dr John Gunther, its Vice Chancellor. The papers were entitled 'Pidgin's Progress' (Laycock), 'An Educational Balance Sheet' (Smith), 'English, Pidgin and What Else' (Wurm), 'More English, More Teachers' (Gunther). Briefly, Dr Laycock argued that Pidgin is already established as New Guinea's national language; Mr Smith that this might be so but that the notion that you could have Pidgin *now* followed by English *later* was, from his African experience, a dangerous delusion; Professor Wurm, that there was no alternative for Pidgin which was already becoming a vehicle for nationalist expression and Dr Gunther who argued much as he had done in 1958, pointing out that with sufficient teachers and expenditure English could replace Pidgin for half New Guinea's people within a decade. The papers are reprinted in *New Guinea*, No. 2, 1969.

Development, but in the absence of the conditions that led to the semi-spontaneous emergence of these symbols in Netherlands New Guinea in 1961, assisted by the Dutch Administration, there might be advantage in pushing the committee to further effort in seeking suitable designs. One of the dangers in waiting for symbols of national unity to arise spontaneously is that the differences between people and districts become more firmly entrenched as time goes on and therefore harder to reconcile. It is particularly urgent not only to clear up the status of Papua, for example, but to find a name for the Territory and its people. Mr Oala-Oala Rarua, for instance, suggests that the country be called New Guinea and the people, Papuans. While this idea may be acceptable now, if imposed, it may not be so later on.

However, if the old House was not a focus for nationalism the provision of sixty-nine open seats in the new House at least recognised the communications problems—as had Sir Hugh Foot five years earlier—facing members whose electorates were either very large and sparsely settled or, if smaller, relatively heavily populated. The ten official seats remained the same. The most important change was the translation of the ten Specials into fifteen Regionals, and the replacement of the former Special seat racial qualifications by Regional seat qualifications of an Intermediate Certificate or its Territory equivalent—a piece of paper that still relatively few indigenes in the right age groups possess even at this stage. Only twenty-three members of the former House were returned including four Europeans, three of whom, Messrs A. Voutas, R. Ashton and R. Neville, won Regionals. The total number of Europeans including official members is twenty-eight. The House is now overwhelmingly native in composition and New Guineans comprise not quite three-quarters of the elected members and more than two thirds of the total House.

The most important political development of 1967 was the Constitutional Select Committee proposals for semi-ministerial government for 1968. They were somewhat more conservative than expected and followed on the Committee's visit to all parts of the Territory in which it found that a large minority wanted no constitutional changes until 1972, a small minority wanted far reaching changes amounting to limited self-government by 1968 and that the majority 'maintained an intermediate position . . . wanting a further step forward so that members could participate more in the government'. The Committee recommended reorganisation of the Administrator's Council into an Executive Council comprising the Administrator, three official members of the House and seven elected members who are ministers. The Administrator could also nominate one other member from the House. The Committee recommended that all Council members should hold office at the pleasure of the Minister for Territories and should be appointed by him on the advice of the Administrator. The Administrator is not bound, under Committee recommendations, to accept the Council's advice but merely to report to the House those occasions where he is bound by ordinance to consult the Council and has not accepted its advice. Conservatism indeed!

Under the original proposals there were to be seven members elected from the House as Ministerial Members of Departments who, because of their inexperience, would share responsibility with the respective expatriate Departmental Head of policy and actions. Each Ministerial Member would represent the Department in the House by answering all questions relating to the Departmental views. Any disagreement between Ministerial Member and Department Head would be referred to the Administrator for resolution. In departments not represented by full Ministers, Assistant Ministerial Members elected by the House would work within the Departments helping them prepare bills, answering questions in the House, 'meeting official visitors', helping prepare budget estimates, participating in departmental information and so on. Neither ministerial members, assistant ministerial members nor members of the Executive Council would publicly oppose government policies.

The method of election was to be through the formation of a standing Ministerial Nomination Committee comprising five members of the House. The Committee would consult with the Administrator, agree with him on nominations and submit them to the House for approval. When approved the House would nominate Ministerial Members and Assistant Ministerial Members to the Administrator for transmission to the Minister for Territories for approval. A similar procedure would apply for the termination of a ministerial appointment. The Committee's reply to motions in the House for control by the House over all internally raised revenue was similarly cautious in recommending that the budget should remain indivisible and that members of the Executive Council 'by virtue of their executive duties in the government, would be in the best position to understand, and give informed advice on, budget matters'. It also recommended a Budget Standing Committee elected from within the House comprising elected members in non-ministerial positions which would channel House proposals or criticisms to the Executive Council or relevant department.

Although the Select Committee's recommendations were adopted by the House both House and Committee reckoned without the watchful conservatism of the Minister and his Department in Canberra. In May 1968, a fortnight before the new House convened, the Administrator, Mr D. O. Hay, on instructions from Canberra, announced that the four major policy making Departments of Law, Lands, District Administration and the Treasury would have only Assistant Ministerial Members. While Local Government, Forests, Information and Extension Services, Technical Education and Training, Rural Development and Co-operatives, would have Ministerial Members. The participation of the former, therefore, in the policy aspects of these departments was to be correspondingly reduced. The remaining Departments of Agriculture, Education, Public Health, Labour, Posts and Telegraphs, Trade and Industry and Public Works would carry full Ministerial Members presumably on the grounds that the policy making processes of those departments could sustain the shock of indigenous ministerial activity. Of the major departments to date only Treasury and Lands have Assistant Ministerial Members.

Canberra's decision to exclude Ministerial Members from the chief policy making departments was received with considerable anger by a number of indigenous politicians, especially members of the Pangu Pati and, in particular, by Mr John Guise, Chairman of the Constitutional Select Committee, who had been returned at the elections with an overwhelming majority and elected Speaker of the House. Pangu party members were also angry over other matters, principally the fact that four of the ten official members were serving *kiaps* appointed from the Department of District Administration obviously to reinforce the natural conservatism of the Highlands bloc and to discourage the unwelcome appearance of Highlands 'rebels' if they should emerge.

When enabling legislation was brought down in the Federal House there were other surprises. The Governor-General, in addition to his right of veto over ordinances reserved for his assent received additional power of partial veto. The Government's ostensible argument was probably that by this means ordinances, which were generally acceptable, but contained objectionable clauses, could now be salvaged by use of a partial veto. The answer to this among Pangu Pati politicians was that the power of partial veto would allow the Government to enact bills it wanted without benefit of clauses wanted by elected members.

On 5 June, Pangu Pati's Parliamentary Leader, Mr Michael Somare, a thirty-two years old former teacher and journalist, announced that no members of the Party would accept ministerial posts on the grounds that acceptance would pose a conflict of loyalties between the Executive Council, the business of which ministers had to swear not to reveal, and the Party which, Mr Somare said, wanted to act as a co-ordinated opposition. This decision neither prevented Mr Guise accepting the Speakership of the House, as a solution to his own particular problems of a conflict between loyalty to Pangu or choosing political independence, nor Mr Siwi Kurondo (Kerowagi Open), a Pangu Pati foundation member, from becoming Assistant Ministerial Member for Forests. Mr Guise accepted his nomination, in fact, shortly after a spirited public address in which he claimed that the Government had failed to implement a proper or thorough public programme of political education in the villages, that it had deliberately frightened the people by telling them that independence or self-government meant desertion and that in any case the level of political sophistication in the villages was a good deal higher, and frustrated nationalism a good deal more widespread, than the government supposed.

Nominations for ministerial posts were decidedly conservative even allowing for the fact that the Government was now openly fighting a rear-guard action against too rapid development of radical feeling in the House and among the *évolués*. Of the seven members of the House nominated and approved as full ministers by the Minister of Territories, one was a European, Mr Roy Ashton (East and West New Britain Regional).

The first meeting of the new House was scarcely explosive and indicated how far away nationalistic politics still were while indicating the continuing power of the Europeans to manipulate New Guinea's endemic regionalism. Even though Pangu Pati had shown at the polls that it had retreated a considerable distance from its earlier demands for early home rule, its ten members were obviously the subject of mounting indigenous suspicion in the House. Its atypical solidarity as a Parliamentary party, the relatively skilled debating capacity of its members and their general political sophistication, aroused something between envy and despair in most indigenous members of the House and among European members, apprehension. The result was a determined European-led effort by some fifty members of the House to teach Pangu a lesson. The moment of truth came when Mr Somare moved for a commission of enquiry into electoral procedures—a motion which did not intrinsically lack the sympathy or interest of most members of the House. The House in effect refused to allow Pangu to adjourn debate on the issue and forced the lesson home by obliging Mr Somare to withdraw the motion. The emergence of the Independent Members' Group was an anti-Pangu response. Nevertheless, despite its current setbacks, Pangu's superior skills in the House, its very cohesion in fact, represents the looming shape of coming New Guinea politics—those of the *évolués*. Mass, democratic politics are simply not a reality. In the end, which may be sooner rather than later, where the parliamentary and urban élites go the villagers will eventually follow. For this reason one has to question the wisdom of Mr Barnes on the opening day of the new House, 4 June 1968, in stating that the Federal Government would not necessarily take a resolution of the House of Assembly in favour of self-government as a true reflection of the wishes of the people and that a referendum of the New Guinea peoples might be necessary before Canberra was satisfied.

As a piece of political infighting the Minister's statement had its points. From the government's point of view, at the present stage of New Guinea's political development, self-government is fraught with uncertainties. The majority of New Guineans, especially the Highlanders, at this stage do not want independence and many are frightened of self-government. They would almost certainly vote against it at a referendum especially as most white settlers and perhaps many *kiaps* would probably represent it in terms of Australian desertion.

## The *évolués*

Quite obviously the Government fears too rapid development towards self-government, let alone independence, in a country where communications, in the broad sense, are so undeveloped. Quite obviously, too, the Government would ideally like to see a more general upward levelling on the part of the masses in education, economic capacity and political understanding before moving towards self-government. However, the emphasis in the World Bank Report, and in the Five Year Plan, on the concentration of investment where it will obtain the greatest return in the shortest period of time indicates by its very nature that economic development, and hence political development, will be extremely uneven. The Highlands and New Britain, for example, will do very much better than the Sepik or the Western District. They do now. Both the World Bank Report and the Five Year Plan also emphasise that economic development can only be obtained through intensive expatriate investment and management. While this will result in accelerated economic activity in particular fields it also means that New

Guineans benefit in the role of employees rather than as entrepreneurs. A combination of these factors including growing
land pressure through increasing population must mean an
inevitable growth in political tensions, secessionist tendencies
and considerable problems in maintaining law and order.

For these reasons Australian Governments will understandably tend to restrain, as long as possible, moves towards self-
government which will come primarily from certain types of
politicians and the increasing number of *évolués*. Nevertheless
to insist on a popular referendum before granting self-government runs the risk of frustrating the articulate minorities which
seek active participation in the political administration of the
country and which believe that they can only learn the arts of
government and administration through active involvement. In
any case government ultimately depends upon them. For these
groups self-government or home rule is a first goal. The fundamental error in the current emphasis on gradualism, under-
pinning the Westminster dream, is the assumption that delaying
tactics will ensure that there is sufficient time for the 'bushies'
to catch up with the political urban and semi-urban *évolués*
now beginning to emerge with increasing rapidity, and that
the confrontation between urban radicalism and rural conservatism can be contained in such a way as to strike an ultimate
balance between the two. This is surely unlikely as in the end
the *évolués* will lead the country. There is a point, requiring
nice political judgment, at which it will be wise to allow New
Guinean élites to run their own affairs and manage the
primitive electors of the villages in exactly the same way as the
Australians in New Guinea have done, that is, simply by telling
village electors what is to be done. Expectations that in New
Guinea, Australia has the time and the basic material to repro-
duce institutions and political practices similar to those in
Australia seem increasingly unrealistic. It is true that for some
time to come the average New Guinean will remain dependent
upon Australian aid, skills and presence. But he is increasingly
aware of colour and expatriate domination and the time is
coming when he will listen to his own leaders rather than to us.
If his own leaders become soured by being made to wait too

long for the chance to participate in and ultimately make, real political and administrative decisions, and to accept responsibility for them, their resentments and frustrations will inevitably communicate themselves to the bush electorates and Canberra will have gained nothing.

Who are the *évolués*? Recognisable by their inevitable uniform of shorts, long white socks and black shoes they do not in the strict sense comprise an *élite,* although the term is widely used. As yet, there is no single class of educated New Guineans clearly bound by common political convictions or common frustrations. The wages question is perhaps the only thing to have united them. The parliamentary political sophisticates, for example, include younger New Guinean politicians like Mr Somare, a former schoolteacher and Administration journalist and older New Guinean politicians like Mr Paul Lapun, who taught for many years in a Catholic Mission and Mr John Guise, the Speaker, who was a pre-war Burns Philp *bosboi* and former Police Sergeant-Major who went through the particular mill of mission education and political frustration provided by growing up in Papua and the students.

It is nearer the mark, perhaps, to say that the urban political sophisticates are in the process of being manufactured now. They are the young men, and to a lesser extent, young women, now in secondary school who are being trained for jobs that for many won't be available, either in the Administration, in private enterprise or in self-employed ventures.

The skills of senior school leavers and university graduates will not be sufficient for some time to come to fill the top jobs in administration which quite clearly will continue to require expatriates unless in some quite unpredictable way politics radically change. The World Bank Report noted as far back as 1964 that 'increased educational opportunities . . . create manpower problems as well as progress—it is clear that . . . there will soon be more youngsters aged thirteen and fourteen than can be taken into the training programmes or absorbed into the economy as skilled and partly-skilled tradesmen'. Those youngsters are now seventeen and eighteen. In his 'Development

Planning'[14] Sir Arthur Lewis warns that 'When, as a result of crash programmes, the number completing primary school is raised from 10 to 50 per cent of the age-group, frustration is inevitable.' That percentage now applies to New Guinea. The three year period 1967–70 will see an average increase of 13 per cent per annum in the number of children completing primary schooling, total numbers rising to 17,900 students. About 9,000 of them will seek employment at the end of 1970. It seems likely that there will be a wide gap between the number of available jobs and the number of applicants. The same situation applies to secondary school leavers as 'localisation' of the public service will tend to be slow if mainland administrative standards are persisted with.

Perhaps the most serious warning in this regard comes from the former Director of Education, Mr Les Johnson, now Assistant Administrator (Services), when he told members of the House in 1967 that they 'must realise, too, that the capacity of the country suitably to employ people with higher education is limited.'[15]

Over the next five years those school leavers unable to get the sort of employment they want will in increasing numbers comprise a social and political problem of considerable magnitude. They will almost certainly prefer semi-employment in urban centres to a return to an alien village life which can only offer them unacceptable restrictions and mixed subsistence and cash crop farming as a means of sustenance. Their personal and political frustrations are therefore likely to be considerable.[16]

For these reasons it is unwise to overestimate current student conservatism in New Guinea. Alan Gilbert[17] reported remarkably conservative opinions in a survey of student attitudes in 1967. On the subject of independence, for example, student

[14] Sir Arthur Lewis, *Development and Planning*, Allen and Unwin, London, 1966.
[15] House of Assembly, March 2, 1967.
[16] For a useful examination of the school leavers' problems see W. D. Stent and J. D. Conroy, *New Guinea*, No. 1, 1968.
[17] 'Meanwhile at Waigani', *New Guinea*, No. 4, 1967.

consensus opinion was that 'at least fifteen years must pass before autonomy is feasible.' While conservative attitudes may be true today, they are likely to change when graduates seeking jobs in the Administration or in private enterprise become subject to natural promotion barriers and other restraints. On one level they will be impatient for normal, careerist reasons and on another will wish to hasten the day when they can participate as New Guineans in political decision making.

To some, as for many of the school leavers, it will inevitably appear too, that their education has failed to give them an expected access to power, possessions and privilege. They may therefore turn to more radical politics as a solution to personal problems. A political link between frustrated or impatient 'haves' and the outright 'have nots', like unemployable school leavers, is surely inevitable.

## The Future

It is axiomatic that any metropolitan power will only introduce its own political institutions and assumptions into a colony of radically different racial and cultural composition. This has been true of all the colonial powers. From Africa to Asia the political systems of newly independent countries are a hodge podge of European political institutions and practises tempered in greater or lesser degree by the demands of indigenous culture and custom. In some places the influence of former metropolitan political institutions and expectations has all but disappeared. In others the influence has remained, persistent if attenuated. In no former colony have transplanted institutions long remained unmodified. Often they have been subjected to severe political distortion.

Few countries, one suspects, have transplanted to backward dependencies their political institutions, as has Australia in New Guinea, with such unquestioning belief that they were both suitable and acceptable. While there are now some questions asked as to wisdom of the course being pursued by Australia in New Guinea, the fact remains that nearly three generations of Australian administrators in New Guinea have been concerned with purely Australian solutions to exotic administrative problems. Those engaged in the past administration of the country, but more particularly in the creation of contemporary policy in Canberra, have seen no need to ask the vital question as to whether the nature of imposed political development in New Guinea has been suitable to the culture and people of New Guinea. The indigene has been neither allowed nor really encouraged at the cost of mistakes to participate in grass roots processes of administration. Others have told him what to do in the belief that they had to tell him if he was to become a brown-skinned Australian. He has been told by the *kiap*, by the Local Government Council Officer, by the Co-operatives officer, by the missionary, and by the planter. He has been looked after, cared for and, in a very particular sense, ultimately dismissed by the white administering establishment. Paradoxically the notion that he should now be looked after, cared for and perhaps ultimately dismissed by a black administering establishment is anathema in Canberra. Having run the country on the principle of a necessarily remote, omnipotent, expatriate administration we seem to object to the same principle in respect of an indigenous administration on the grounds that it would prove not only 'incompetent' but 'undemocratic' as well.

In view of the whole range of Australian institutional and public support for the democratic experiment in New Guinea it may no longer be possible for Australian governments to consider political alternatives in New Guinea even though there are clear indications in New Guinea itself that parliamentary democracy is not taking root. In the 1964 elections 72.8 per cent of the total number of eligible voters went to the polls. In the 1969 elections the number had dropped sharply to an estimated 62 per cent. It was immediately claimed by some in the administration and in Canberra that the reduction was due to the growth of greater political sophistication and discernment in the intervening four years; that the naturally apolitical had dropped out including those who had confused voting in the elections which is optional with census registration which is compulsory. The argument of increased sophistication might be true but what sort of sophistication? Disillusionment is a form of sophistication. In areas of long contact, economic frustration and other factors influenced voters to ignore the elections. Voting was very low along the New Guinea coast for example while voting percentages in the electorates in general were in inverse proportion to the length of contact—the longer the contact the lower the number of votes recorded.[18]

While those members returned to the House from urban areas, or from areas of lengthy contact had some knowledge of what politics were about, it was quite apparent on the basis of campaigning, and the criteria governing the election of members in many electorates, that the majority of voters and a very large number of elected members did not. In terms of Australian political practice and expectations the 1964-68 House of Assembly was a failure for electors and elected. The position seems little changed for the new, enlarged House of 1968. A majority of members do not know what they are doing in the House or what is expected of them any more than they can explain its mysterious processes to their constituents or deliver to them anything more in the way of cargo than the Administration is already delivering, e.g., schools, bridges, roads and hospitals. If the House started out by appearing to most electors, and large numbers of the elected, as representing some new and special way to knowledge and possessions, it has perhaps ended up identified with other administrative and political processes in the Territory, as *samting bilong gavman,* in which the whites have the assured answers that come from power and knowledge.

The question at stake is whether in view of all the problems and experience elsewhere we should not be looking at alternatives to the Westminster experiment.

Parliamentary democracy may quite possibly suit New Guineans best, provided that Australia has, say, thirty years left in the Territory with unfettered capacity to keep the brakes on increasingly frustrated élites. Over a long period of time it is possible that with a number of fundamental modifications the currently baffling procedures of Westminster might be accepted,

---

[18] See E. P. Wolfers' revealing diagram, *New Guinea,* No. 4, 1968, p. 22.

accompanied by the sort of grass roots political understanding and participation that seeks, if not guarantees, an independent, incorruptible civil service, that surmounts regionalism, resists fragmentation, observes the rule of law and insists on a non-political army and police force. This involves nothing less than the total transformation of a culture. In New Guinea where the central government has been effectively cut off from village life in all but a narrow range of specific administrative contacts the notion of grass roots participation in 'national' politics remains unreal. While necessarily incomplete, there is a persistent relevance to the likely political shape of post independent New Guinea in George McT. Kahin's 1952 description[19] of politics in Indonesia in 1950. As with Soedjatmoko's description of the basis of Javanese political beliefs, he says, in part, that the central tasks faced by the Republic's leaders after independence were to organise 'a new and effective state administration' to carry out 'an extensive program of socio-economic change' which would require strong government. This involved a 'basic question' as to whether 'it would prove possible to develop such strength while at the same time promoting a democratic system of government. Although the Republic's leaders were sincerely devoted to the attainment of both objectives, some of the most prescient of them feared that the temptation might become strong to resort to authoritarian methods. Kahin refers to 'the still surviving authoritarian tradition' for which, in a New Guinea context we may substitute the tradition established by an omnipotent, expatriate Administration backed by an omnipotent Australian government. Despite Indonesia's 'awakened national consciousness', after independence, 'and the much increased vigor of its political life at the village level, peasant society was still not effectively linked with the national government in a mutually activated and mutually responsive relationship. The existing relationship was still predominantly a one-sided affair—from the top down . . . (*the*) *parties floated as vague shapes above the peasant masses* . . . if the scope of the program which the Republic's leaders

[19] *Nationalism and Revolution in Indonesia*, Ithaca, New York, 1952.

undertook to carry out were too limited, or the pace too slow, they might forfeit their popular backing, and those more disposed to employ more authoritarian techniques might displace them at the helm of government.' What is now needed are native managerial élites of the maximum attainable capacity within the shortest possible time merely to administer the country on a day-to-day basis,[20] working within a government run by tough-minded New Guinean political administrators. The Westminster system at which we are allegedly aiming with its sophisticated notions of cabinet responsibility and separation of powers based upon widely accepted conventions is a long germinating growth and the time does not look to be available.

If Canberra were fully concerned with the atomised nature of New Guinea's society it might conclude that New Guinea will be better managed politically on a Presidential-Congressional system. There are numerous models, including some in Africa based on the separation of the executive, legislative and judicial powers and providing for the election of a President for a fixed term. In New Guinea in the first phase, he might be elected for a four year term by the House from among elected members and perhaps made removable only on a two-thirds majority vote of the House. The President should not be obliged, in short, to resign because of failure to secure passage of a bill.* He should be empowered to appoint as ministers the most able New Guineans and possibly expatriates (but only if they have New Guinean citizenship and the political climate is congenial), from inside and outside the House that he can find. The executive should not be responsible to the House which should have a different role. Elected members should be responsible for interpreting the government's policies to the elector-

[20] The 1968 UN Visiting Mission's *Report*, that mildest of documents, on p. 109, reports that 'some departments may not yet be facing up to the need for a steady increase in the responsibilities carried by local officers'. The Mission recommends fixing a date after which no more expatriate officers are recruited below a certain grade.

* Since writing these lines, Mr John Guise, the Speaker, has publicly voiced similar views. See *The Australian*, 11 October, 1969.

ates and in turn representing the wishes of the people, which will necessarily be inchoate in many instances but nevertheless of supreme political importance to the government. At a later stage the President might be elected by popular vote. A congressional system of government as practised in the United States has its own problems; it can suffer from periods of deadlock between executive and legislature leading to excessive parliamentary irresponsibility. Its advantages lie in the fact that it is designed to obviate party instability especially where there is a multiplicity of parties, (a phenomenon yet to make its appearance in New Guinea), or equally in a situation where there are no real political parties, such as is the case in New Guinea at this stage, and where elected members can do little more than express electoral desires and reactions while looking to a strong executive for guidance and direction. In any case, as we have said, various presidential government models exist and as Mr Paulus Arek, Member for Ijivitari, remarked (at the June 1969, session of the House) in his capacity as chairman of the House Select Committee on Constitutional Development: 'We New Guineans must look at various systems and see what is best for us.' Nevertheless to avoid too insistently begging the question of a constitutional change of direction at this stage we may ask conversely what problems confront us by continuing with the Westminster system, the values of which the Minister for External Territories, Mr C. E. Barnes has so strongly espoused. 'If it is to be persisted with in the evolution of a New Guinea constitution,' writes Mr Justice J. R. Kerr,[21] 'then one of the difficult problems requiring careful and continuous discussion will be the expression in the Constitution of the rules for selecting the Governor-President and the statement of his powers in respect of the dissolution of the House, the obtaining of alternative governments in some circumstances on the defeat in Parliament of a government in office, and the dismissing of a Prime Minister either because of loss of confidence in the legislature or because the machinery of

[21] 'Some New Guinea Constitutional Problems', a paper read to the Queensland Branch of the Australian Institute of International Affairs, June 1969.

parliamentary government is threatened with disruption by the Prime Minister's improper conduct. One problem which is dealt with in some new Commonwealth constitutions is the power of the Governor-President where the Prime Minister is defeated in the House and refuses either to resign or advise dissolution.

'But should the Westminster experiment in New Guinea be persisted with? . . . it may be already almost too late to consider any alternative based on some adjusted Presidential system appropriate to an emerging country. S. A. de Smith refers to the popularity of the Westminster system in the new Commonwealth countries. He says:

> In short, the Westminster model of responsible government has been adopted primarily because it has been persistently and insistently demanded. It has been demanded partly because it is familiar to colonial politicians, partly because they genuinely admire the way it works in Britain, partly because they have sometimes been told that they lack the political maturity to operate it effectively, partly because it makes for very strong government if a single party is dominant.[22]

'If the only risk were what might be done to the classic Westminster model by a strong authoritarian single party headed perhaps by a leader who managed to combine both the offices of Governor-President and Prime Minister in his own person, it might be as well to leave the Westminster developments to take place despite the possibility of ending up with an authoritarian state, though one slightly less authoritarian than might otherwise have been the case.

'Where, however, the risk is of basic political instability in the Legislature due to the lack of a strong party base, with frequently changing governments and frequent elections, alternative systems need investigation. Now is the latest time for doing this because, if the movement along the Westminster path goes much further it may become irreversible, with a real consequential risk of serious political trouble of the kind which

[22] S. A. de Smith, *The New Commonwealth and Its Constitutions*, London, 1964.

invites army intervention and military government such as we have seen in some newly independent governments.

'One reason for preferring a unitary to a federal system is the lack of experienced indigenous leaders to man the more complicated federal structure. Even in a unitary system New Guinea will face a very real shortage of educated and experienced persons to administer at the top level the various departments of government. The electoral process will not necessarily throw up for some time educated or reasonably experienced indigenous people, in significant numbers, as representatives in the House of Assembly. Although in an emerging country like New Guinea many young educated persons may aspire to politics over the next five to ten years it does not follow that many will succeed in getting elected in a predominantly rural country of atomised social groups such as New Guinea. A future cabinet, in the early stages of evolution to self-government and even later, if it is to be found amongst the members of the House of Assembly, may not be able to be put together from literate persons of sufficient political and administrative capacity. In these circumstances and on the basis that the House of Assembly may be politically ill-disciplined, is it necessary for cabinet members to be members of the House, or can a modified presidential system be evolved which would enable a President-Prime Minister to select his cabinet from the available talent outside the House?'

It can not only be evolved, if New Guineans 'wish' it, but it may prove absolutely necessary. On present indications the sort of political talent, necessary to the efficient functioning of a Westminster system, is simply not available in the House of Assembly. For all the reasons advanced in this book, where they concern the fundamental nature of New Guinean social concepts and assumptions, it will not be there for a very long time to come. In the meanwhile, the pace of New Guinea's political development, however disparate, is gathering speed. Despite delaying tactics such as those employed by the official members of the House through the manipulation of the linguistic and regional divisions of the country, there is increasing New Guinean demand, expressed in various ways and at various levels, for greater participation in politics. In short, ready or not in our eyes, they want to run their own affairs in increasing numbers. It is almost certain that the politics of the 1972 elections will concern self-government. In that event it is highly probable that those of the 1976 elections will be about independence. For reasons also advanced there is not a great deal of evidence to suppose that New Guinea will be or can be democratically governed although there is hope that democratic features of government will be retained and perhaps formalised in a written constitution. But on the whole pessimism is more justified than optimism and one is inclined to agree with E. P. Wolfers' observation[23] that: 'It may well be that a division of powers and a neutral judiciary are essential to the existence of democracy, but it may well be that a democratic New Guinea may be an ungovernable one, unless the system of government takes account not only of the formalities of democracy but of the realities of social control, too.' Mr Wolfers was writing in 1965, before the redistributed electoral boundaries and increased number of electorates, but his observations retain their pungency. He goes on to say, 'It might be argued that the present open electorates for the House of Assembly provide for democratic government in the sense that each MHA "represents" a similar number of people, but it may equally well be that many of them represent very little at all except through the accident of where their electoral boundaries happen to have been drawn. Through the accidents of boundary-drawing, many of the electorates represent very little indeed, as many of the most powerful and influential New Guineans . . . were excluded from the legislature either because their appeal is too diffuse, as in the case of a few leaders of the educated elite, or too small quantitatively, if not in absolute power terms, as in the case of the Motu people, or because their particular group was divided up among two or more electorates so "swamped" by other groupings.' Assuming, as a conclusion to the arguments given here, that a modified presidential system is desirable for New Guinea—how is it to be done? Earlier I had written that it should be done if New Guineans

[23] 'Let's Kill All The Lawyers', *New Guinea*, No. 4, 1965-66.

'wish' it. But who are they? The notion of the Select Committee on Constitutional Development consulting the people on change—a delaying tactic of colonialism if ever there was one—is quite ludicrous, however democratic it may sound, for there is simply no criteria by which the villagers of New Guinea can really make constitutional choices. One may as well ask them if they prefer Locke to Montaigne. They may say that they want more self-government or even independence but the various forms will be, for most villagers, remote and incomprehensible. While it is true that when the great figures of American independence got around to constitution making, they expressed deeply felt popular feelings about the liberty of the individual, they did not actually consult the people as to the details or form of the constitution. Neither did the Australian constitution makers in the 'nineties of last century. How could they? In both cases they sought to secure through the constitution certain fundamental political rights and freedoms inherent in Western democracy, that people obviously wanted. But the constitution makers themselves really consulted nobody but each other. There are two ways in which a presidential system could be established in New Guinea. One is to allow the New Guineans to establish it themselves after independence which would mean undoing the whole Westminster structure. On present indications they will probably do this. But would not a second course be far better? To allow the House of Assembly, indeed deliberately stimulate it, to appoint a new Select Committee on Constitutional Development, or enlarge the present one, to include people from outside the House, and charge it with the task of finding and formulating a system of government suitable to an independent New Guinea? This would mean the Committee taking a long period of time, travelling extensively and calling upon experts the world over—even appointing expert sub-committees—to help it reach conclusions and make recommendations to the House. Part of the attraction of a modified congressional system for New Guinea derives from the discomforting assumption that the government of an independent New Guinea will only be relatively democratic, that its civil service will remain neither impartial nor incor-

G

ruptible, that the country itself will tend increasingly toward fragmentation after the Australian withdrawal and that even in the most favourable circumstances it will present unusually difficult problems in the maintenance of law and order. The handling of these problems seems to demand a strong central executive backed by force. If this is true the future role of the army, and to a lesser extent, that of the police force, are paramount to New Guinea's cohesion as a self-governing and ultimately independent state. And so therefore is the focus of army and police loyalties.

Currently there are two battalions of the Pacific Islands Regiment and a third is projected[24] when sufficient training officers and NCO's are available from Australian Army sources. The Army will probably prove an eventually unpopular institution in New Guinea. It is already understandably suspect among many of the newer generation of civil servants and university students which sees it as a possible contender for political power.[25] It is élitist in the sense that it is well housed, well paid and well looked after and in the sense that many of its members regard themselves as 'better men' on the whole than civilians and often display a contempt for 'civil' political processes. It is planned completely to indigenise the PIR and make it the principal security force of the future. In the course of training, all men attend lectures stressing the soldier's responsibilities as a citizen and the role of the PIR as a 'citizen army'. Lectures, and exercises in road and bridge building similar to the 'civic mission' of the Indonesian Army, are aimed at making all members of the PIR aware that the role of the national Army of a future,

[24] There is some evidence that in Canberra there is opposition to the notion of a third battalion on the grounds that a large New Guinea 'army' might get exaggerated ideas as to its future role and powers.
[25] For an indication of some indigenous fears of the future role of a New Guinea Army see Basita Heatu, *New Guinea*, No. 3, 1967, and Kokou Warubu, *New Guinea*, No. 2, 1967. For an equally interesting assessment, among other things of the attitudes of native members of the PIR, see Major Harry Bell, *New Guinea*, No. 2, 1968. Interalia, he says, '. . . nothing less than the standards of a fully qualified Australian will satisfy (indigenes) —an attitude that could breed contempt towards fellow civilian indigenes holding senior government appointments . . .'

independent New Guinea is to be a strictly 'non-political' military force, loyal to the authority of the duly elected and constituted New Guinea government.[26] This emphasis on political neutralism for New Guinea's coming army accords well with Australian preconceptions of the role of the armed forces in a western, industrial democracy, a role painfully hammered out over centuries. Reality may prove very different. More persuasive analogies suggest themselves between what an independent, or even self-governing, New Guinea is likely to be, and Indonesia, than between New Guinea and Australia. Like Indonesia, New Guinea faces future problems in *sukuism* (tribalism), incipient secessionism, in rural drift to the towns and in correspondingly rapid growth of urban political problems and in the resentment of the rich, outlying islands for the greedy mainland.

Future New Guinean governments will face great difficulty in maintaining national unity. In Indonesia the principal instrument by which unity has been maintained has been the Army, which is both a 'political party' ensuring administrative continuity, or internal security, and also a defence force. It is in short intensely political in its activities which it regards as essential to maintaining national cohesion. This is not to suggest that the Army in Indonesia *is* the government. The Indonesian Army has never sought, although it might have been tempted at times, to take over government in Indonesia, but rather to maintain it and to give it the strength to resist internal subversion, e.g. the eventual PKI confrontation. It is *in* government simply because of the weakness of civilian politics. It is also the repository of a wide number of managerial skills and has thus been a stabilising factor in administration in Indonesia. Whether it might one day be tempted to take over government in Indonesia is another matter. It seems doubtful. I once wrote elsewhere that the Indonesian Army, with distasteful memories of its unpopular role in Indonesia's martial law period from 1957 to 1963, has been sharply appreciative ever since of the distinction between 'holding the ring' and 'carrying the can'.

[26] See P. R. Lynch (Minister for the Army), 'New Guinea's Future Army', *New Guinea*, No. 1, 1969.

The New Guinea Army of the future may be no less concerned with the difficult task of maintaining national unity and effective administration and it will be obliged to become a political organisation in order to do so. Under circumstances of rebellion or sporadic secessionism, of which New Britain's and Bougainville's separatists are straws in the wind, it may well be called upon to make tough minded political choices between alternative governments in the interests of national unity. It may very well under some circumstances disavow the legally constituted government of the day in order to support another. While this may sound alarmist, it would be unwise to dismiss the possibility that situations of this sort could arise or that the Australian government might not be in a position to intervene. Given these possible conditions a congressional system with a strong President exercising wide powers might more easily canalise the loyalty of the Army, by sharing the political spoils, than a Prime Minister responsible to cabinet and parliament. These are problems of the future which cannot be wished away simply by adherence to the optimistic belief that Australian parliamentary democracy will take root in New Guinea simply because we wish it.

Canberra is after all very remote from events in New Guinea. Despite government telex, daily telephone conversations and occasional visits to the Territory by the responsible Minister and his officers, it can have little knowledge of the enormous cultural and political problems posed by native understanding and assumptions with which the Administration must grapple each day. It is paradoxical and Australian that as political development in New Guinea slowly gathers momentum, Canberra exerts increasing control over the day to day conduct of the administration by detailed, often minute, instructions. This practice is in marked contrast to that of the British in the past in similar situations in which, within the overall framework of general policy as laid down in the Colonial Office, the colonial governor was given increasing discretion in handling problems of which London could have little knowledge.

Room for great flexibility of administrative and political policy making on the ground exists under the Papua and New

Guinea Act as Mr Justice J. R. Kerr pointed out in his 1968 Roy Milne Lecture—'Law in Papua and New Guinea':[27]

There is, of course, a true state in existence in New Guinea. This is so despite its very numerous stateless societies. This apparatus of the state is superimposed upon the New Guinea societies. It consists of legislative, executive and judicial arms and within the executive are the peace-keeping and law enforcing agencies of the army and the police. The latter have indigenous people in their ranks and some among the officers but they are controlled by and are the instruments of the Australian-dominated Executive. The legislature has a majority of indigenous people and is constructed according to a model which anticipates ultimate though gradual change to the full Westminster scheme. It has so far been effectively dominated by the Australian executive. The New Guinea State as it now exists has been designed in Australia and power within it is still almost exclusively exercised by Australians. This state has not in any sense emerged from indigenous institutions. The stateless societies have no part in it.

A feature of this state system is that it is effectively and in detail controlled from Canberra. Under the Papua and New Guinea Act it is provided that there shall be an Administrator of the Territory, who is charged with the duty of administering the government of the Territory on behalf of the Commonwealth (Section 12). The Administrator is appointed by the Governor-General by Commission under the Seal of the Commonwealth and holds office during the pleasure of the Governor-General (Section 14). Section 15 is as follows—

(15) The Administrator shall exercise and perform all powers and functions that belong to his office in accordance with the tenor of his Commission and in accordance with such instructions as are given to him by the Governor-General.

[27] AIIA nineteenth Roy Milne Lecture, 27 November 1968.

The administrator is also given various discretions and powers under local Ordinances.

However, detailed decisions are made in Canberra, both at the departmental level and at the ministerial level, and the Administrator appears to be under close supervision from Canberra.

This is possible because of the development of techniques for rapid communication between Port Moresby and Canberra but it inevitably causes delay and means that the exercise of executive power within the New Guinea state occurs outside New Guinea. The system has worked well enough in the past whilst a true colonial state of affairs persisted, but as the time for self-government approaches it becomes necessary to reconsider this system and to allow administrative discretions to be exercised, within broad policy directives, in New Guinea itself. Such a change could readily be brought about within the existing legal framework of Section 15 of the Act. If it is to become possible for a local executive to be brought into existence under indigenous control and for the art of politics and administration to be learnt through real experience leading to self-government, the balance of power, on the executive side, as between Port Moresby and Canberra, will ultimately have to be altered. The alternative, involving long-term maintenance of the present system, would add enormously to the difficulties being faced by an emerging political leadership as it comes to see that all the important decisions are made in far-off Canberra.

The gradual evolution of a Westminster system within the legislature, itself almost incomprehensible to most native members of the House, will continue to mystify them when they see detailed executive power on a day-to-day basis being exercised in Canberra.

The Ministerial members under the present system may be learning something about administration and politics and will probably come to see that the views of the New Guinea Administration are often accepted or confirmed in Australia and this may occur more and more frequently with Administration views being increasingly influenced by the Administrator's Executive Council. Ordinary members will, however, continue to be mystified by it all and ministerial and ordinary members alike can hardly fail to see where the reality of power lies.

All this proves that the Australian government does not regard New Guinea as comprising a colonial problem, but as something far more intimately bound up with Australian defence, security and aspirations for a special relationship. There is now a marked inflexibility on the part of the Minister and his department over New Guinea matters notwithstanding that there are departmental officers who are well informed and knowledgeable about New Guinea development. But this sort of knowledge can only be of a general nature and not concerned with the complex nature of cultural and political change in New Guinea itself. Nor is this inflexibility merely an expression of personal convictions.

Despite the very broad powers given the Administrator under the Act it is clear that Australian popular indifference to the real nature of New Guinea problems and the weight of popular assumptions that what we are doing in New Guinea is the best that can be done, make it institutionally very easy for governments to refuse to entertain, even by way of examination and debate, any alternative courses. Any suggestion of a change in direction, especially a radical change, would suggest in public terms that we were preparing for the worst even if it were reasonably to be argued that we in fact were hoping for the best.

On the face of it any real enquiry by government as to the actual nature and ultimate value of what we are trying to achieve in New Guinea, any real recourse to outside criticism especially that of members of the administration itself, seem very unlikely until 'something happens'. It may be that the right course is the present one towards an eventual Westminster parliamentary system. The evidence to date does not suggest this. It suggests that Australian democracy will not take root except under a very long period of tutelage, if ever. It suggests that we might be sensible to look towards 'guided democracy', to a presidential system, to a strong army loyal to a strong,

central executive. While it is true that whatever political structure we leave behind when executive power is effectively in the
hands of New Guineans themselves may not long go unmodified, that should not prevent us, or the government, from
realising that the present system is largely uncomprehended
and possibly unworkable or thinking of modifications—however radical or 'un-Australian'.

## Secessionism

One of the most intractable problems to face an independent
New Guinea government will be secessionism, a potentially
strong, if undirected, force in New Guinea's disparate politics,
as the Bougainville and New Britain confrontations with
central authority demonstrate. The former was precipitated,
broadly speaking, through the disruptive and distorting effects
on a traditional landowning society by the relatively sudden
appearance and monstrous inexplicable demands of twentieth
century industrialism; the latter through the Gazelle Peninsula multi-racial council dispute which has acted as a catalyst
for four generations of resentments and frustrations arising
through a particular contact situation involving early severe,
and so far unredressed, alienation of land.

Copper was discovered at Panguna, in south central Bougainville, in the early 1930's but it was not until 1968, four years
after exhaustive proving operations by Conzinc Rio Tinto of
Australia (Bougainville Copper Pty. Ltd.) and an expenditure
of $16 million, that the size of the ore body was established—
a huge, workable, low grade deposit of 750 million tons of ore
containing 0.47 per cent of copper and 0.4 dwt gold per ton.
With a life expectancy of somewhere between 25 and 50 years,
the mine's exploitation will require $300 million working capi-
tal. As from 1972-73, copper royalties accruing to the Administration, and a later independent government of New Guinea,
will amount to between $1 million and $2 million per annum.
CRA will also commence to pay company tax to Port Moresby
in 1981-82, estimated at somewhere between $30 million and
$50 million yearly depending upon world copper prices. In

addition, the Administration has an option on 20 per cent of Bougainville Copper's shares.* Direct benefits to Bougainville, through CRA and the Administration, excluding those flowing to landowners, include construction of a new town at Arawa, a portside at Loloho, a major all-weather bitumenised road from portsite to minesite in addition to ancillary roads, power and fuel storage installations, schools and a major base hospital. Over the years in rising levels of skills, hopefully at all events, hundreds of New Guineans will be employed in various categories in replacement of expatriates.[28] This is a brief and incomplete summary of the Administration case over Bougainville—an unexceptionable blue print for western conceived 'development' and undoubtedly essential to New Guinea's future economic viability. But Bougainville is not so easily susceptible to this sort of rationalisation. Discovered by the French explorer of the same name some twenty years before the First Fleet sailed into Port Jackson, it has had a long and mostly unhappy history of European contact. It was a blackbirding source in the nineteenth century. In 1898 Britain detached it from the Solomons, with which it has distinct geo-biological and ethnic ties, and traded it to Germany in return for withdrawal of German claims to Tonga and other areas. The Germans added it to the Bismarck Archipelago for administrative purposes. Some Bougainvilleans know about the exchange and resent it in a vague fashion.[29] The people are mostly blue-black Melanesians and in south Bougainville have kinship and trading ties with the black Melanesians of the Shortlands and the Solomons. Before the Pacific War, Bougainvilleans (Bukas) were much sought after as plantation labour throughout New Guinea. The post war development of cash cropping, especially in cocoa, on their rich, Gauguinesque, volcanic island has

* Taken up by the Administration 14 November 1969.

[28] There is an additional aspect to the CRA problem on Bougainville, examined with considerable insight by R. G. Crocombe in *New Guinea*, No. 3, 1968. What happens when the copper is finished? Bougainvilleans will be left, in my own words elsewhere, 'with the second biggest hole in the world.'

[29] See 'Down Kieta Way' by Leo Hannett, a Bougainvillean student, *New Guinea*, No. 1, 1969.

meant that they now travel far less. Much of Bougainville's own plantation labour is in fact Highlands. In general Buka people do not like mainland New Guineans, especially Papuans, of whom they use the descriptive racial term, 'redskins'. Brown New Guineans cordially reciprocate the compliment by calling them, *arse bilong sospen* (saucepan). During the German regime—missionaries settled in Kieta in 1902—and in the ensuing Australian one, Bougainville was comparatively neglected and there was little development. Such as there has been was consequent upon CRA's coming to the island.

In German times there were numerous and frequently savage punitive expeditions mounted from Kieta. Contact and control were limited. Between the wars the Australian writ did not run very far back into the mountains—the long, narrow spine of the Crown Prince Range which runs down the centre of the island—and were seldom visited by more than one or two patrols a year. Control was more in name than in fact even by 1941. The Japanese occupation brought with it the usual complicated background of shock, payback, cruelty and exposure of the myth of white supremacy. Some Bougainvilleans accepted the new *mastas*, others fought them. Apparently in the southern part of the island the Japanese actually attempted to conduct schools with indifferent success but one occasionally meets a Bougainvillean who recalls them with a wistful, reproachful gratitude.

It is difficult, perhaps impossible, to pinpoint where and how the Bougainville crises began. There was, as there always is, the problem of understanding, involving not only the difficulties of linguistic communication but those of differing cultural assumptions. Pidgin is widespread on Bougainville but at best is a *lingua franca* incapable of conveying the exact meanings of the vernacular and there were bound to be misunderstandings when *kiaps* tried to explain what CRA was trying to do and what it would mean. In the second place, at a later stage, there were bound to be misunderstandings over CRA's promises of schools, roads and medical services which would involve the New Guinean's concept of giving. His pleasure at the thought of hospitals, roads and schools which he craves is not without ambivalence. Giving, as we have seen earlier, is a method of imposing obligations on others. Where the gift given to a person is reasonably commensurate with his capacity to repay, in goods or services, a state of reasonable equilibrium is created between giver and recipient. Huge or culturally immeasurable largesse, however welcome, may impose a repayment obligation which it is impossible to meet, arousing deep anxiety and consequently even deeper hostility in the recipient.

In the third place, there was the problem of land, which to the New Guinean is not only an economic asset, received from past generations, but the ancient source of being. The minesite people probably did not understand what was required of their land and quite possibly still don't, believing it to be on loan or to be returned. I have spoken to Bougainvilleans with customary claim to an area through which the major CRA road will pass. They quite patently believe that they own the portion of road traversing their land.

There were also political mistakes. The early and unheeding insistence of the Minister, Mr C. E. Barnes, that all royalties must in conformity with British practice accrue to the crown, led to a political crisis which was solved only by an amendment to the mining ordinance introduced by the persistent and intelligent member for South Bougainville, Mr Paul Lapun. Through this five per cent of the royalties, in addition to normal occupation fees and compensation, were paid to landowners in the minesite area. Approximately 1,000 of these people will now receive $100,000 annually for the next forty-two years. But while they appeared to become reconciled, other native landowners were not, namely the Arawas (650 acres of whose undeveloped land added to 1,000 acres of the highly developed Arawa Plantation belonging to Mr Kip McKillop, were wanted for a permanent townsite) and the Rorovanas (145 acres of whose land were required on a forty-two year lease, firstly as a construction campsite for CRA workers and at a later stage, as a possible site for smelting ore concentrate prior to shipping overseas). The first move was made by the Administration which, after a great deal of hard negotiation under threat of compulsory acquisition, forced Mr McKillop to sell Arawa Plantation, an old German freehold property, which contributed $500,000 annually in copra and cocoa to New Guinea's export income. Mr McKillop finally reached an agreement in August 1969 whereby he was paid $600,000 in cash of which $200,000 was placed in trust against fluctuations in cocoa price movements over the next five years. His world famous orchid collection was valued separately as were other improvements to his beautiful estate while a productivity panel is to determine actual productivity over the next five years. In all probability he will receive close to $1 million for the estate. At the time he was finally closing with the Administration the Arawas were manifestly reluctant to part with their land and the Administration was on the point of serving known landowners with notices to treat, a prelude to compulsory resumption.

At the same time it was seeking to lease the Rorovana land. The Rorovanas comprise Rorovana Village No. 1 and No. 2. Most people in Rorovana No. 1 wished to lease the land. Most in Rorovana No. 2 did not. This made the problem of general Rorovana agreement extremely difficult. At the expiration of the lease, the land will revert to the Rorovanas who may extend the lease if the land is still needed; Arawa land will be permanently alienated. In the event, the Rorovanas refused to lease their land—for which they were being offered $105 an acre plus individual tree compensation and other compensation and new land—and the Administration unwisely sought compulsory leasing, sending police to occupy the land and use force and tear gas to eject angry landowners. There was a pause in activities while a visit was made to Australia by Mr Paul Lapun and Mr Ralph Bele, a Rorovana landowner and former schoolteacher, who, with the active guidance of members of Moral Rearmament, had interviews with CRA executives, the Prime Minister, Mr J. G. Gorton, and the Minister for External Territories, Mr C. E. Barnes. The upshot of the visit was that CRA made a direct offer to the Rorovanas that in addition to the price offered per acre it would plant undeveloped Rorovana land to the same number of coconut trees, 3,000-5,000, and supply the people with free coconuts, to the same number as the annual harvest, for a period of ten years—three years beyond the period when the new trees would be bearing. The Rorovanas were plainly not interested and negotiations continued. Then, unexpectedly, one of those strangely fortuitous events occurred which changed the whole scene. Some time in 1968 the Administration had purchased about 100 acres of St Michael's, a Roman Catholic mission, between Kieta and Aropa airport, comprising choice flat land, at about $450 an acre. In the first week of September the Administration inexplicably, in view of its anxieties over Rorovana, sold the land to private bidders at sums believed to be close to $2,000 an acre.

Apparently the Rorovanas or their advisers took the hint. The Rorovanas agreed to negotiate on the basis of an annual rental of five per cent of the unimproved capital value (normal practice) which they estimated at $2,000 an acre. They eventually settled at a valuation of $1,000 an acre. CRA's offer at this stage of negotiations was to pay the Rorovanas approximately $7,000 per annum (145 acres x $50) for forty-two years (with the possibility of a renewed lease at the end of that time) plus—$30,000 in compensation, 7,000 Bougainville Copper Pty. Ltd. shares and new houses. It was agreed that the leased land would be revalued every seven years. At the time of writing the deal had not been formalised as not all the necessary Rorovana signatures had been fixed to the agreement between the two parties. The effects on the Arawas have yet to show themselves. Although Arawa land is undeveloped, there is more of it, but more importantly, it is to be alienated permanently, which will undoubtedly lead the Arawas to seek a higher price. After the Administration's backdown over seeking compulsorily to enforce the lease over Rorovana and the Federal Government's urgent pre-election inspired endorsement of direct CRA-Rorovana negotiations, it would not be altogether surprising if the Administration sought to avoid the political dilemmas inherent in compulsory acquisition of Arawa land and again left direct negotiations to CRA even though the Administration is the purchaser of the land. The eventual settlement may involve high prices. At all events, the escalating

prices paid for land on Bougainville, either for lease or purchase of land, are bound to have an effect throughout New
Guinea on all native landowners whose land is needed for
development.

However, in so far as Bougainville is concerned, it is possible
that indigenes who have already sold land, however favourable
the prices, will feel free to seek readjustment in the prices paid
and that, in fact, some of them do not necessarily believe that
their land has either been permanently sold or is on long lease.
Among New Guineans living in areas where there has been
ruthless, early alienation of land, as in Rabaul and the area
around Madang, there is not only a sense of deprivation but
the firm belief that the land still rightfully belongs to their
people.

The relatively very high prices paid to Bougainville landowners together with other benefits accruing to them from
the copper project, are undoubtedly a big element in secessionism. Combined with Bougainvilleans' general dislike of mainland New Guineans, especially Papuans, the ethnic ties between
South Bougainvilleans and some Solomonese and their general
long contact dislike of *gavman*, there is now the sense that they
would like to keep the benefits of the copper operation, about
which they are otherwise so ambivalent, for themselves.
Bougainville's wealth may well spark a viable independence
movement. If Nauru has its phosphates . . .

In New Britain secessionism is probably more developed
although, as on Bougainville, it is a feeling, a growing sentiment, rather than an articulated plan of political action. The
current multi-racial council dispute has tended to bring secessionist feelings more strongly into evidence although a year ago
there was considerable support among some Tolai for the
Melanesian Independence Front, a political organisation, white-
managed, which advocated an eventual 'federation' of the
main islands of Manus, New Ireland, New Britain and Bougainville. The multi-racial council dispute has ostensibly arisen
over the Administration's determination to keep the Gazelle
Peninsula Local Government Council multi-racial (there are
87 multi-racial councils in Papua/New Guinea) in accordance

with the Council's own original decision—and to extend the
franchise to an additional 5,000 Tolai (of whom there are
60,000 in the Gazelle Peninsula) and to European and Chinese
planters and businessmen in the area who would swell the
council's coffers by paying council taxes. The dissident Tolai
have formerly resolutely opposed inclusion in the entirely native
run council. In fact those under council jurisdiction have
always objected to the fact that they have paid tax while those
outside council jurisdiction have not. Opposition to the multi-
racial council, of whose sixty members three are Europeans and
one Chinese, was led by the articulate Mr Oscar Tammur,
Member for Kokopo Open, who headed a large protest march
in May 1969. His campaign against the council was apparently
so effective—the Administration claimed it was intimidatory—
that when Council elections were held, of 24,000 eligible voters
less than 7,000 polled, although one could not infer from this
how many non-voters were necessarily anti-council. After the
Administration's decision on 15 May that the council had
already in fact been lawfully established, despite a Council
resolution reversing its earlier decision, Mr Tammur formed
an anti-council organisation, the Mataungan Association,
pledged to resist the inclusion of non-indigenes in the council.
The Administration claims, with some justification, that the
Mataungan Association has failed to argue its case democratically by contesting it at the polls but has resorted to threats of
violence and to intimidation. While this may be true it ignores
very real apprehensions on the part of many Tolai that a multi-
racial council will be captive to superior Chinese and European skills. One result of Mataungan activities is that only half
normal council tax has been collected. Matters came to a head
in September, 1969, when in answer to increasing threats of
violence over the Council, the removal of heavy geodetic
survey pegs and the unlawful closure of the Council chambers,
the Administration moved 1,000 armed police to Rabaul with
riot trucks, set up road blocks and used a chartered helicopter
to spot native ground movements, even those in outside villages,
which it radioed to police. Administration fears of violence
were genuine enough and probably well founded as they had

been over the Rorovana affair. At the time of writing the Administrator has agreed to a House of Assembly recommendation to appoint a Committee of Enquiry whose composition is unknown, but may hopefully include overseas members with African or Pacific experience.*

Causes of Tolai unrest are many and varied. The chief one seems to be that the Tolai, more advanced and better educated than any other people in New Guinea, are suffering from a severe land shortage combined with a rapid increase in the birth rate.

More than 40 per cent of Tolai land has been alienated, mostly in German times but also in post World War One Australian times, the greater part of it the best land available. As far back as 1912 land was so short around Kokopo, German administrative headquarters, that the administration found it difficult to obtain land on which to erect government buildings.[30] The rich volcanic soils of the Gazelle Peninsula have been sufficiently productive until recent times to offer the Tolai a comparatively good living from mixed subsistence and cash crop farming. Today, with an annual 3.8 per cent increase in the birth rate, there is urgent need for land. While the Administration is seeking to buy back estates for Tolai subdivision it is inadequate for Tolai needs and increasing numbers of Tolai are beginning savagely to resent unused alienated land and past alienations. Some will seek redress through the courts for alienated land originally purchased at bushranger prices and others are actually threatening violence. There are other contributing factors to current resentment, chief among them a power struggle between older, prestigious, generally more *gavman* oriented elders and younger, better educated, frequently jobless radicals with increasing political aspirations.

It is in situations like this that separatism has its beginnings,

---

* In the event the Commission comprised two Tolai, one a bishop and the other a student, and as chairman, a Brisbane Q.C. Their report was released in mid-November, 1969, and resulted in a 7,000 strong Tolai protest march in Rabaul and a number of tough, anti-Administration speeches threatening 'civil war.'

[30] Scarlett Epstein, op. cit.

although the point of time at which resentments and aspirations of the sort mentioned above become politicised in a cohesive separatist movement is almost impossible to predict. In September 1968, in Port Moresby, twenty-five Bougainvilleans, including the two open electorate members, signed a petition to the Administration demanding a referendum in Bougainville in 1970 to decide whether it should remain part of Papua/New Guinea or become independent with or without including the Solomons.[31] This may be the shape of things to come.

The most frightening, and at the same time perhaps the most hopeful, implication of the Gazelle Peninsula affair, is the alternatives it poses emerging, youthful, Tolai élites. Are political solutions to political problems to be sought through the ballot box or by threats, and perhaps the actual use, of violence? The way in which the Tolai solve their problems will have a profound effect on New Guinea's other élites. At the same time the confrontation of Administration strength and Tolai 'intransigence' begs an entirely different question as to whether the government is wise deliberately to seek confrontations—the Administrator's decision of 15 May insisting that the Gazelle Local Government Council remain multi-racial despite known, strong opposition to it, even if only from an influential minority, is a case in point—when it may not have the resources and the will to carry through with tough methods. Just how many police are available to cope with a Gazelle type situation breaking out in five different centres, spontaneously or at some point in time, by design?

This is not yet a real problem, but it is incipient and may become as real as it has been, and to a large degree remains, in Indonesia where a strong, Javanese-dominated, centralist oriented army has been the major factor in maintaining national unity. Another element in Indonesian unity has been the relatively large number of men and women, of varying ages, in whom common interests, a common language and shared nationalism have been sufficiently strong to resist the

31 Leo Hannett, op. cit.

regional ties of their particular ethnic origins. It is here, perhaps, that New Guinea's best hopes of cohesion lie—in the
schoolteachers, the doctors, the engineers, the lawyers, in short,
in the members of the élites who intermarry across linguistic
lines, whose children have no *plestok* but speak English and
perhaps Pidgin, and whose self-interest as well as their ideology
will be best served by national unity. Their problem will be,
even if they have the desire, to participate in the politics of the
regions from which they come, seeking to influence them along
nationalist lines. Their weakness may be that they will become
increasingly divorced from their regional origins, their local
languages and their clan ties, finding their identity in a new
tribe—a relatively well paid but remote bureaucracy. In Indonesia nationalism by and large has been strong enough to cut
across regional loyalties. In New Guinea there is no nationalism.

Who then can maintain national unity in New Guinea? If,
as is quite possible, there are serious secessionist movements in
the islands in the post-independence period requiring police or
military action, the Australian Government of the day may
have no inclination and may be in no position to take action
involving white soldiers and brown New Guineans even at the
request of a friendly, independent New Guinea government.
This leaves only New Guinea's own security forces, the police
and the army. While they may have no qualms in putting
down a rebellion, say, in Bougainville or Manus, they will not
be numerically strong. Secessionism under these circumstances
may well prove almost impossible to stop, especially if it should
occur spontaneously in more than one area at the same time.

After all, the people of the outer islands with varying degrees
of sophistication are aware of the insular nature of their homes,
of the seas that separate them from the mainland. They are
also aware that while they may dislike each other they probably dislike mainland New Guineans more, especially Papuans.
They are increasingly aware that the four main island groups
produce more than 60 per cent of New Guinea's export income.
When Bougainville's copper is added to island agricultural produce the figure will be nearer to 90 per cent. There is also a
tendency to regard Port Moresby as a distant, hungry capital

which takes their produce but gives far too little back. An increasing number resent paying out for their more unfortunate 'brothers' in the Sepik, in the Western District or in the Southern Highlands. In fact there is a growing similarity between the attitudes of the people of the islands to Port Moresby —the productive periphery and the greedy centre—and those of the people of Sumatra and Sulawesi to Djakarta, just as New Guinea's Highlanders may become as distasteful and threatening, because of their relatively vast numbers, to the people of the islands as the Javanese appear to the people of Indonesia's outer islands. This is not yet a real problem but it may become one slowly. It will certainly be a very real problem after independence, as big a one as secessionism has been in Indonesia where at least a strong Javanese-dominated army has been able, if at times barely, to maintain national unity. It would also tend to invite foreign meddling. At the very least it would be a threat, in ways difficult to predict in all their consequences, to the peace and stability of the south-western Pacific area. There may be a case, therefore, in beginning to think seriously now, rather than later, of the benefits as well as disadvantages of deliberately promoting secessionism in Bougainville, New Britain, New Ireland and Manus with a view to forming some loose federation or union. It might prove best in Australia's national interests, and in those of New Guinea, deliberately to seek separatism and start building on it. Certainly it would be easier for an Australian government to promote it before independence comes, in the hope of building more stable political units, than it will be for a sovereign New Guinea government to contain it after independence comes.

Quite apart from the fact that the suggestion that we should deliberately fragment New Guinea, runs counter to Australia's political culture—Australians, after all, are overwhelmingly homogeneous, with one language, who comprise in fact the only nation in the world to inhabit an entire continent and who adopted a federal political structure to deal with their own political problems—it simply may not work in practice. The island peoples might not accept each other any more readily than they accept mainland New Guineans. It would mean setting up a federation perhaps something like the Caribbean Federation which broke up in a relatively short time. It would mean creating a separate government, civil service, customs, police and security forces. It would mean dividing the Australian grant in two, one subsidy for mainland Papua and New Guinea and the other for an islands federation. It would prove costly and politically difficult, not only in Australia and in New Guinea but in finding ways of creating a separate dependency [destined for independence] within the Trust Agreement under which New Guinea is administered. It would mean carving up the present Papua-New Guinea local officer bureaucracy and coming to special arrangements about schools, technical and agricultural colleges and the university. It would raise special difficulties for business companies with New Guinea wide interests. It would mean having to unscramble the omelette, which is not easy. Not least it would almost certainly create great resentment among mainland New Guineans —at all events the politicians, civil service and student *élites* —who would see the principal sources of New Guinea's income disappearing over the horizon. There is also the problem of *how* it could be achieved; especially if the House of Assembly, in defiance of established Canberra policy to allow separation, refused people in the outer islands the right to a referendum on the issue or, if feelings were strong enough, the unilateral right to secede. Thus while secessionist feelings in Bougainville are quite strong and likely to grow stronger, the island's three members of the House are simply not numerically strong enough to force the issue. In alliance with the other islands' six members for open electorates and two members for regional electorates however, they would be arguing a different sort of case from a position of relative strength—that of the 11 members representing the New Guinea Islands electorates.

However if the sum of island peoples' interests proves greater than that of their differences then neither the Government nor interested Australians should dismiss the idea simply because it runs counter to our normal political grain.

The gravest problem in a secessionist, separate state comprising the present New Guinea Islands is that it may in turn fragment. Bougainville might almost certainly secede from it unless, at some later stage, the Solomons were not included. As it is, 'political' feeling in Bougainville is not as responsive to the notion of some form of political amalgamation with Manus, New Ireland and New Britain as it is to the notion of union with the Solomons, and even that sentiment is mostly confined at this stage to more populous south Bougainville.[32] There is also the problem of what form such an amalgamation should take. If Papua/New Guinea should at independence comprise its present territorial boundaries one can see little hope of it remaining intact under a federal structure which has been suggested in some quarters. Quite apart from the relatively enormous costs of a federation, only a unitary state, its army at the disposal of a strong central executive, could possibly cope with post-independence fragmentation as Indonesia discovered in its post-independence stage when it dissolved its Dutch-inspired federal structure. An independent state comprising the outer New Guinea Islands might, on the other hand, comprise some federal structure on the grounds, stated above, that the sum of the interests of the member island states would hopefully be greater than the sum of their differences—even if for a long time to come, only just. On New Britain, for example, there is a rankling traditional dislike between the people of East and West New Britain. However the principal factor in inter-island unity may prove to be the more or less unanimous and growing dislike of Port Moresby, not only as a disagreeable town in detested Papua, but as a symbol of future mainland domination. This dislike is shared fairly equally among blacks and whites, for more or less the same reasons of economic and political self-interest, and extends even to many missionaries, especially Catholics, who tend to see the eastern islands as a religio-temporal unit. Indeed it is. The ecclesiastical jurisdiction of the Archbishop in Rabaul extends to the Solomons.

One of the probable advantages of a two island state policy is brutally practical. It might make mainland Papua and New Guinea dependent for a longer period on Australian aid and

[32] Leo Hannett, op. cit.

skills. The longer the time the better the political structure we can leave behind, provided we use the time to do that and not merely to extend and prolong the present style of Australian administrative control. Nor does the suggestion that two separate New Guineas, a unitary mainland state and possibly some form of outer island federation, preclude the possibility that the two might come together again in the future although this is unlikely. Separation of this sort tends to set in train, or confirm, attitudes that harden with time. There is little doubt that a unitary state of New Guinea comprising its present boundaries is for many reasons preferable to two states with the risk of further fragmentation. However as fragmentation may be inevitable after independence, [or the threat of it so severe a strain on central government political resources and morale] we will be wise to examine the possible benefits of allowing, or promoting, secessionism well beforehand, especially if it should appear to provide the basis of more viable political entities.

However any tendency to fragmentation in New Guinea carries unpredictable problems. The future of Papua is one such. One of the more unpleasant possibilities that must occasionally haunt anxious External Territories officers is the thought that one day a Papuan, resident in Australia for one purpose or another, will stay beyond the duration of his permit and refuse to go home on the grounds that he is an Australian citizen, as distinct from a New Guinean who is an Australian Protected Person.

However while such an event would cause the Government acute political embarrassment, especially if there were High Court injunctions and appeals, the fact seems to be that Australian citizenship is separate and distinct from a person's status. Latham C.J. in O'Keefe v. Calwell, 77 CLR, (p. 271) says: 'There is nothing in either the Immigration Act or the Nationality and Citizenship Act which shows that the inclusion of a person within the class of Australian citizens affects the application of the Immigration Act to that person.' The 1958/ 1966 Migration Act, which superseded the Immigration Act, applies the same principle. In short, a Papuan without a valid permit to be in Australia is probably a prohibited migrant and liable to deportation.

Papua's position as an Australian Territory, and that of its people (ranging from Hanuabada sophisticates to Southern Highlands primitives, all of them Australian citizens with no automatic rights of entry into Australia) is anomalous. The Federal Government has never moved to change Papua's status, as an intermediate and necessary step towards Papua/New Guinea independence, because, apart from legal considerations successive Cabinets in the past may always have had lingering doubts that Papua might have a different destiny from New Guinea, or they may have been too lazy and lacking in foresight to do anything about it. The situation is now different. In view of increasing signs of fragmentation in New Guinea and because of the increasingly dominant position of the New Guinea Highlanders, whom they fear along with New Guinea coastal people, many Papuan sophisticates are tending towards the view that Papua might be better off in the same constitutional relationship with Australia as it now has. Undoubtedly behind this sort of thinking is the ultimate hope that Papua can become Australia's seventh state. Any Australian government whose policy is unequivocally that of independence for Papua/New Guinea, and which seeks to avoid the complications of New Guinea's continued dependency upon Australia, commits a tactical blunder by leaving Papua's legal status as it is now. Papuan sophisticates continue to hang on to their special status as Australian citizens, discriminatory though it is, with a special and fearful nostalgia mixed with anger and resentment for there is no doubting that many Papuans feel different from New Guineans because of their special status and that many believe that it in some special way affords them protection. The longer Papua remains a Territory of Australia and the greater Papuan fears become of being 'done over' by New Guinea, the more difficult it may prove for an Australian government to cast Papuans off by changing their legal status.

# 6 West Irian

'. . . the territory of our state comprises the entire former Netherlands East Indies . . . from Sabang to Merauke. Thus . . . Irian is also Indonesian territory.'

President Soekarno, 17 August 1950

'I tell you it can be done to make a single country of New Guinea from Sorong in the west to Samarai in the east.'

Nicolaas Jouwe, April 1961

'. . . effective security conditions (in West Irian) are likely to require many things besides economic development and modest improvements in consumption. Security also depends on widened participation, including expanding opportunities, for the local population in the decision-making structure, and responsible, selective and effective use of the instruments of control by a locally based and locally manned force, whether police or military.'

A Design for Development in West Irian, the FUNDWI Report, November 1967

Before World War II, Netherlands New Guinea was a lonely, Dutch colonial outpost administratively under the *Governement* of the Moluccas, which comprised part of the *Provincie* of the Great East formed in 1938 to govern all Dutch territories east of Madura. West New Guinea's administrative headquarters were in Manokwari. In 1946 the territory became a separate *Residentie* with administrative headquarters at Hollandia where the Americans had left a huge wartime infrastructure.

In Djakarta in May, June and July of 1945, prior to the declaration of Indonesian independence, there were several meetings of the BPKI (Body to Investigate Indonesian Independence) which discussed the territorial limits of the new state. Some territorial claims put forward by members like Professor Mohammed Yamin were extravagant versions of old but tenuous historical links with Javanese outliers. One, supported by Dr Soekarno and passed by thirty-nine votes out of sixty-four, included in addition to the entire territory of the Netherlands East Indies, British North Borneo, Brunei, Sarawak, Malaya, Portuguese Timor and 'New Guinea'.[1] Definitions of New Guinea were imprecise. To Dr Hatta it meant specifically Dutch New Guinea, which he was in any case inclined to leave to the 'Papoeas'. Dr Soekarno, in somewhat ambiguous terms, apparently referred to all of New Guinea when he used the word Papua. At all events the decision of the meeting was clearly that as Netherlands New Guinea formed part of the NEI, to which Indonesia was the successor state, it therefore clearly came under the jurisdiction of the new Republic of Indonesia.

Thus, by 1950, as Herbert Feith[2] says

Irian was in a sense the same kind of cause that unification had been earlier. It was directly related to the central values of nationalism. It was something on which nearly everyone agreed (indeed, more so than on unification). It enabled issues to be focused in terms of Indonesians versus enemies of Indonesia, thus rallying all-Indonesian sovereignty. It provided a central leadership role for 'solidarity makers'. And it helped to absorb some of the restless energies of former revolutionaries who wanted to be active participants still in a political movement (and who threatened to give their support to anti-governmental organisations if the government did not offer them outlets.)

But, like the unification issue, the Irian issue was also in an important sense divisive. Its divisive effects within the political élite were in fact a central aspect of the issue. Indeed, all groups in Indonesian politics were committed to the 'national claim,' and all favoured the inclusion of Irian in the Republic by 27 December. But there were important differences between groups in intensity of their commitment and the political reasoning that lay behind it. For Soekarno and other 'solidarity makers' whose nationalist convictions provided them with their most strongly held

[1] Brian Beddie, 'Indonesian Attitudes', *New Guinea*, No. 3, 1965.
[2] Herbert Feith, *The Decline of Constitutional Democracy in Indonesia*, Cornell University Press, 1962.

views, the Irian claim was intrinsically of great importance. At the same time it served to provide them with a cause in which they were peculiarly well placed to provide leadership. For the 'administrators' who dominated the Natsir cabinet and who tended to place less value on the symbols of national unity and national identity, the intrinsic importance of the claim was not as great. But the current temper of nationalism demanded that they establish a vigorous 'me too'-ism. Their response to this demand found its rationalisation in their belief that only after the Irian issue was settled would it be possible to proceed with the practical administrative and economic tasks they regarded as all important.

Professor Feith's description of general attitudes to the Irian question were to pertain, by and large, throughout the ensuing years with one important qualification. In the period he was describing the PKI (Communist Party of Indonesia) was split between two wings, the older established of which, in line with the Dutch Communist Party, opposed Indonesia's claims to West Irian and the wing containing the younger, rising stars like Aidit, Njoto and Lukman which feared taking too strongly a 'negative position on a popular nationalist claim.' In the ensuing years under Aidit's leadership the PKI supported and urged the return of West Irian to the Republic. As the years went by, too, the emphasis on symbols of national unity and national identity became all pervading and in inverse proportion to the decline in administrative capacity and of pragmatic values. In the end West Irian was an *idée fixe* in 'A period of collective hypnosis. Thus Adam Malik . . . recently characterised the Soekarno era in his country. The climate came closer and closer to madness, yet an old discredited politician, quoting Hamlet, remarked "how much System there was in this Madness." '[3]

In West New Guinea itself there was an early pro-Indonesian Papuan organisation, the PKII (*Partai Kemerdekaan*

[3] J. M. van der Kroef, 'Sukarno, the Ideologue', *Pacific Affairs*, No. 2, Summer 1968.

*Indonesia Irian*), founded by Silas Papare who, along with Frans Kaisieppo (the present Governor of West Irian), Johan Ariks[4] and other West New Guinean mission-educated leaders attended the Malino Conference in the Celebes in 1946, at which some Papuans took a pro-Indonesian line and others a pro-Dutch one. It was Kaisieppo who first employed the word Irian, a Biak word meaning 'hot place', to describe the mainland and as an alternative to West New Guinea or West Papua. At the following conferences between the *de facto* Indonesian government and Holland, at Pangkalpinang and Den Pasar, significantly unattended by any West Papuans, there was an inconclusive argument between the two as to whether West New Guinea should ultimately be included within the constituent states of the United States of Indonesia and, if so, at what point of time.

At the Den Pasar Conference in December 1946 (which had followed the Linggadjati Agreement and had formally provided for the establishment of a United States of Indonesia), the Netherlands Lieutenant-Governor, Dr van Mook, again argued delay for West New Guinea's inclusion in the new Indonesian state on the grounds of its special ethnic, economic and geographical difficulties, but clearly indicated that ultimately it would be included within the 'compass' of the new state. Over the next two years Dutch attitudes distinctly hardened. In December 1948 the Netherlands Government, in legislating for the proposed Netherlands-Indonesian union, made specific provision 'for any part of Indonesia [that] shall not form part of the United States of Indonesia'. In Holland a combination of right wing anti-Indonesian nationalist interests, the forlorn hope that West New Guinea might make a suitable home for Indonesia's reluctant Eurasian population, a genuine conviction that Indonesia was not up to the task of administering the island and the concern of Christian mission institutions with the spiritual welfare of their New Guinea converts, was shaping a different Dutch policy for New Guinea. At The Hague Round Table Conference of August 1949, West New Guinea was not included

---

[4] He reportedly died in prison in Manokwari sometime in 1967.

in the discussions leading to the Transfer of Sovereignty. In the actual Transfer instrument, West New Guinea was specifically excluded on the grounds that 'the *status quo* of the Residency of New Guinea should be maintained with the stipulation that within a year of the date of the transfer of sovereignty . . . the question of the political status of New Guinea be determined through negotiations between the Republic of the United States of Indonesia and the Kingdom of the Netherlands.' The talks never took place. Through a Netherlands administrative decree, New Guinea was changed from a Residency to a Territory with a Governor and four Residents. Thus began the long and bitter political argument between Indonesia and Holland over the Territory, ending only with the Netherlands' transfer of sovereignty through the United Nations in 1962. Throughout the dispute, Dutch and Indonesian claims both rested on sovereignty. The Dutch claimed they had never actually transferred sovereignty, so the Territory was theirs. The Indonesians refused to litigate before the World Court and claimed that the Republic was successor state to the entire Netherlands East Indies, so the province was theirs, insisting, in any case, that the issue was a political one, not legal. Both accused each other of bad faith.

Dutch arguments that Indonesia did not possess the capacity or resources to govern and develop West New Guinea were undoubtedly true. However, the validity of ancillary Dutch arguments that West New Guineans should have the eventual right of self-determination depended upon how their claims to sovereignty were regarded, for self-determination is not only an act *towards* something but *from* something. One implication of the self-determination argument was inescapable. As West New Guinea developed politically and economically its coastal people, at least, came to believe in that right and to organise politically around it so that the Dutch were obliged increasingly to force the pace of decolonisation. It was the latter that worried Indonesia's Foreign Minister, Dr Subandrio, more than anything else. If West Papuans became politically articulate in the cause of their own independence in an anti-colonialist world, then Indonesian claims based on legitimacy, even if legally valid, stood increasingly little chance of finding favour among the Afro-Asian states. In West New Guinea itself, the Dutch administration with varying degrees of emphasis at different periods, set upon a policy of rapid Papuanisation with self-determination for West New Guinea as the ultimate goal.

The notion of self-determination for West New Guineans was in itself novel. In the preceding fifty years West Papuans had been regarded as the more or less negligible inhabitants of an unlovely piece of Dutch real estate. During that period there were four attempts to purchase West New Guinea of which Gavin Souter[5] mentions three. In 1921, a proposal by Queen Wilhelmina's German brother-in-law, the Duke of Mecklenburg to form a *Nieuw Guinea Compagnie* to acquire and exploit the Territory fell on deaf ears. The second attempt was a formal proposition put by the Australian Government in June 1903 to the United Kingdom Government that it should purchase Netherlands New Guinea. The Australian Governor-General, Lord Tennyson, wrote: 'It appears that there is reason to believe that the Dutch authorities are disappointed at the poor results which have followed their attempts to develop New Guinea and in view of this feeling it has been suggested that there may be an inclination on the part of the Dutch Government to dispose of their interests in that country to some other power, and I am informed that Germany has been mentioned in that connection. It is not known whether this inclination really exists or not, but my Ministers are of the opinion that, if the Dutch do intend to relieve themselves of the responsibility of governing the Territory, it will be well, in the interests of Australia, that it should fall into the hands of Great Britain rather than of Germany, and I am desired to submit the suggestion that an effort should be made by His Majesty's Government to secure a pre-emptive right in the matter.'

The Colonial Office received the suggestion with noticeable hauteur and one of the Principal Clerks, Sir John Anderson, in minuting Lord Tennyson's suggestion for Foreign Office

[5] Gavin Souter, op. cit.

action, noted: 'This is rather "cool." Ask FO if they have any information. We can then explain to Australia that it will have to pay if it wants Dutch New Guinea'. The following October, the British Ambassador to The Hague reported that 'the Minister for Colonies told me this morning that there was no foundation for the rumour that the Netherlands Government were inclined to dispose of Dutch New Guinea, and His Excellency added that no Cabinet could possibly approach the country on such a question.' There the matter rested.

The third attempt to buy West New Guinea was Japanese. In 1936 the then Prime Minister, General Hayashi, supported a suggestion from one of the committees of the Diet that Japan should approach the Netherlands with a view to obtaining a perpetual lease over the territory. The approach was never made. The Japanese presumably hoped to settle West New Guinea with Japanese migrants to develop it as a source of tropical raw materials and, possibly, as a strategic base. The notion that the Netherlands Government would agree was curiously naive, as South-West Pacific governments were by that time already alarmed by Japanese actions in China and apprehensive about Japanese intentions in the Pacific as the 1934 Latham Mission to Batavia, Singapore, Bangkok, Manila and Tokyo already indicated.

The fourth suggestion of a Louisiana Purchase came from none other than Dr Herbert Evatt in 1950, only a year after his term as President of the UN General Assembly, and when Deputy Leader of the Opposition. In replying to a statement (in the House of Representatives on 8 June of that year) by Mr (now Sir Percy) Spender, then Minister for External Affairs, on the problems posed by growing Netherlands-Indonesian hostility over the future of West New Guinea, Dr Evatt described the dispute as comprising a 'situation of peril.' He went on to say, ' . . . but suppose the Netherlands Government is anxious or agreeable to part with sovereignty over Dutch New Guinea, I suggest also to the government it may be possible to arrange for the purchase of that territory by Australia.' Dr Evatt added that ' . . . there is in that situation the possibility of the future of New Guinea being assured not only for the security of Australia and the preservation of peace in this important area of the world but also in the interests of the native people of New Guinea, which . . . are our primary consideration.' The suggestion was in itself surprising enough, in 1950, but even more so was the quarter from which it came. One would have thought that Dr Evatt's experience at Lake Success would not have allowed him to suppose that member countries of the United Nations would have countenanced an attempt at undisguised purchase of 800,000 humans even if it was successfully argued that they would be better off for it.

To the end, the departing Dutch in West New Guinea remained insistent that they were leaving behind them an embryonic West Papuan nationalism of which more would be heard. In 1963, both the incoming Indonesians and the on-looking Australians largely discounted it, even if for quite different reasons: the Indonesians because of the needs of state propaganda and because they not unreasonably believed that any nascent Papuan nationalism could be smothered and eventually oriented towards Djakarta; and the Australians for reasons peculiarly their own. Senior officers in the Australian Administration and the Department of Territories had little knowledge of the history of West New Guinea development. Few would have known about the notorious 'Mansren Myth' cargo movements in the Geelvink Bay area which had flickered and flared in the 1890's and again, more strongly, from 1938 to 1943 and which in 1942 led to various anti-Japanese activities including the formation of the AB Army, a declaration of independence defining the territorial limits of an independent Papua Barat (West Papua) as bounded by Sorong in the West, Hollandia in the East and Merauke in the South, and to the adoption of a national flag.[6] Many Aus-

[6] The 1942 flag was the Dutch tricolour reversed, blue, white and red, featuring a white five-pointed 'morning star of Biak' (involved in the Mansren Myth cargo cults) and a small white cross denoting Christian influence. The 1961 flag also combined the Dutch flag colours—a red third featuring the star of Biak plus six horizontal white stripes for the six West New Guinea districts, on a blue field. The cross disappeared.

tralians, including senior Administration officers in New Guinea, were strongly ambivalent towards the Dutch—an attitude also reflected in the Department of Territories. They disliked the Dutch administrative and cultural style. They distrusted the pace of political development set by the Dutch in the late 1950's in creating the 'dynamic few', and profoundly distrusted its implications for Australia's policy of 'uniform development' in East New Guinea. They disliked being associated with the Dutch 'colonialists' image—'300 years of exploitation'—and, a powerful if irrelevant factor, they were contemptuous of Dutch military performance in the Netherlands East Indies in 1942.

Distrust of the West New Guinea élite—all of it nominally Christian in education and outlook—was carefully nurtured in East New Guinea leaders, whom the then Minister for Territories, Mr Hasluck, in view of increasing indications of the Dutch position collapsing, not unreasonably hoped would look south to Australia and east to the Pacific. In 1961 last minute personal attempts by the West Papuans to capture the imagination of East New Guinea leaders in support of an eventual one island state only partly succeeded, even though the political possibilities of this policy had been officially encouraged in the Australian-Netherlands Co-operative Agreement of 1957 and spelled out in J. R. Kerr's 1958 suggestion of a Melanesian Federation.[7] I was the only Australian present at an impromptu meeting of East and West New Guinea leaders in Hollandia in April 1961. Both Nicolaas Jouwe and Herman Womsiwor—the two principal West Papuan spokesmen—argued persuasively in English. While Governor Platteel's yacht cruised the blue, expansive waters of Humboldt Bay far below our verandah, John Guise, now Speaker of the House of Assembly, translated Jouwe's statements into Pidgin to his compatriots. Jouwe spoke enthusiastically and imaginatively of a united New Guinea from 'Sorong to Samarai', a somewhat pathetic adaptation of the Indonesian slogan 'from Sabang to Merauke'. The discussion itself, of course, was futile as West New Guinea's future was being decided else-

7 See Chapter 7.

where—in Washington, Djakarta, London and in Asian capitals. It was, nevertheless, a significant conversation in that a few of the West Papuans were displaying a good deal of political initiative and imagination which was by no means entirely Dutch-inspired. Most of the older West Papuan élite retained vivid memories of the 1942 Biak declarations which had gained considerable currency along West Irian's north and west coasts. Stirring in them was an embryonic sense of Papuan nationalism.

The speed with which the Dutch created a politically conscious élite, mainly the product of the missions but also of a peculiarly Dutch-Indonesian political hot house growth, by the early 1960's was surprising. No less surprising was the early adoption by the coastal Papuans of a national anthem, coat of arms and flag,[8] readily given them by the Dutch in November 1961, the relative effectiveness of the regional councils, the emergence of political parties and the creation of the National Council or *Volksraad* despite the presence of strong semi-traditionally pro-Indonesian Papuan groups in Japan, Sorong, Merauke and other west coast centres. At the time the Indonesians took over West New Guinea, some thousands of coastal New Guineans, including students, firmly believed that by 1970 or later they would be able to determine their own future—even though many were vague as to just what 'self-determination' or 'independence' implied, and for the most part were utterly ignorant of the economic implications.[9]

The Dutch moved at first unevenly and then with gathering speed in the fifteen years between the immediate post-war administrative period of Resident Commissioner J. P. K. van

[8] Together with a national flag, mentioned earlier, West Papuans adopted a national anthem, *Hai Tanahku Papua!* (Hail Papua our Motherland), a name for their country, Papua Barat (West Papua) and a national coat of arms featuring the *kroonduif* (crown dove) and the motto, identical with Indonesia's, *Bhinneka Tunggal Ika* or Unity in Diversity. A Dutch wit said it should have been Disunity in Perversity as it applied with impartial accuracy to both countries.

[9] Pau lvan der Veur, *Questionnaire Survey Among the Potential Elite in 1962 in West New Guinea*, Koninklijk Instituut, s'Gravenhage, 1964.

H

Eechoud and the terminal phase of Governor P. J. Platteel's administration which ended in late 1962, after the New York Agreement was signed. In 1958 only about half of the territory was fully under Dutch administrative control, but nevertheless Papuans held about 38 per cent of lower grade administrative posts (many of them equivalent to those held in Australian New Guinea by administrative servants). Three years later, in 1961, Dutch administrative control was extended over three-quarters of the country and about 51 per cent of all administrative posts in the country were held by Papuans of which 77 per cent comprised lower and some middle grade positions. Even though most Papuans in administrative positions were being carefully guided by their European counterparts, they were nevertheless being involved actively in administrative decisions.[10] Papuanisation was accompanied by rapid expansion in crash political and educational programmes. The number of Papuan junior high schools increased from one in 1957 to seven in 1961. The *Volksraad* (People's Council) established in 1961 had thirty-eight members, of whom sixteen were elected, including thirteen Papuans, and twelve were appointed, including ten Papuans.

Nevertheless there was an urgent, makeshift character to Dutch efforts in West New Guinea reflecting not only expedient haste, but considerable ambivalence of intention. One Dutch motive in hanging on to West New Guinea was clearly to embarrass Indonesia and to use their continued presence in the Territory as a possible means of leverage against Indonesian actions against Dutch commercial interests in Indonesia. This failed. However there was another motive, apart from nationalistic desire to avoid being pressured out of the area, and that was the welfare of the Papuans themselves to which many interests in Holland, including powerful Christian ones, subscribed. In the end the Netherlands was on the hook,

---

[10] The Dutch were still privately sceptical. Dr Platteel described political development in April 1961 in these terms: 'There is a large round table with a pile of money on it. Around it are seated a number of black men. Behind each is a white who tells him how much money to ask for.' (Private communication).

finding that the faster it forced the pace of Papuan decolonisation the more urgent, the more inescapable, became its
responsibilities. However Dutch actions were to breed terrible
consequences in frustrated Papuan hopes. Over the years
relatively huge sums of money were expended in an inhospitable island to provide a large, efficiently run, coastal infrastructure—docks, towns, roads, airstrips, cold storage chambers, power generators, telecommunications, schools, hospitals,
aircraft and coastal shipping, administration buildings and
housing—but relatively little was spent on development of
the interior or on base industries other than the rice project
at Kumbé, the timber mill and dockyard at Manokwari,
various small scale industries at Biak and some copra and
spice development. But in the central highlands, for example,
with the highest concentration of population in the Territory,
there was not a single road and at the time of the Dutch
departure, little or no economic activity. In 1962 the Netherlands grant-in-aid to the Territory was $A60 million (the
Australian grant to TPNG in the same year was $69 million)
and was necessarily used in large part to maintain a high rate
of urban employment with high wages. This unavoidably
created indigenous expectations of more or less permanent
subsidisation and made the task of the incoming Indonesian
administration extremely difficult for no matter how dedicated Indonesians might be in the task of administration their
material standards were bound to be lower. General Nasution
astutely described the increasing social and economic expectations of the West Irianese in the late 1950's and early 1960's
as a 'Dutch time bomb' which it was indeed to prove. Nevertheless, a sense of economic deprivation, 'stomach politics' in
the Indonesian phrase, has not been the only factor in West
Irianese resentment of Indonesian rule.

Diplomatically Holland and Australia suffered a savage and
humiliating defeat not only over Indonesia's final acquisition
of West Irian, but through the methods employed which
ultimately involved the use of force by Indonesia despite
categoric assurances from President Soekarno that force would
never be used; assurances which were specifically and solemnly

repeated by General Nasution during his visit to Australia early in 1961. The broad chronology of events leading up to the transfer was a fairly dismal commentary on Australian and Dutch incapacity to manoeuvre without great power support. In 1960, the Netherlands Minister-in-Charge of New Guinea, Dr Th. Bot, visited Canberra with a proposal to implement the full implications of the 1957 Netherlands-Australian Administrative Agreement,[11] which had envisaged the possible, ultimate union of the two sides of New Guinea as a single political unit. After consideration, the Australian Cabinet, mindful of its future relations with Indonesia, rejected the approach. By early 1961 Indonesia had broken off diplomatic relations with Holland and had ordered $400 million worth of military equipment, a squadron of Badgers and a *Sverdlovsk* type battle cruiser (the *Irian*) from the Soviet. In April 1961 neither the United States' nor the British representative attended the opening of the New Guinea *Volksraad*, People's Council, in Hollandia, an act which closed off all Dutch hopes of great power support for its proclaimed principle of self determination. In September of the same year the Netherlands Government made a last desperate attempt to salvage the position and its increasingly damaged international prestige, by proposing to the General Assembly that operating under the authority of the United Nations 'an organisation or international authority' should take over West New Guinea to 'prepare the population for early self-determination under stable conditions.' Holland's Foreign Minister, Dr J. Luns, had made his last dash by proposing the plan. Indonesia fought the proposal with considerable diplomatic skill in the United Nations by pointing out that although the plan appeared to conform to the General Assembly's 1960 'Declaration on the Granting of Independence to Colonial Countries and Peoples' it contravened it in one highly important regard. Dr Subandrio made the point that while the Declaration insisted on the rights of colonial peoples to self-determination it also clearly qualified this by insisting that implementation of these rights must not

11 See Chapter 7.

lead to any attempts to achieve 'partial or total disruption of national unity and the territorial integrity of a country.' Indonesia's case, as we have seen, rested on its sovereignty and integrity as successor state to the entire territorial possessions comprising the former Netherlands East Indies. A final attempt to retrieve the situation came from the Brazzaville Thirteen—the group of central African states—which had close sympathies with emerging West Papuan nationalism and sought to establish an interim international administration for West New Guinea pending resumption of Dutch-Indonesian negotiations. The motion was lost fifty-three votes to forty-one.

In December, 1961, President Soekarno issued his famous *Trikora* command for the liberation of West Irian and Indonesian air force and paratroop units moved to East Indonesian air fields. On 4 January, Sir Garfield Barwick, then Minister for External Affairs, issued a statement in the third person emphasising Australia's neutrality in the dispute and accepting the results of any Dutch-Indonesian negotiations provided they were 'arrived at freely, not under duress or the threat of force.' In the ensuing week President Soekarno appointed as liberation force commander the man destined to be his presidential successor, Brigadier-General Suharto. On 12 January the Australian Prime Minister Mr (later Sir) R. G. Menzies issued a somewhat bitter statement saying in part that ' . . . no responsible Australian would wish to see any action affecting the safety of Australia on the issues of war or peace in this area except in concert with our great and powerful friends.' It was an admission of political impotence. Curiously, it was the Leader of the Opposition, Mr Arthur Calwell, who, without quite urging Australian military aid to the embattled Dutch, advocated resistance saying very plainly at the time of the Menzies' statement that ' . . . in this crisis we must oppose Indonesian actions which are flagrantly in breach of the UN Charter. Further, if Indonesia seeks to deny the principle of the UN Charter and to use force to create a potential threat to Australia's security, then I say, with all due regard to the gravity of the situation, that the threat

must be faced.' Mr Calwell was intensely and fearfully aware
of the possible eastern extension of the interests of an unstable, potentially Communist, Indonesia into Australian New
Guinea.

Two days after Mr Menzies' statement three heavily armed
Indonesian patrol boats headed by the *Matjan Tutul* which
carried Commodore Jos. Sudarso, second-in-command of the
Indonesian Navy, were picked up by radar by a Dutch
reconnaissance aircraft and shadowed by the frigates *Kor-
tenaer* and *Evertsen*. The *Evertsen* opened fire on the *Matjan
Tutul*, sinking it. Commodore Sudarso, to whom, in Biak,
there is a somewhat dubious memorial, was not among the
fifty-two survivors. The other two patrol boats returned to
Indonesia. It was a humiliating blow to Indonesian prestige
and led President Soekarno to order a number of paratroop
and other infiltration operations against West New Guinea.
The Dutch had little trouble in handling these attacks and it
is now known that the Indonesian Government's greatest fear
was that the Dutch might stand firm in a war of skirmishes
tempting Indonesia into a major military operation for which
it was unprepared and would have lost. It was this fear that
led to renewed Indonesian political and diplomatic pressures
to remove the Dutch. In February the late Mr Robert
Kennedy, then United States Attorney-General, on a visit
to The Hague made it clear that the United States would
not support Holland in the event of an Indonesian attack. In
March, bending to the inevitable, the Dutch sat down with
the Indonesians near Washington under the chairmanship of
a United Nations Special Representative, Mr Ellsworth
Bunker. In July they sat down again to discuss the substance
of the Bunker proposals which called for the transfer of
Netherlands sovereignty over West New Guinea to an interim
United Nations administration which in turn was to hand
'full administrative responsibility', not sovereignty, to Indonesia after an agreed period with the stipulation that West
New Guineans would exercise free choice over their future
relationship with Indonesia in a formal act to take place
before the end of 1969.

The formal Netherlands-Indonesian Agreement was signed at the United Nations on 15 August 1962 and provided for transfer of Dutch authority to a United Nations Temporary Executive Authority (UNTEA) and for the establishment of full Indonesian administrative control by May 1963. The provisions of the Agreement calling for an act of free choice and the conditions under which it was to be carried out are dealt with later in this chapter.[12] Of the shattering events which led up to the enforced transfer of Netherlands sovereignty over West New Guinea to Indonesia, the Dutch Prime Minister, Professor de Quay, was to say with great feeling, 'We are ashamed before the world.'

The Indonesian takeover in 1963 caused confusion and dismay in West Irian. For prominent native Council members like Elizier Bonay, who had turned from the notion of Papuan independence to that of Indonesian co-operation, there seemed no alternative. After all, apart from Indonesia's fervently pressed legal claims to West New Guinea, much seemed in favour of Indonesian absorption. 'Market' Malay, a less developed version of Bahasa Indonesia, was the *lingua franca* of the coast and was the language of primary education and of administrative contact. The Dutch had used Moluccans and other Indonesian ethnic groups in their pre- and post-war administration. Administration structure—even working hours—was that of the former Netherlands East Indies and Indonesia, as was the Dutch, and some coastal Papuan, style of living. There had also been a long, if frequently bloody, historic association between the west coast, the Bird's Head and the eastern islands of Indonesia, the courts and sultans of which had for centuries sought New Guinea slaves and birds of paradise plumes. If West New Guineans could have been said, on the coast at least, to have had an outlook, it was to the west, not to the east. To anyone travelling in West New Guinea in the last half of the UNTEA (United Nations Temporary Executive Authority) period in 1963, the people seemed sadly bewildered. UNTEA itself was a makeshift and largely inefficient administration intent on effecting a hand-

[12] For the relevant articles of the Agreement see Appendix.

over as quickly and peacefully as possible.[13] In a country ostentatiously occupied by large numbers of Indonesian troops and which the Dutch administrative service had almost completely deserted, UNTEA was in no mood, lacking the capacity or the authority, to be tender about Papuan sensibilities. The departing Dutch were sad, humiliated and relieved by turns. The Indonesians were triumphant and uncompromisingly nationalistic, although for the most part—the one quite enjoyable irony of the situation—a decade of irredentist propaganda was not proof against disenchantment with the island's terrain or people. The Irianese were mostly confused. In Hollandia, Biak and Manokwari especially there were quite sizeable groups of sullen Papuans who, while complaining about the Indonesian takeover and resentful of Dutch 'betrayal'[14] showed quite plainly they had neither the capacity nor the strength to organise politically. Demonstrations were quickly broken up by the Indonesian Army, and although there was vague talk of 'rebellion' and 'guerilla' warfare and an abortive attempt by the Biak-Numfoer Regional Council to get the United Nations to listen to its complaints, the majority of Papuans decided to wait and see.

While there were numerous cases of Indonesians manhandling the native population, of beatings and intimidation and substantial, and entirely credible if largely unproved, rumours of shootings, the Indonesian authorities on the whole handled firmly and sympathetically a difficult situation in which they were not yet landlords over their own domain. The new Indonesian administration, in collaboration with the Army, started on the formidable task of developing the Territory with energy and dedication. Special Presidential decrees ordained how the Territory should be governed, Elizier Bonay was appointed Governor, an energetic programme of primary

---

[13] The official UN Booklet describing UNTEA's activities is brashly entitled, *An Unprecedented Story*, (UN, New York, November 1963). As a description of a sell out, it is certainly that.

[14] Herman Womsiwor happened to be in my office the morning the Dutch had announced acceptance of the Bunker proposals. His voice choked with emotion, he said, 'I spit on the Dutch.'

and secondary school education was instituted, and a number of economic and developmental plans were inaugurated—in addition to those founded or recently instituted by the Dutch, for which special funds had been earmarked from Dutch and Indonesian sources. There seemed no shortage of adequate Indonesian administrative and technical skills to implement them. For a few months, at least, it looked as if Indonesia might prove a benevolent guardian. It was an illusion. Papuan disillusionment swiftly set in at two levels—economic and political. Consumer goods, including clothes, cameras, bicycles, household necessities, beer, transistors and outboard motors to name a few, rapidly disappeared from shop counters, mainly into the hands of Indonesian troops and Administration personnel, who swiftly traded them into the black markets of Djakarta; food became scarce and Papuans in the towns, many of whom had long become dependent in greater or lesser degree on bread and imported foodstuffs began cultivating their subsistence gardens again. Many were obliged to leave their houses which were commandeered by the incoming Indonesians and today, apart from a few high ranking Papuans, few occupy the houses they lived in in 1963. Bonay, on the one hand subject to the pressures of Djakarta and, on the other, to Papuan demands for restoration of their former prosperity and a greater say in their internal affairs, either resigned or was removed and replaced by Frans Kaisieppo (mentioned earlier), the nephew of Marcus Kaisieppo who chose exile in Holland along with Nicolaas Jouwe and Herman Womsiwor. Confrontation with Malaysia, inopportunely draining Indonesia of needed skills and resources, was followed by Indonesia's departure from the United Nations. This led to the temporary suspension of a Dutch grant of $US30m. —the equivalent of the Dutch grant-in-aid to its colony in 1962—which in conjunction with a similar amount furnished by Indonesia was to be expended on economic development through the agency of FUNDWI (Fund for the United Nations Development of West Irian) set up for the task. Indonesia was in fact unable to find its contribution and cannot do so now. Indonesia's departure from the United Nations also left up in the air the question of the 'plebiscite'[15] which, under the terms of the 1962 New York Agreement signed by Holland and Indonesia, was to be carried out before the end of 1969; an act of self determination which it is doubtful if President Soekarno or Dr Subandrio would ever have attempted to honour. By the end of 1964 the whole momentum of Indonesian administration had slowed down. The obvious facts of Indonesian administrative failure, ranging from empty shops, a lack of paper, chalk and books in schools to a scarcity of typewriter ribbons in administrative offices, was a matter on which Indonesians became understandably sensitive. West Irian was in fact a casualty of the worst and most selfish excesses of the Soekarnoist regime. In 1964 the province was closed to foreign journalists and to all but selected members of the domestic press.

Seen from Djakarta the perspective was, of course, different. West Irian had been rightfully restored to the Republic and its people who had suffered under the yoke of Dutch imperialism had been reunited with the Indonesian motherland. At the same time it was a particularly underdeveloped part of the Republic demanding more than its fair share of central government funds. In future it would have to wait in the

[15] The Agreement did not once mention the word plebiscite, but variously referred to an 'act of self-determination', 'freedom of choice', 'freely expressed will of the people', etc. I suspect that the word plebiscite, which has more specific legal implications, achieved its early currency in two ways: It was assumed as inherent in the document, for in Keesing's Contemporary Archives a brief description of the Agreement and the events leading up to it contains the word plebiscite several times; the Indonesians themselves loosely used the word for several years until they realised its 'one man, one vote' implications and hastily dropped it. Mr Hasluck, at least, was not confused. On 23 March 1965, in the House of Representatives, in answer to a question by Mr E. G. Whitlam, he said: 'I think self-determination does not mean the holding of some sort of plebiscite or direct consultation with the people in that manner. I am doubtful whether the documents would justify that view. There certainly has to be an act of ascertainment—some sort of attempt to consult the people—but the documents are not, perhaps, as strong on the means of self-determination as originally we would have liked them to be.' Mr Hasluck's statement, made more than four years ago, had a decidedly wistful quality to it in view of the actual method and conduct of the act of self-determination.

queue along with other claimant provinces for funds and aid from the hard pressed government in Djakarta which had other and more important matters to concern it such as confounding Nekolim through confrontation. However after the counter coup of October 1965 the view from Djakarta changed again. In the four years that have elapsed since then Indonesia's foreign policy has taken close to a 180 degrees turn. The first major change was the immediate and thorough destruction of Djakarta's links with Peking, the second was ending Confrontation and the third was rejoining the United Nations. In corollary actions Indonesia turned to the west, to foreign loans and to foreign investment. Its relations with the Soviet perceptibly cooled, it left the Afro-Asian anti-colonialist camp of which it had been chief spokesman and it preached regionalism through its espousal of ASEAN—the Association of South East Asian Nations. In short the precarious ideological edifice erected by President Soekarno was carefully dismantled.

Not least among the foreign policy initiatives of the new, highly intelligent and energetic Foreign Minister, Mr Adam Malik, was a statement that the Indonesian government would abide by a major stipulation of the New York Agreement that an act of self-determination should take place before the end of 1969. It was not an entirely popular decision in Djakarta, despite some genuine liberal and press criticism of Indonesia's disastrous administration of West Irian since 1963, where the retention of West Irian in the Republic was an *idée fixe* with the political parties and *élites* and the Army alike. For most politically minded Indonesians there was the simple conviction that the Republic had 'fought' for the restoration of the lost province to the Republic for nearly two decades and there could be no question of allowing it to choose to depart. In any case the notion of secession was repugnant in a unitary state which had suffered two serious secessionist rebellions in Sumatra and Sulawesi. Mr Malik, like most in the new order government, was in a quandary. The reactivation of FUNDWI depended on rejoining the United Nations and in honouring the Agreement. At stake was Indonesia's international credi-

bility and therefore its eligibility for international loans. However there were many shoals ahead. To open the question at
all was to open Pandora's Box and no one could safely guarantee what might emerge although there were some constants
on which Djakarta might rely, chief among which were two.
Neither the Soviet nor the United States, the super powers,
were likely to show any interest in trying to make political
capital out of West Irian; the Soviet because it was busy trying
to maintain its now waning influence as a Communist power
in the wake of the Sino-Indonesian rupture and possibly
with the thought of Indonesia's $400 million debt in mind;
the United States because of its involvement in Vietnam and
its passionate corollary interest in the stabilisation of Indonesia
as a pro-western power. The other and more immediately
involved powers, Holland and Australia, were in a similar
position in not wishing to query Indonesia's sovereignty over
West Irian. The Dutch certainly did not want, and in any
case could not have retrieved, West New Guinea. They were
far more interested in maintaining their greatly improved post-
coup relations and in re-establishing at least some of their
commercial interests in Indonesia once again. Both the
Netherlands Government and many institutions, especially
the churches, had come to believe that they could best help
the Irianese, for whom they palpably continued to feel a
sense of responsibility, by making sure that West Irian remained within the Republic and by ensuring that Dutch
funds were available for the reactivation of FUNDWI. Australia's position was similar, its interests even more sharply
defined. Relations with Indonesia had improved dramatically
after October 1965, Australian aid, skills and personnel were
welcomed in Djakarta, Indonesian politicians, academics and
students were welcome in Australia. Now it seemed was the
time, if ever there was, to build for the future. In the interests
of building friendly relations with a populous underdeveloped
and uncertain neighbour, West Irian, by comparison, was a
small matter. In addition Canberra was becoming, at long
last, aware of the problems posed not only to Australia but
to Australian New Guinea by any diplomacy aimed at ensur-

ing that the act of free choice, looming over the horizon of 1969, was a genuine ascertainment. Canberra pragmatically accepted the obvious fact that in Indonesian eyes the act of free choice was a legitimating device and nothing more as Indonesia's leaders made clear. There was also a moral argument involved—the future welfare of West Irian and its people.

Quite obviously without great power support and large subsidies it would not make a viable, moderate entity even in an age of fragmented, formerly colonial, mini-states. Lacking material resources and human skills to an unprecedented degree it would also, as an independent state, have had to pay the penalty of Indonesia's enduring hostility as would the nations subsidising it. This would have been especially so had, as many of its urban élite hoped, West Irian been able to form a union with Australian New Guinea under Australian subsidisation and protection. That train, Melanesian Federation, had gone—forever. On any rational examination of the situation the most hopeful future for the West Irianese—a majority of whose estimated 800,000 population were un-sophisticated Highlands people—lay in their being reconciled to permanent incorporation within the Republic of Indonesia. Reconciliation nevertheless was easier said than done, especially in the urban centres where anti-Indonesian feelings were strong and there were lively memories of relative economic affluence under the Dutch and of Dutch promises of self-determination.

Throughout 1964, 1965, 1966 and 1967 conditions in West Irian steadily deteriorated. The local administration was primarily a refuge for largely incompetent old order sympathisers and, in any case, was without either funds or facilities. The infrastructure, especially sea and air communications, left by the Dutch deteriorated and until recently both the civil administration and the Army became dependent for about eighty per cent of their air movements on the Missionary Aviation Fellowship, a voluntary body serving many of the Protestant missions, creating a curious ambivalence of feeling between Christian missionary in the field and nationalist official in the Administration. This situation was not rendered any easier by the fact that a number of missionaries were plainly anti-Indonesian in outlook while too many of the senior administration officials were Muslim and unsympathetic, at best indifferent, to the strongly Christian sentiments of much of the population in the urban and coastal areas—Protestant in the north and Catholic in the south. Economic decline was rapid. In 1966 in Biak, for example, townspeople were cooking vegetables, when obtainable, in salt water because of a salt shortage while work was still sporadically being continued on the erection of a prestigious mosque—on an island less than seven per cent of whose 50,000 population was Moslem and mostly non-Irianese—on which the Soekarno Government had spent two billion rupiah. In most centres markets had closed down through lack of produce while cigarettes, soap, textiles, cooking oil, imported foods and finally rice, had become virtually unprocurable.

Moreover if the civil administration was inefficient it was also, like the TNI (Indonesian Army), politically repressive. Small traders and businessmen, for example, could not move even if transport was available, between one centre and another without travel documents. Political meetings, other than those of the strictest ideological purity and promoted by the Administration were banned and former indigenous political parties were proscribed. The regional councils established by the Dutch from elected and appointed members ceased to be the means by which the people, in varying degrees of development, could voice opinions and became instead channels of official instruction and propaganda and the objects of increasing Papuan suspicion. Large numbers of West Irianese, comprising now dissident leaders from the period before 1962 to dissatisfied students, were gaoled from time to time. In 1966 there were probably 369 political prisoners in Sukarnapura, Biak and Manokwari. There was also considerable evidence, much of it exaggerated, but too well attested and persistent to be dismissed, of armed uprisings in the territory and of tough Indonesian reprisals. One of the first publicised stories of Irianese armed resistance was that of an attempt by Biak dissidents, including some 'school-children'[16] to sabotage the Shell oil installations at Mokmer Airport in August 1965. Between 1965 and the present day there have been a number of uprisings of which, apart from urban unrest, three have been serious—two rebellions by the Arfak people around Manokwari and continuing skirmishes between police and paratroop units and numerous tribespeople in the area around Enaratoli and Waghete, in the far western Highlands of the Wissel Lakes region. In the first Arfak uprising in 1967 there were sustained reports of continuing Indonesian Army activity and an alleged but unproven report that the Indonesian Air Force machine gunned and bombed in low level attacks several thousand Arfak people killing 1200. The report is almost certainly greatly exaggerated, if only by reason of terrain and the scattered nature of Arfak settlements, but it was sufficient for Silas Papare, who had chosen Indonesia in preference to the Netherlands after the 1949 Round Table Conference, to complain in the MPRS (Provisional Consultative Assembly) in Djakarta shortly afterwards that 'my people are being mistreated.'

The most serious revolt took place about April of 1969, and was still continuing in August of that year, among various tribes people of the Waghete area. The revolt significantly began with a request that the *bupati* (District Commissioner) should be removed and that all Javanese officers of the Administration should leave. Officials of other ethnic origins could stay. This request was followed by the defection of 95 Papuan police, all armed with Mauser carbines, taking with them two bren guns, over a dispute involving wages and conditions. Since then more than half have returned but as late as mid August 1969 it was estimated that some 40,000 people in the area were still disaffected. It should be remembered that 'revolt' does not mean either that it is armed or concerted. It is more likely to be sporadic, largely unorganised and largely unarmed. However as an indication of enduring resentments it was serious enough. There were alleged Air Force sorties against the dissidents but it is unlikely that there

16 *Sinar Harapan*, 19 August 1965.

were. Paratroops were certainly dropped in the area but mainly to restore law and order rather than to carry out punitive operations.

Conditions improved slowly after a visit to the province in August 1966 by the Minister for Foreign Affairs, Mr Adam Malik. Accompanied by foreign newsmen and two Australian journalists[17] he was extremely frank with his guests and bitingly critical of the Administration and the TNI.

Nevertheless the improvements were only marginally noticeable as I verified from a quick trip in August 1968 to Sukarnapura, surrounding areas and Biak. In both places there was an efficiently run typical *bung* or Papuan market, instituted by the former *panglima*, Brigadier-General Bintoro, an eccentric and unpredictable figure, but in both prices were high. Three small tomatoes cost 50c[18] and half a smoked fish, $2. The most significant feature of the market-area was armed Indonesian guards. In the surrounding *pasar*, consisting of small stores run mainly, it seemed, by Makassarese, there were as many goods, and as great a variety, as anywhere else in Indonesia but the prices were extremely high. Shirts, trousers and coats varied between $30 and $45 and an aluminium cooking pot was about $45. While Indonesian civil servants on special regional salaries could cope, [notwithstanding that West Irian has a special currency arrangement to prevent currency speculation the official rate of 10 Irbar (Irian Barat) rupiah to the US dollar did not prevent a flourishing black market in Chinese shops of between 30 and 40 Irbar rupiah to the US dollar] if only just, skilled Papuans for whom a top wage, with a family to support, was no more than $14 a month, found it hard to make ends meet. Heineken's beer at $1 a can, and imported cigarettes the same price per packet, were well out of the reach of all but the most affluent. In the circumstances, despite the geographically fragmented nature of West Irian, its extreme tribalisation and lack of communications it was not altogether surprising that loosely disciplined

[17] Frank Palmos, 'A Visit to West Irian', *New Guinea*, No. 7, 1966.
[18] All values, unless specifically described otherwise, are in United States dollars.

if firmly committed resistance groups should spring up. What was surprising, and one might have thought food for thought in Djakarta, was the fact that they were able to organise at all.

The West Irianese resistance movements were loosely controlled by the West Papuan government-in-exile in Delft, Holland, headed by Nicolaas Jouwe, Marcus Kaisieppo and Herman Womsiwor. The principle organisation was the *Organisasi Papua Merdeka* (OPM) or Free Papua Organisation. Financed by various private, non-governmental sources including those supporting the South Moluccas Republic organisation, the OPM ran a small office in New York—whose main job was to lobby United Nations members, particularly the Brazzaville Thirteen—and maintained from there and from Delft a voluminous correspondence with interested parties worldwide and published an occasional magazine in Dutch, Indonesian and English entitled *Fadjar Melanesia*. It also provided Free West Papua flags, emblems and other propaganda.

Since the act of self-determination there is some doubt as to how active the OPM has remained or either of its two sister organisations, the *Gerakan Papua Merdeka* (GPM) or Free Papua Movement and the *Gerakan Nasional Papua* (GNP) or Papuan National Movement. To some extent all three were only paper organisations, despite the spate of typewritten documents with impressive stamps that they distributed, mainly across the Australian New Guinea border, and despite a number of photographs showing young guerillas with tommy guns, dark glasses and side levers. The OPM and other nationalist organisations in West Irian lacked not only arms and communications, to be effective, but away from restricted and widely separated urban centres, they had no politically organised indigenous community among which to operate. While large numbers of West Irianese varied between being vaguely or even intensely anti-Indonesian, they had no concentrated, collective, political goal at which to aim.

Nevertheless Djakarta regarded the OPM as a political danger and there were several official complaints from Djakarta, including one made to me on 30 May 1969, by the

Foreign Minister, Mr Adam Malik, that the OPM was receiving privately organised finance from the United States, Japan and Australia apart from that received from Holland. He also maintained that dissident Irianese camps inside the Australian border were tolerated by Australian Administration officials and had become illicit training camps for OPM guerillas. This was not true but it certainly was true that more activist dissidents[19] coming across the border into Australian New Guinea were frequently not so much anxious to obtain permissive residence as to establish camps near the border from which they could freely travel into West Irian to distribute propaganda and letters—either from Irianese refugees in the Australian Territory or from Holland or New York—and take part in subversive activities, including armed insurrection, returning later to the 'sanctuary' of East New Guinea. Indonesian fears of this, as well as incomplete central control of Indonesian mobile police operations along her border, led to a series of Indonesian incursions into Australian New Guinea and the shooting, on two occasions, of Irianese refugees in Australian territory. This situation was quickly adjusted by meetings between Australian and Indonesian administration representatives in what had become Djajapura and the establishment of efficient radio links between that town and Vanimo.

In July and August the Indonesian Government conducted

---

[19] The government in Djakarta has never really appreciated the traditional concepts of political asylum in Australia which led the Commonwealth Government to offer permissive residence to West Irianese dissidents. The criteria used by the Papua/New Guinea Administration, laid down by Canberra, are that those seeking permissive residence must be able to show that they would be in personal jeopardy if they returned to West Irian. If granted permissive residence, they must also undertake not to indulge in anti-Indonesian activities—an obligation more observed in the breach than otherwise. As of August 1969, there were 267 Irianese residing in Australian New Guinea comprising some 75 families. More than four thousand Irianese have crossed the border since 1963 of which in 1969, between January and August, there were not quite 1700. The vast majority of those returned failed to satisfy government requirements for permissive residence. The remainder, a small number, returned to West Irian voluntarily for personal or political reasons.

the act of free choice, *Pepera*, (an acronym for *Penentuan Pendapat Rakjat*) in the capital of each of its eight administrative districts, in compliance with the New York Agreement. The articles of the Agreement covering the conduct of the act and the eligibility of those taking part in it are fully quoted in Appendix F. In brief, they: required the Secretary-General's (United Nations) Representative and staff to 'advise, assist and participate in arrangements which are the responsibility of Indonesia for the act of free choice'; established that there would be 'consultations (*musjawarah*) with the representative councils on procedures and appropriate methods' for the act; established that the question to be asked would allow 'inhabitants to decide (a) whether they wish to remain with Indonesia; or (b) whether they wish to sever their ties with Indonesia'; established 'the eligibility of all adults, male and female, not foreign nationals, to participate in the act of self-determination to be carried out in accordance with international practice'; required the Secretary-General's Representative, and Indonesia, to report on the conduct and results of the act to the Secretary-General, who, in turn, would report to the General Assembly; finally bound both Indonesia and Holland to abide by the results of the Act.

The Secretary-General's Representative was a former Bolivian diplomat and journalist, Fernando Ortiz-Sans, who took up his post in 1968 with a staff of six where he needed at least fifty. He will undoubtedly tell his story one day but it was quite obvious that he met with passive and open resistance from the Indonesian Government throughout the period of his mission. It was also obvious that he was deeply sympathetic to Papuan aspirations and deeply conscious of two other important facts—that there was no possibility of international support for a true referendum and that the incorporation of West Irian into Indonesia was essential to the continued stable government of the Republic. He did however suggest early in 1969 that there should be a 'one man, one vote' principle employed in any *Pepera* in the urban centres, allowing for ascertainment through consultation, in the 'traditional' or undeveloped areas. His suggestion was rejected on logistical grounds. He was successful in inducing the Indonesian Government, mainly through the efforts of the Foreign Minister, to release most of the 195 political prisoners, held in Djajapura, Biak and other Irianese centres and to accord more humane conditions to others.

The method of ascertainment chosen was predictably that of *musjawarah*, or consultation, which is part of the traditional Indonesian (and New Guinean) process of *gotong royong* (all together) once *mufakat* (consensus) has been reached. The mechanics of *Pepera* were simple. The regional councils were formed into a Consultative Assembly and such members, representing traditional, democratic, functional groups and religious groups interests, added as were necessary to the number of permanent members of the Councils to bring the total to 1025. The number of delegates, which included women and Christian and Islamic pastors, varied with the size of the regency. Thinly populated regencies like Manokwari had 75 delegates representing 50,000 people while Djawidjaya (central east Highlands) had 175 delegates representing 168,000 people ranging from semi-primitive to uncontacted people. At each of the *Pepera* the proceedings were the same, prayers by Christian and Islamic ministers, followed by statements by the Minister for Internal Affairs (Lieutenant-General Amir Mahmud), by the Special Assistant for West Irian Affairs, Dr Sudjarwo Tjondronegoro (who was responsible, on the Indonesian side, for drawing up the 1962 Agreement in New York), by the local District Commissioner, (*bupati*) and then by spokesmen among the delegates. All statements from the official party or from delegates were, where necessary, translated into local dialect.

The results of the *Pepera*, in each regency, comprised an absolute acclamation for Indonesia's continued sovereignty. There was simply never any doubt of the outcome. As a purely impressionistic estimate it is probable that if there had been a free, one man one vote referendum, that four of the eight regencies would have voted for Indonesia and four against. The four that appeared to be pro-Indonesian included Merauke, Fak-Fak and Sorong which have had long histories of Indonesian contact and the Baliem Valley where those polled did not, because of their short contact history and traditional village life on which neither the Dutch nor Indonesians had made much impact, have very much notion of what was at stake. The four northern regencies of Biak, Manokwari, Djajapura and Nabire which is capital of Paniai Regency and includes the far western highlands and the Wissel Lakes area, would have voted almost overwhelmingly against.

The various *Pepera* were conducted with all the familiar instruments of Indonesian political persuasion and intimidation. There were free cigarettes, cheap plastic brief cases and food and goods specially flown into all centres for the occasion combined with heavy handed police and security activities, gaily decorated towns, endlessly exhortative posters declaring solidarity from 'Sabang to Merauke', 'one nation, one people, one language', the 'final act' of the Indonesian revolution and so on. Perhaps, looking back, one's clearest memory of the atmosphere was thousands upon thousands of fluttering Indonesian national flags, the *merah putih* or red and white. Of the various *Pepera* one's clearest recollection after the endlessly repetitious appeals for national solidarity, the cheering and the slogans, the armed guards and suspicious police, were the delegates themselves many of whom, women as well as men, rose to say, in effect, that the question of Indonesia's sovereignty was not at issue but that they hoped, in front of the distinguished visitors from Djakarta and the Dutch and Australian Ambassadors, for a pledge that conditions would not be as bad as they had been in the years of Indonesia's administration and that broken promises would now be redeemed. Time and again they were assured that this was, indeed, the beginning of a new road although they would have to be patient and work hard themselves. For a picture of the intensity, colour and confusion of those few weeks I cannot do better than quote a despatch I sent from Manokwari:

'At Manokwari everything came together and somehow, for the first time, the complicated picture was complete—the sullen Arfak people brought down from the hills, the thousands of fluttering red and white flags, the slogans, the heavily-armed police, the neurotically nationalist young Indonesian goon squads, Christianity and Islam, promises and expectations. Manokwari, the oldest West New Guinea centre, is quite stunningly beautiful. From early colonial streets, cool under avenues of giant raintrees, one looks over the immense, shimmering, blue harbour to the Arfak Mountains soaring sheer 5000ft into a cloudless sky. It is a dissident centre where the splendid dockyard and sawmill established by the Dutch, and the agricultural station gifted by FAO, await rehabilitation through FUNDWI. It is also a centre where West Irian's capable, energetic Panglima, General Sarwo Edhie, has built clean, functional villages for Arfak tribesmen who come down from the hills to accept the authority of the republic. At the *Pepera* centre, a large, modern community centre hall built by the Dutch, right on the water's edge several thousand people must have gathered. Beautiful young Indonesian girls in the costumes of Java, central Sumatra, Sulawesi and Bali formed two rows through which dignitaries walked under a cascade of flowers. Chinese Christian schoolchildren in black shorts, white socks and shirts were drawn up like a battalion —scrubbed and impassive. Moslem political groups gathered under green flags bearing the sickle and crescent of Islam, holding small *merah putihs*—Indonesia's national red and white flag. The principal Protestant pastor wore a formal black robe and a well cut black suit. The Catholic Bishop wore a white cassock and purple sash. In true Indonesian fashion everything was noisy and colourful and Indonesian soldiers were everywhere. Trucks were drawn up in alleyways, in side streets and anywhere they could find room. Two fast motor patrol boats nosed up and down along the waterfront.

'But it was the Papuans that attracted most attention. They were Arfaks, small and slightly wizened, curious, frightened and uncomprehending, sitting or standing in clumps with Indonesian *kiaps*, holding *merah putihs* and chewing betel nut. This was New Guinea *true*, embattled and baffled. Something big was happening and something was amiss. In the hall, speakers indulged in a range of emotions quite contrary

to the organised cheering, sloganising and singing outside.
There was seriousness, acceptance, anger, joy and resignation
among the representatives of the people of the Bird's Head,
who have had extensive contact with Europe and the Malay
world, with Islam and with Rome, and have been in sporadic
revolt against the civilising intruders since the days of earliest
contact. They all spoke, the religious and the functional
groups, the women's clubs representatives, the democratic
representatives of the urban areas and the representatives of
the traditional groups and even those of that handful of West
Irianese who fought against the returning Dutch in 1945. And
then it happened. Outside one sensed rather than saw the
movement of people, ungainly and uncertain, towards one end
of the road. Suddenly there were soldiers running and Papuan
police looking shocked and resentful. Outside an Irianese had
been arrested. A soldier motioned me back and police cor-
doned off the road from Arfakkers who suddenly appeared
from everywhere. I walked through the cordon to see a little
Papuan break free of his captors. Then I saw another two
Papuans start to fight with an Indonesian soldier. What followed happened very fast. The New Guinean nearest me was
overpowered by plainclothes police, hauled struggling into the
back of a lorry and thrown violently to the floor. I saw a fist
pound down. There was a cry and the truck moved on. An
Arfakker walked up to an Indonesian policeman and spat in
his face. To my surprise the policeman merely headlocked
him and dragged him off to another truck. Down at the
other end of the road a similar incident was taking place.
As my friend Bobby Gibbes and I moved down towards a
struggling knot of people we were surrounded by Indonesians.
What we had seen, they said, was only an incident, the Irianese were drunk or crazy or both.

'We walked up and down the roads of that beautiful town
in the fantastic heat followed at every turn by Indonesian
Administration and plainclothes police officers. Wherever we
went there were silent Irianese walking along the roads,
standing in the shade of giant trees and wherever they were
there were Indonesians watching them. It was quite bizarre—

the watchers and the watched, the blaring, distant PA system, the flags, banners and slogans, the distant menace of nosing gunboats, the trucks, the guns, the shimmering, fantastic harbour, the brooding wall of mountains, the saturating heat. Back in the hall a delegate detached himself and came and sat with me on the large stone verandah overlooking the harbour. I was sitting with Indonesians and he had a short while before delivered a short, firm speech resounding with *merdekas* and peppered with references to the 1945 Constitution, to Sabang to Merauke and to the indivisibility of the republic. He was a Protestant minister and carried a short, natty little cane. I picked it up and he took it back from me. Pointing to himself he made mocking gestures with the cane, probing it through the air, bringing it down on some imaginary person's back and sticking it in his ribs. The message was clear enough. My Indonesian companions sat with frozen, polite smiles or looked away. He got up and returned to his official seat. A young information officer from Java looked at me. "He will be all right," he said gently. I hope he will be. And yet at the same time one of the star turns of the Manokwari *Pepera* was Lodewijck Mandajatan, the rebel leader who returned to the republic earlier this year by surrendering. He spoke earnestly and sincerely, expressing his willingness to accept the republic on behalf of himself and thousands of Arfaks, and expressing his hopes for the future.

'That night there was, as at every *Pepera*, a victory parade. For the top Indonesians, the ministers, the members of the special task force teams, the *Bupati* (DC), wives and delegates, there was a meeting at the *Pepera* centre. There were speeches, exchanges of gifts and in that unexpectedly talented Indonesian way, quite suddenly, Dr Sudjarwo—*Pepera's* "mastermind"—was at the microphone singing the special *Pepera* song. Soon a giant crocodile had formed and was dancing its way around the hall to rhythmic handclaps. It comprised Indonesians and West Irianese, Christians and Moslems, bishops and *bupatis*. This was Indonesia *true*. One noted not only the gorgeous girls of Java and Sumatra but Irianese girls in sarong and kebaja, their headdress each a single, stunning

bird of paradise whose brown wing tips matched the choco-
late of their skins. Out in the square where frightened Irianese
had run that morning there was also a celebration. It was
half Indonesian and half Papuan. Primitive Arfaks were holding a sing-sing for which pigs had been killed. There was the
smell of roast pig meat and the stench of sweating bodies in
the languid, starry night. Indonesians were holding small
parties and dancing and singing and watching the New
Guineans and eating spicy foods. One group surrounded a
Papuan woman as ugly in face as she was handsome in dress
of sarong and kebaja. Suddenly, in the darkness, she sang the
pop songs of Indonesia in throaty, tuneful voice while an
electric guitar band played. Indonesians from the great islands
to the west clapped and cheered her and sang the choruses.
She was one of them and accepted. But did she accept them?
As I turned away into the darkness, so did she. I turned to
her in the gloom and she bowed gracefully and said something. *Wel, nu is het allemaal voorbij!* Well, now it's all over!
Is that what she said? A group of Arfaks ran by half naked
in the night beating drums, chanting and dancing. One turned
and a voice in the dark in guttural English said, "Sir, we do
not like Indonesia." Back at the hotel an Irianese waiter
brought us some rare, cold beer. Members of the special
*Pepera* task force from distant Djakarta played domino, a
card game. On the radio a talented pop singer spoke softly,
caressingly in Dutch before singing in English, *People Will
Say We're In Love.* An idiot, troubled night if ever there was
one.'

And what now? West Irian is now confirmed, except for
the last and probably the least of its hurdles, the 1969 General
Assembly, as part of sovereign Indonesian territory.* It has

* The Secretary-General's report together with that of Ambassador
Fernando Ortiz-Sans and the Indonesian Government became available
to members of the General Assembly on 6 November, 1969.

Mr. Ortiz-Sans' report was careful, reasonable and, in parts, critical.
Although the UN Special Representative decided that 'an act of free
choice has taken place in West Irian in accordance with Indonesian
practice,' he was critical of the Indonesian Government's refusal to grant
free assembly of movement and speech according to the Agreement and

been given autonomous provincial status although in Biak
the Home Affairs Minister, General Mahmud, was anxious
to explain that this did not, and could never, mean self
government. There is undoubtedly a new awareness of West
Irian as a problem in Djakarta, and as a special problem in
relation to East New Guinea and Australia, evidenced by the
fact that in 1968 the central government spent five million
US dollars on reconstruction in West Irian and is in the
process of spending another seven to eight million US dollars
in the 1969-70 period. Both sums represent precious foreign
exchange, and more important, a greater expenditure per
head than on any other part of the Republic. In fact present
Indonesian plans for the economic and social development of
West Irian are potentially unpopular in Indonesia where many
areas of the Republic are in much greater want than West
Irian. The problems nevertheless remain considerable. Apart
from an extension of primary schooling Indonesia has done
little in West Irian. It has not been just a matter of past
neglect. A lack of resources combined with one of the world's
most difficult terrains and a fragmented people has made the
task almost impossible. For example, in the central highlands,
there is on average about one patrol officer per sixteen thousand people where as in the Australian administered highlands
the ratio is one patrol officer for six thousand people in
addition to numerous officers representing agricultural extension services, medical services, information and so on as well
as an extensive role now assumed by local government council.
In Australian New Guinea uncontacted people number at
most a few thousand. Two days walk from Wamena in the
central Irian highlands there are valleys comprising twenty
thousand uncontacted people. Indonesian patrol officers, some
have told me, rarely spend more than three nights out on

---

of the Indonesian Government's rejection of his request for a 'one man
one vote' poll procedure in the urban areas. Mr. Ortiz-Sans said that
'certain elements of the population of West Irian held firm convictions
in favour of independence.' At the time of writing the vote had been
postponed in the General Assembly a week to give four of the Brazzaville
nations time to study all three reports.

patrol. On the Australian side in comparable circumstances *kiaps* rarely spend less than three weeks out and often make patrols lasting two and even three months. In West Irian's central highlands there are no roads, no cattle, no peanut plantings to supply cheap protein, no coffee, no tea and no agricultural experts other than those among the various missions. They have not changed at all since I first saw them in 1958. Seeing the area again for the fourth time in August, 1969, I was reminded of Goroka or Hagen in the 'fifties when control and development were first being established. Nevertheless despite the formidable problems confronting Indonesia in West Irian there are hopeful portents that Indonesia may yet win Irianese acceptance of their place in the Republic despite the observations of Alfred Russel Wallace, that astute observer of the Malay Archipelago, who wrote in his book of the same name in 1859, that ' . . . if a tide of colonisation should be turned to New Guinea, there can be little doubt of the early extinction of the Papuan race . . . (for) the Malays and Papuans differ(ed) radically in ever physical, mental and moral character.'

Now that the uncertainty of Indonesia's formal tenure of West Irian has been removed, Djakarta has all the time it wants, provided it has the will, to bring West Irian within the mainstream of Indonesian political, social and cultural life. This will undoubtedly take a long time but in the end the process of acculturation into a great and richly varied society may well overcome the resentments of the present and the memories of the past. After all Irianese children will attend Indonesian schools, learn Indonesian as the principal *lingua franca* of discourse and become educated by the standards laid down for the rest of Indonesia. Eventually the political institutions and cultural norms of Indonesia will become those of West Irian just as they have for a dozen other, frequently dissident, ethnic groups in the Indonesian archipelago. In the end Indonesia may be far more successful in its self-appointed task of giving to the West Irianese a sense of belonging to a greater political and cultural entity, something through which they may gain a sense of identity, than

Australia may prove in trying to create an independent state out of two and a quarter million people speaking seven hundred different languages. However the success of Indonesia's efforts to reconcile the reluctant inhabitants of its seventeenth province will depend not only on sustained effort but upon the uncertain and unpredictable course of future relations between West Irian and Papua and New Guinea.

There has been a growing, if formless and imprecisely oriented pan-Papuanism at work ever since the Australian-Netherlands Co-operative Agreement in 1957. The Dutch deliberately fostered it in West New Guinea and the Australians in East New Guinea had always more or less tried to inhibit it. The problem has been to gauge how real a force it has become. In 1965-66, for example, a number of anti-Indonesian and pro-West Papuan questions were asked about West Irian in the House of Assembly but were mostly concerned with the failure of the United Nations to intervene. The questions were sufficient, however, for the Administration allegedly to ask members to refrain from asking questions in the House about the situation in West Irian or to make statements critical of Indonesia. With the border crossings of 1968 and 1969 the situation changed and New Guinean politicians were openly criticising Indonesia's activities in West Irian and Australian and United Nations refusal to intervene on behalf of the Irianese. By and large members of the House did not understand the role of the UN representative in West Irian or the function and interests of the United Nations in the act of self-determination. Matters came to a head in June, 1969, with a House resolution moved by the Member for Port Moresby Open, the Rev. Percy Chatterton, deploring Indonesian repression in West Irian, condemning the United Nations for not actively intervening on behalf of the West Irianese and requesting that the forthcoming act of self determination should truthfully reflect the wishes of the people. The House moved that the resolution should be passed to Canberra for transmission to the Secretary-General of the United Nations. This put the Department of External Affairs in an awkward position. While Australia retains external powers relating to defence and foreign policy in respect of New Guinea it had on a previous occasion unwisely encouraged, and later transmitted to the United Nations, a House resolution condemning the Soviet's intervention in Czechoslovakia. There were also two student demonstrations in Port Moresby in the first half of 1969 and general student unrest both in the University and in the Goroka Teacher Training College over events in the western part of the island. The danger in the resolution in particular, and in student protests generally, was that both encouraged the West Irianese to believe that 'deliverance' from Indonesia was on its way.

During that period I spoke to a number of students, to many local officers in the public service and to numerous politicians. Feeling ran strongly, against Indonesia just as it did among younger (as well as older) people in the urban centres of West Irian, and one frequently heard New Guineans use the phrase 'our brothers in the west.' However, New Guineans always gave a much less enthusiastic reaction to the notion of future, possible union with West Irian when one started to propound some of the financial problems involved. Few New Guineans, even the most emotional on the subject, relished the notion, in a hypothetical situation, of sharing their national income or the Australian grant-in-aid to help the West Irianese. This attitude was reflected along the border at village level where, in more than one area, there was marked reluctance to allow Irianese dissidents, unrelated by language or kinship, to make gardens, except on a temporary basis. In West Irian pan-Papuanism, like that of East New Guinea, was based on a common ethnic dislike of Indonesians but on the vague hope that union with Australian New Guinea would not only rid the Irianese of Indonesians but allow them to share in Papua/New Guinea's relatively immense affluence—stories of which had motivated many West Irianese, the economically dispossessed of the new dispensation, to cross the border in the hope of finding the same sort of jobs, incomes and goods, they had enjoyed under the Dutch. This common element of a shared dislike of Indonesia and the vaguely emerging feeling, restricted to the *élites*, of a common ethnic origin, should not be underestimated despite notable differences in *lingua franca*, administration, imposed political institutions, legal system and economic levels between the two sides of the island. The most potent factor in West Irianese unrest may yet prove to be New Guinea's comfortable and subsidised march to independence which can only remind West Irianese *élites* of the independence which the Dutch had promised them in the 1970's. Eventual independence for Papua and New Guinea is regarded with considerable and well warranted misgivings by Indonesia.

The fact that West Irian is now confirmed as an integral part of Indonesia has so far settled little except West Irian's legal status. Unless Indonesia can combine its acculturation processes in West Irian with a fair degree of local autonomy and a solid and sustained effort to develop the western half of the island economically, the West Irianese will probably continue in a state of sporadic, semi-rebellion, the results of which are likely to overflow into Papua and New Guinea in ways yet to reveal themselves and over the years tend to crystallise pan-Papuan thinking into more concrete and positive political forms. Pan-Papuanism will, under any circumstances, be provoked in various and unpredictable ways. It is interesting to note, for example, the numerous references in the FUNDWI[20] (Fund for the United Nations Development of West Irian) report advocating contact between West Irian and New Guinea through scholarships, study tours and through that most potent of all common interests, the development of trade. It seems inevitable that in the future both students and politicians on both sides of the border will seek contact with each other, if only in the spirit of friendly curiosity and broad ethnic identity. The fact that the border is currently marked and patrolled, that the people on either side of it live in stone age villages, and that Australian authorities apply strict criteria to the admission of refugees, will not prevent the increasing flow of ideas between Port Moresby and Djajapura by letter, by pamphlet and by newspaper— and by direct exchange of Papuan personnel if FUNDWI

[20] United Nations, New York, 1968.

recommendations are adopted. In short, strict border control cannot guarantee immunity from the ultimate impact of new and exciting political ideas on East and West New Guineans alike from the great world outside. Increasing *élite* literacy in English on both sides of the border will be the most potent factor in this.

On either side of the border overt moves towards union, or even towards close and sympathetic forms of future Papuan co-operation, will undoubtedly be viewed by Indonesia with suspicion if not active resentment, thus placing a strain on Australian-Indonesian relations. As both new order Indonesia and Australia will regard the preservation of good relations between the two as being of primary importance, both are likely to exercise tact and discretion in their separate and joint handling of New Guinea and its problems. And great tact and discretion *will* be required on the part of Australia and Indonesia to handle the problem. One line of action should be to discourage any attempts by East New Guinean politicians, students or others to visit West Irian and to discourage the West Irianese from visiting Papua and New Guinea for educational tours or for other reasons. There is currently the quite reasonable hope in Djakarta and Djajapura that there can be a steady exchange of officials, University lecturers and others between the two sides of the island and that Irianese students, for example, should attend technical and other institutions in Australian New Guinea. This notion should be most carefully examined. Irianese students visiting Papua and New Guinea are almost certain to be impressed by the material standards, growing political fervour, and coming independence of East New Guinea and to return to West Irian severely dissatisfied if not entirely disaffected. Similarly, visits by East New Guineans to West Irian would probably act as a focus for West Irianese discontent thus stirring up the very problems that it is as much in New Guinea's interests, as in Australia's, to avoid. There are understandable hopes in Djakarta, now that *Pepera* is over, that Administration experts in various fields in East New Guinea can make regular visits to West Irian to advise on various matters, such as agricultural development in the Highlands. Visits like these will need very careful thought if they are to become part of a regular pattern. While at this stage the Australian Administration would perforce send European officers this situation will change in a few years time as local officers replace them. It will be far better, until such time as New Guinea is independent when it will have to become responsible for its own foreign policy towards Indonesia of which West Irian is inalienably part, to minimise contact between the two sides of the island, diverting, if possible, New Guinean interest in West Irian towards the nature and structure of Indonesia, the immensely powerful and populous neighbour with whose ultimate goodwill New Guinea's future well being is so largely involved. By the same token it will be more fruitful, in every sense, to take West Irianese students into Australian rather than Territory institutions.

At the same time it is obvious that Indonesia will not be able by itself to maintain the momentum of economic and social development in West Irian necessary to ensure that its people will reconcile themselves to being Indonesian citizens which is so obviously in their best interests as well as in those of Australia and New Guinea. Australia must, therefore, consider ways and means of giving aid to West Irian, the primary purpose of which is to dampen political tension and anti-Indonesian feeling.

The most important economic activity in West Irian comprises the current operations of FUNDWI—an organisation set up by the United Nations to implement the economic plans recommended to the Indonesian government by the UN survey mission and to oversee the expenditure of $US30m. granted by the Netherlands in 1962 as a 'farewell' gift towards West Irian's economic development. Equal to the Dutch grant-in-aid to West New Guinea in 1962, it is, as the reporting mission emphasises, 'a modest sum in relation to West Irian's problems'. Of the $30m., very nearly half is being spent on refurbishing transport, particularly coastal and river transportation which has deteriorated spectacularly through the Indonesian Administration's incapacity to maintain vessels left by the Dutch, or to replace unserviceable craft. Seven million dollars is being spent on river and coastal transportation and $4m. on small aircraft to maintain administrative contact with outlying stations and on strip repair and maintenance. New aircraft already purchased, or being purchased, include three Twin Otters and spares, and spares for currently operating DC3s. Other sums are being used for infrastructure repair—roads, trucks, electrical generative power, telecommunications, water purification plants, and so on—and for agricultural and livestock programmes. As will be seen from the table in the Appendix, relatively large sums are suggested for vocational training and education, as well as for forestry and fisheries exploitation. See Appendix G.

Possibly the most fruitful suggestion by the FUNDWI team is that of a Joint Development Commission, to which is allocated $4.5m. of the total fund. The Commission's functions include overseeing development in all sectors and acting as a development corporation. The JDC finances development activities through loans and equity investments 'in accordance with appropriate criteria'. The function of the Joint Development Commission has obviously been conceived, perhaps hopefully, as an ongoing institution. While most of the Netherlands loan will have been expended by the end of 1970, and FUNDWI have phased out by the end of 1973, the Commission by its very nature will still have funds at its disposal because it will have made a large part of its activities concerned with loans to small enterprises for self-liquidating ventures. Djakarta is very much aware of the cut-out date of FUNDWI's operations, and is conscious of both the political problems that will arise in the province when aid money is no longer available for limited development and of its powerlessness to do much about the situation. From the point of view of the West Irianese, it could prove yet another Indonesian failure. In 1961 the West Irianese were enjoying the benefits of Dutch subsidisation which ended in Dutch withdrawal, seen by many as 'betrayal'. In 1962 they were showered with Indonesian promises and in subsequent years exposed to Indonesian performance. In 1966 they again received Indonesian promises, which were in part fulfilled by the commencement of FUNDWI operations in 1968. If, in 1970, after the promises made during *Pepera*, renewed economic activity, limited though it is, virtually ceases, West Irianese political resentments and tensions will become acute. Mr Malik, in several conversations in West Irian, during *Pepera*, made it clear to me that the Indonesian Government had considerable reservations about the economic planning and actual fund expenditures carried out by FUNDWI. So did the *panglima*, Brigadier General Saruo Edhie, and the Special Assistant for West Irian Affairs, Dr Sudjarwo. The general feeling was that there were no results for FUNDWI expenditures, that the Asian Development Bank might be better suited to lend money and carry out economic surveys and that, in any case, the Indonesian Government felt that the FUNDWI charter and style was 'a reflection on Indonesian capacities,' which indeed they are. Nevertheless from the point of view of potential donors it is precisely FUNDWI's autonomy, combined with the expertise of its staff that makes it attractive. On 7 September Mr Malik told journalists in Bangkok that he still felt that Development Bank aid was desirable. Whether the ADB's charter would extend to aid for West Irian is a moot point. FUNDWI, after all, is *in situ*.

The ongoing nature of the JDC therefore presents the Australian government with an excellent means of contributing to West Irianese development through small annual aid grants, for an indefinite period. There are good reasons for doing so if we wish to avoid the political problems inherent in the increasing disparity between economic development in East and West New Guinea. As suggested earlier, one of the political problems arising from this imbalance is its unsettling effect on educated West Irianese, who are increasingly aware of East New Guinea's relatively rapid and extensive economic development. This awareness only feeds their resentment of their Indonesian bondage while creating in many the manifest desire to seek union with East New Guinea. The maintenance of steady economic activity in West Irian would undoubtedly take a great deal of heat out of the current situation of political unrest and resentment, although it would by no means remove all of it.

I have previously suggested through the editorial columns of *The Australian* that it is very much in Australia's national interests to help dampen down tension in West Irian if ways and means can be found compatible with Indonesia's sense of sovereignty and nationalist sensitivities. Unilateral gifts to the Indonesian government with the stipulation that they must be used only for West Irian's economic development raises many problems and would, moreover, cause the Indonesian government embarrassment. In any case it is unlikely that an Australian cabinet or treasury would view with favour a suggestion of special direct aid to Indonesia for use in West Irian, especially as Australian aid to Indonesia is now close to $20m. yearly. FUNDWI presents a different proposition for Australian aid to the province. It is a United Nations organisation which can oversee fund disbursements rather than the Indonesian government itself. This in itself obviates many practical and political problems. It also avoids any chiliast expectations that might follow in West Irian if aid were directly identified in any way with the donor country —a special problem where Australia is concerned. FUNDWI can also call upon international experts and, as it is now established in Djajapura, it can also operate on a fairly continuous basis through its Joint Development Commission if ongoing funds are available. Australia should therefore contribute to the operations of the Joint Development Fund either by direct grant or through an agreed amount over and above the present level of aid given to Indonesia, in conjunction with the Netherlands and the United States. Japan might also be approached as a donor country, and West Germany. There are many powerful institutions in the Netherlands, including the Protestant and Roman Catholic Churches, which have a continuing and dedicated interest in the progress of the people of the lost Dutch colony. In fact the $30m. Dutch gift-in-aid, to oversee the expenditure of which FUNDWI was created, is an indication that the Netherlands government might view Australian initiatives in this direction with considerable favour. The United States interest in the proposition would be of a different order, but no less important. The United States is directly concerned with the economic and political regeneration of Indonesia on the stability of which it regards in large part the security of South-East Asia as resting. Part of that security is closely involved with continuing good relations between Australia and Indonesia which will greatly depend in the future on the degree to which New Guinea does not become a matter of contention between the two countries. To this extent the United States might be persuaded to become a donor country. Any notion of foreign aid funds for West Irian through the agency of FUNDWI's Joint Development Commission is based on the assumption that Indonesia will continue a grant-in-aid to its Administration of not less than its current subvention of $7m. yearly. It is impossible to suggest the size of foreign government donations to a scheme of this sort, because there are a number of technical problems to be considered. For a number of reasons, however, including the need to avoid a degree of development in West Irian far in advance of that in other parts of the Republic, the overall amount of foreign aid should be modest—possibly not more than $US8 million annually which added to Indonesia's contribution should ensure $17m. yearly. The desirable characteristic of this form of aid should not in any case be its size, beyond a certain level, but its continuity according to a fixed plan of economic development drawn up and administered by FUNDWI in conjunction with the Indonesian government.

Aid for West Irian will not solve all the problems of the future and may actually create some, for economic development in West Irian will not necessarily remove political unrest. Unaccompanied by more liberal Indonesian attitudes to greater political autonomy for Djakarta's reluctant seventeenth province, economic development by itself could easily lead to even greater dissatisfaction than there is at the moment. Increased economic development means increased social and inter-ethnic mobility. It means more education. It means more overseas travel for West Irianese and consequently greater opportunities for comparisons, some of which will inevitably be invidious. It may mean future trade between West Irian and Australia's rapidly developing hard currency markets. This in turn implies an inevitably closer future interest in West Irian's affairs on the part of Australian and New Guinean governments and people for developments of this sort have their own momentum. However, the alternative is to leave a resentful Indonesian province next door to two and a quarter million people of similar ethnic composition subsidised to relatively immense affluence and destined for independence. If, therefore, contact between the two New Guineas, with all of its inherent risks to Australian-Indonesian relations, is inevitable, sometime in the future, if not at the present time, then it is surely best that it occur under conditions in which West Papuans are a good deal better off economically than they are at present. A further positive aspect of the suggestion above is that ongoing aid to West Irian, whether through FUNDWI or by other means, is likely to ensure continued Indonesian interest in the province's overall development. Indonesia has made a start on redressing past wrongs and in an awakened mood of enlightened self-interest has instituted against formidable odds a new deal for West Irian. There is undeniable evidence of new Indonesian attitudes and intentions which are substantial straws in the winds of change. The question is whether the same winds will continue to blow since the successful conclusion of the 1969 act of self-determination. Preoccupied with numerous, difficult, perhaps intractable problems in all parts of the archipelago, the Indonesian government might, in the absence of outside incentives, or aid, decide to leave West Irian to its fate.

In these circumstances it will be an ironic comment on the age of decolonisation that relatively huge annual sums of money, at present nearly $A10 a head for every Australian, will have been spent in East New Guinea to prepare it for independence only to make it the envy and despair of its captive neighbour and the possibly enduring object of Indonesian resentment.

# 7 The Future

*And when you are seeking the answer to the question of what is good for the people, do not overlook the fact that they will claim and will have their own identity. They are not going to be imitation Australians but will want to be real Papuans.*

—Hon. Paul Hasluck, Minister of State for Territories, 'The Future in Papua and New Guinea', 6 January 1964

*Independence for Papua-New Guinea will not be achieved for very many years, if at all.*

Hon. C. E. Barnes, Minister of State for Territories, 5 March 1967

Proximity, with its defence implications, has been the principal influence on Australian attitudes towards New Guinea, inhibiting rather than promoting clearly defined metropolitan policies on the end status of Australia's colonial dependency and obscuring public discussion.[1] Geographically almost part of the mainland, culturally in large part one of the world's last primeval redoubts, New Guinea has posed particular problems for Australia unlike those facing other colonial powers whose colonial possessions were in most instances thousands of miles distant.

Queensland's border, for example, extends north from the Great Barrier Reef almost to the Gulf of Papua before turning sharply westward to follow the south Papuan coastline, in some places less than two miles offshore. At this point it encloses three islands inhabited by 800 people of predominantly Papuan stock who are Australian citizens and who vote in the Federal elections but not in those of Queensland. A few miles away on the Papuan coast are Papuans who are also Australian citizens, who cannot vote in any Australian elections and who can only enter the Australian mainland by special permission.[2]

[1] 'I have been fortunate in having an uninformed electorate,' Prime Minister Sir Robert Menzies said to the author in a discussion on New Guinea, November 1963.
[2] Since writing these lines the Member for Fly Open, Mr Elia Olewale, brought the anomalous boundary position to the attention of the House at the June 1969 sitting, demanding that the boundary be redrawn— further south.

These anomalies, like that of the Queensland border, are the heritage of early Australian preoccupations with New Guinea as the first line of defence. As we have seen in Chapter 2 it was defence rather than gold, the spice trade or the salvation of souls that brought Australians to New Guinea of which the southern half, at least, was thought indispensable to Australia's continental security.

The belief that New Guinea was essential to Australia's defence, promoted in the 1880's and asserted in the Australian occupation of German New Guinea in 1914 was confirmed, in Australian eyes, by the Japanese invasion of 1942. It remained firm government doctrine well into the post-war decades. In 1950, in response to Indonesian claims to West New Guinea, then then Territories Minister, Mr (now Sir Percy) Spender said that ' . . . experience has shown to the Australians how strategically vital to Australian defence is the mainland of New Guinea.' His successor in the Territories portfolio, Mr (now Sir Paul) Hasluck, said late in 1951 that '. . . to Australia [New Guinea] is sure to be recognised as a strategic barrier or possible battleground' over the 'next half century.' In 1954, Sir Percy Spender as Australian Ambassador to the United States, told the UN General Assembly, when opposing Indonesian claims to West New Guinea and voicing Australian alarm over militant Indonesian attitudes, that '. . . there remains the bitter lesson that New Guinea will forever be a potential invasion springboard to Australia.'

However, while defence remained a major preoccupation of Australian governments in this period, it was no longer the only one. Post-war Australian governments faced social, political and economic problems undreamt of in pre-war times. Australia was now charged with the development towards self-determination of New Guinea under the UN Trust Agreement to which it added its sovereign Territory of Papua in an administrative union. Elsewhere the colonial world was collapsing. In Asia the imperial powers had all but gone. In Africa they were soon to depart. Could Australia expect in its primitive colonial dependency the early emergence of nationalist movements such as those which had swept Asia and were beginning to appear in Africa? Just what were Australia's long term responsibilities in Papua and New Guinea? Was the preparation for independence, in Australian eyes always likely to be premature, among them?

It hardly seemed so. On assuming office in 1951 the new Minister for Territories, Mr Hasluck, had said that Australian aims in New Guinea were 'to retain what is best in native life and blend it with western civilisation so that, while gaining the advantages of western civilisation, they will not lose pride in the fact that they have an identity as Papuans and so that, when in the generations to come, they may be required to manage their own affairs to a greater degree, they may feel a common bond among themselves as a people.' *In the generations to come!* Even eventual independence was unthinkable. What then was thinkable?

Among some Australian intellectuals and others interested in New Guinea and problems of decolonisation there were voices advocating that Papua and New Guinea should become Australia's seventh state. The chief motivation seemed to be that of defence combined with paternalism and the fact that statehood seemed as good a way of tidying up unfinished business as any other. Statists seemed particularly evident among those who lived in or had served in New Guinea. At the 1958 Australian Institute of Political Science Summer School on 'New Guinea and Australia', Mr Ian Downs, a forceful Territorian personality and Goroka planter, a former District Commissioner and a subsequent MHA, advocated in strong terms that Papua and New Guinea should become a state of Australia and urged 'the granting of Australian citizenship and nationality to all the inhabitants who wish to become Australian.'

Downs' statement, and others like it,[3] signalled the beginning of a very long debate in this country, only recently, and

[3] At the same seminar, Mr Arthur Calwell, then Leader of the Opposition, said, 'we have an obligation to prepare these people for the day, which may be thirty or fifty years ahead or more, when they will choose freely and without duress whether they wish to become an independent nation or a member state of the British Commonwealth or a state or states of the Commonwealth of Australia'.

reluctantly, concluded, on statehood, a special relationship and various other forms of close association between Australia and New Guinea. In every way it has been one of the most unreal debates ever carried out in Australia, even if historically it has been curiously significant because of the manner in which it has revealed the fundamental and continuing reluctance of Australian governments to set clear constitutional goals—let alone target dates—for New Guinea and to plan accordingly.

The general argument for statehood in the 1950's was based on proximity, historical association and the necessity to secure New Guinea in the interests of Australia's defence. Subsidiary arguments were that New Guinea's tropical economy was supplementary to Australia's, that underpopulated Australia needed New Guinea's manpower and that New Guinea in the final analysis was too fragmented and unstable to become a viable, independent state and would merely form, in J. P. McAuley's pungent phrase another 'coconut republic'.[4]

The statehood proposition was interesting in two respects. It came from almost entirely conservative intellectual quarters and in a curiously romantic way it represented a virtual rejection of white Australia affirming that as large scale Asian (coloured) migration to Australia seemed inevitable where better to begin than with New Guineans, a people of known pro-Australian sentiments and for whom Australia had a special responsibility? On close examination statehood was clearly unworkable on the question alone of unrestricted migration of New Guineans into Australia.

Statehood meant, in effect, the admission to Australian citizenship of some two million New Guineans in every stage of development from the uncontacted villager to a then handful of largely mission-educated *évolués*, representing some seventeen per cent of Australia's predominantly white population. It meant that two million New Guineans, whether choosing to exercise their prerogatives or not, were entitled to unrestricted access to Australia, to equal job opportunities, to social services and to the vote. It meant that New Guinea in the Federal Par-

[4] See James McAuley in 'Pacific Affairs', 1953. James McAuley is now Professor of English in the University of Tasmania.

liament would automatically have the same number of Senators as other states and, in the lower House, about the same number of representatives as New South Wales—the most populous state. Quite apart from the enormous costs of subsidising New Guinea to bring it as rapidly as possible to social parity with the other states of the Commonwealth, the notion of statehood for New Guinea's two million black, tribalised people was all the more surprising in view of Australia's traditional treatment of its Aborigines. Nothing in the history of white Australian attitudes to the indigenous people of Australia might have led anyone to suppose that immigrant New Guineans would have been treated any differently if they had appeared in large numbers, or even relatively small ones, in mainland Australia to form inevitable enclaves in its cities and tropical towns. The implied alternative to statehood was 'second class statehood', i.e. limited admission and limited rights until such time as New Guineans achieved cultural approximation. Although the constitutional machinery seemed available—Australia's Federal Parliament has the power to admit or establish a new state and impose such terms and conditions on its admission and its representation 'in either House of Parliament as it thinks fit'—it would have proved politically impossible; acceptable neither to Australians, the United Nations, nor, in the long run, to New Guineans themselves.

The seventh state proposition, or any of its possible variants, in short created many problems and resolved few. It also involved where New Guinea, as distinct from Papua, was concerned, a discharge of the UN Trusteeship. Nevertheless it represented the first attempt to think seriously about the long term future of Australia and its New Guinea dependency. It also remained seriously tenacious in its hold on government thinking. After a brief flirtation with the notion of declaring unequivocal independence as the end goal of Australian New Guinea policies in the early 1960's, the Government returned to various unspecific notions of modified statism which still vaguely persist today as evidenced in Lord Casey's June 1968 address to the House of Assembly although Mr Gorton's more unequivocal statement of July, 1969, must finally end all ambiguity on the matter. The growing crisis of the 1950's between Holland and Indonesia over West New Guinea created pressing diplomatic and political problems over the future of the western half of the island which forced the Australian government to think about a different solution for New Guinea. In the mid-1950's the Dutch began to seek more active Australian support for the Netherlands position which rested, principally, on legitimacy of occupation in West New Guinea, on the ethnical differences between the Papuans of West New Guinea and the other peoples of Indonesia and on the West Papuans' ultimate right to self-determination which the Dutch claimed to protect. Australian responses to Dutch overtures led to the Netherlands-Australian Co-operative Agreement of November 1957, proclaiming the principle of self-determination for both West and East New Guineans and stating that the Netherlands and Australia would co-operate with each other administratively 'in a manner which recognises (their) ethnological and geographical affinity'.[5]

Without spelling it out, the Agreement clearly envisaged the possibility of the two sides of New Guinea becoming one independent political unit in the future. In December of the same year, Mr R. G. (later Lord) Casey, Minister for External Affairs, said in reference to the Agreement that of many possibilities open to New Guineans in the future '. . . a single political unit for the whole island will be one of them'. The Australian Government was inherently uneasy about the Agreement nevertheless. As Mr Casey said exactly one month before the Co-operative Agreement was signed, Indonesian claims to West New Guinea '. . . project Australia into the position of having to oppose a neighbour with whom we have no difference whatsoever,' a sentiment shrewdly echoed by Dr Subandrio at the General Assembly the same year when he said he believed that in the end Australia woud find 'Indonesia as a whole more important than a Netherlands colonial enclave'. It did. The Agreement was not a thoughtful exercise in colonial disengagement but a manoeuvre to keep the island of

[5] See Appendix H.

New Guinea uncontaminated by the presence of an unstable, possibly Communist and probably expansionist Indonesia. At the end of January 1958, at the previously mentioned political science summer school, a Sydney lawyer and noted Australian commentator on New Guinea affairs, Mr J. R. (now Mr Justice) Kerr, in a paper entitled 'The Political Future', attempted to put both Australian Government and some private thinking on the possibilities contained in the Agreement into a theoretical framework by proposing the establishment of a Melanesian Federation which was to include West and East New Guinea and the British Solomons.[6] He suggested this as a positive aim for the future and that active and essential British and US support as well as Dutch, should be enlisted for the purpose. He envisaged the Federation ultimately as a weak but independent state within the British Commonwealth propped up politically and economically by Britain, the United States and Australia.

The proposition, enthusiastically adopted by the Dutch, probably alarmed the Australian Government, partly because of the traditional intellectual inertia of Australian cabinets over any proposals regarding New Guinea's political future but mostly because of the Government's understandable caution over any course of action which might irreparably harm Australia's long term relations with Indonesia,[7]—the effects of which Mr Kerr's paper tended to ignore—now busily mobilising massive Afro-Asian support for its West Irian claims. There was also evidence that the United States and Britain might desert the Dutch who were showing clear signs of internal weakening. While ingenious, the Federation idea was far too

[6] As part of the argument for Federation the paper skilfully rejected other political solutions for New Guinea, including statehood.

[7] In retrospect the gravest political risk of continued great power opposition to Indonesia's claims to West Irian was the possibility of a successful Communist coup. By mid-1962 pro-Western Indonesian politicians and intellectuals were being placed in an impossible situation over a national issue from which it was impossible, except at the risk of personal and political eclipse, to withhold support. The West Irian issue, perhaps more than any other, was one through which the PKI might have arrived at power, either by coup or, under some circumstances, by acclamation.

late. It is just possible that it might have had a chance if it had been advanced ten years earlier.

In a broadcast primarily to Europeans in the Territory on December 4, 1959, from Port Moresby, Mr Hasluck deplored 'a rumour . . . being woven about insecurity . . . as the Prime Minister said when he visited the Territory: "Here we are and here we stay" . . .' Less than a year later this stand was being modified by the Prime Minister, Mr Menzies. On his arrival at Mascot on 20 June 1960, from the Prime Ministers' Conference, he said with special reference to developments in Africa:

'Whereas at one time many of us might have thought that it was better to go slowly in granting independence so that all conditions existed for a wise exercise of self-government, I think the prevailing school of thought today is that if in doubt you go sooner, not later. I belong to that school of thought myself now, thought I didn't once. But I have seen enough in recent years to satisfy me that even though some independences may have been premature, where they may have been a little premature, they have at least been achieved with goodwill . . . *Question*: Would you apply that view to New Guinea, sir? *Prime Minister*: I would apply that to any country.'

Nevertheless in amplification of his statement he added that he did not belong to 'this fancy school of thought that you write a time table and say "in ten years time so and so, and in twenty years time so and so" '.

Two months later, 23 August, in the House of Representatives Mr Hasluck himself referred to independence in cautious terms. Remarking on the UN trusteeship system, and to Australia's share in helping promote and 'embrace it', Mr Hasluck quoted Article 73 of the Charter, which refers to the responsibilities of administering powers, saying:

'The end of the trusteeship comes with self government and independence. One point which should be recognised internationally is that political independence on its own is of limited value unless the people have the capacity to use their independence to their own advantage.' But two years later the Prime Minister was to become much more positive in his views on New Guinea's ultimate political status. On the occasion of his

Jefferson Oration in the United States in 1963, the year of Indonesia's takeover of West Irian he said: 'We look forward to the time when those Territories (Papua and New Guinea) will be completely politically and economically independent...' His statement was quoted by Australia's External Affairs Minister, Sir Garfield Barwick, at the UN General Assembly several months later. For the first time in Australian history ultimate independence for New Guinea was official policy although it didn't arise from any deliberative Cabinet processes. It was a much more haphazard, personal reaction by Sir Robert to external events. Just possibly it was due in part to reaction to the uncertain problems raised by Indonesia's possession of the western half of the island. Mostly it was a reaction to Mr Harold Macmillan's 'winds of change' speech in South Africa, to the pace and fervour of African decolonisation, and to the strong, anti-colonialist sentiments of the United Nations which had been formalised in the 1960 Resolution 1514 xv or 'Declaration on the Granting of Independence to Colonial Countries and Peoples.' At all events the 'independence' policy was remarkably short-lived. With the appointment in 1964 of a new Minister for Territories, Mr C. E. Barnes, there was a return to Mr Hasluck's thoughtful, if implacable gradualism with an added ingredient—complete muddle. Mr Barnes immediately drew back from the idea of unequivocally declaring that independence was the political aim of Australian Government policy in New Guinea. 'Independence', he said in 1965, was not 'the inevitable or predetermined result of political development as some commentators on the Territory would ... assume. The historical and geographical ties between Australia and New Guinea are such that the people of the Territory might seek some closer association with this country.' There were, he continued, between 'self-government' as the 'minimum' and 'sovereign independence' as the 'maximum' a 'variety of arrangements which could be made within these two positions if the people desired a continuing relationship with Australia'. It was a deliberately confusing statement reflecting the old, scarcely concealed, seventh state paternalism.

What made this policy improbable was its very vagueness. What was the 'variety of arrangements' which the Minister had in mind? And why should he have thought that they 'could be made' by New Guineans in some sort of game of political lucky dip? And why above all did he imagine that such choices would be implemented simply by the process of New Guineans opting for them? After all if New Guineans 'desired a continuing relationship with Australia' the people of Australia at some time would have to be consulted. Paradoxically, many basic Australian policies in New Guinea, whether consciously or not, were inimical to the whole conception of statehood or to a constitutionally formalised 'close association' between Australia and New Guinea. Had the Government ever seriously thought through the implications of statehood, for example, it would not have pursued different wage policies for the Territory and Australia. If New Guinea was destined for statehood indigenous public servants' salaries should have been at parity with those in Australia. Instead, they were deliberately fixed at 40 per cent of the mainland rate.

Moreover, the political situation had changed dramatically with the establishment of Indonesian sovereignty over West Irian. If the issue had ever come to be seriously examined it would have been seen that it was one thing to talk of statehood for Australian New Guinea when it bordered a Dutch colony but entirely another to talk of it when West New Guinea was a province of Indonesia, which in 1963 looked as if it might become Communist and certainly appeared to many as expansionist.

The most active adherents of seventh statism or close association, were in New Guinea itself.[8] For many Europeans working in a remote, tropical, provincial society far removed from the realities of Australian political life, let alone those of the anti-colonialist world of the United Nations, the admission of New Guinea as a state of Australia was seen as a purely domestic affair, offering them permanent security of tenure in business, on the plantations and in the Administration and confirming that 'fifty years of sacrifice' were not in vain. For the

[8] See Appendix I.

emergent, native population, fragmented into small, traditional societies, and psychologically and economically dependent on continued Australian protection, aid and skills, statehood, the real nature and implications of which they could not possibly understand, was both comprehensible and highly desirable if represented as an assurance of permanent, large scale subsidy at Australian mainland levels.[9] One of New Guinea's political parties, the United Christian Democrats Party, said plainly in 1967 that a principal plank in its political platform was statehood for New Guinea. The Minister's 1965 statement therefore, with its implied options for some close relationship, short of statehood but of a fairly binding nature between Australia and New Guinea, ran the risk of creating unrealistic hopes among many New Guineans of a permanent political association with Australia—which many Papuans still hope for as insurance against their fears of New Guinea side domination—which more than likely Australians would repudiate at the time of decision. Although subsequent ministerial statements on the subject were to prove a little more restrained, the hinted promise of a future close constitutional tie remained for some considerable time thereafter.

The Minister's statement created other difficulties, in the United Nations and with Australia's Afro-Asian critics. Apart from Sir Garfield Barwick's statement on unqualified independence in 1963, Australia's representatives in the United Nations, while religiously reiterating that New Guineans could have independence when and if they wanted it, never actually stated up till the time of writing in 1969 that independence was the sole Australian political aim for New Guinea. The key word has been self-determination. One of the principal reasons given by Government apologists for the use of this unspecific word has been that New Guineans in their state of dependence on Australia would equate a statement on independence with desertion. Many Europeans in the Highlands push this very view with natives relentlessly. An official Australian declaration that it was preparing New Guinea for independence, it

[9] Especially the Highlanders. See J. T. Gunther, *New Guinea*, No. 6, p. 25, 1966.

was said, would produce panic and chaos among New Guineans especially among the more recently contacted, more conservative and more numerous Highlands populations. It was at best only half an argument. It is undoubtedly true that a bold, unqualified statement on independence without repeated assurances that Australian aid would continue after independence, and that independence would not come before a time of the New Guineans own choosing, might earlier have had serious consequences in New Guinea. However, a general statement on independence as being Australia's firm policy goal such as Mr Gorton's statement in July 1969, with its implications of continued Australian aid has obviously proved acceptable, although there is plenty of evidence to suggest that the thought of losing their special status, which independence implies, is beginning to worry many Papuans.

One of the more curious aspects of government policy in this respect has been its continued failure to see that exaggerated gradualism defeats its own purpose. New Guineans cannot prepare for independence, or any other constitutional settlement, in a political vacuum. If independence is to be the end result why should not New Guineans be told so that they may adjust to the prospect psychologically and prepare for it politically and institutionally by means of flexible, long term target dates? If independence is not the goal of Australian policy then New Guineans—and Australians—should surely be told so. Until very recently the Government simply never availed itself of the opportunity to declare that it has in mind any specific political solution for New Guinea of any sort other than the vague statement that it is preparing New Guineans for 'self-determination'. What does this mean? There are some things which are not open to New Guineans solely to determine, e.g., statehood or any form of close association. These choices are even more a matter for Australians to make up their minds on. One of the Government's unstated reasons for avoiding an unequivocal statement on independence has been its belief, at least in the past, that if the word independence created fear among New Guineans it might induce panic among many in the European private sector on whose business skills and investments the Government has always, if understandably, too heavily relied. In the end, however, it is hard to avoid the conclusion that the main motivation of Government equivocation has been a lingering paternalistic desire, buttressed by the argument that New Guinea is essential to Australia's defence, to maintain in some form or another close ties with New Guinea. In the Territory there are some indigenes and Europeans, comprising politicians and others, as well as some civil servants in the Department of Territories in Canberra who, as an alternative to statehood, have assiduously toiled to promote a future constitutional relationship between Australia and New Guinea along the lines of that existing between the United States and Puerto Rico, Holland and Surinam, Cook Islands and New Zealand and Britain and Antigua.[10] The weakness of these models lies precisely, as in the seventh state proposition, in their migration provisions. In the examples quoted the populations of the dependencies, in some instances with unfettered access to their metropolitan partners, are relatively advanced and comprise only about one per cent of the metropolitan country's. New Guinea's largely tribalised indigenous population already comprises 17 per cent of Australia's. With rapid natural increase New Guinea's population will come within a relatively few years to represent an even higher percentage of Australia's.

Those who used to advocate seventh state, or, more commonly in recent times, some form of special relationship, also ignore the very real objections raised by the anti-colonialist bloc in the United Nations, which until now, certainly, has seen both propositions as mere devices enabling Australia to maintain its 'colonialist' domination of New Guinea. It has been a consistent criticism of African delegates that Australia

[10] On 22 November 1965, a meeting of the Constitutional Select Committee of the House of Assembly in Port Moresby directed its executive officer to obtain details of the history and present status of the constitutional relationship between the United States and Puerto Rico and 'any similar special relationships between countries'. Some time after April 1966, when the Select Committee had returned from Canberra to Port Moresby, it was reported in the press that the Department of Territories was investigating these 'special relationships'.

creates suspicion by its very refusal to announce that New Guinea is destined for independence, and for nothing else but independence. In the 1966 meeting of the United Nations Fourth Committee, Australia could only muster seven votes against a resolution calling for specific, early dates for independence. A Russian delegate to a Fourth Committee meeting the same year put it very succinctly when he said that if Australia did not think New Guinea ready for independence, then it should say so.

Independence as a fixed, target-dated goal, was very far from the mind of the Australian government then or two years later, when the Governor-General, Lord Casey, said in his speech opening Federal Parliament on 12 March 1968, and again, word for word, in his speech to the House of Assembly on 4 June 1968:

> The destiny of Papua and New Guinea is to become a self-governing country developed for independence if and when it is clearly demonstrated that this is what they wish. My Government's policy for Papua and New Guinea is therefore to develop it for self-determination.
>
> Whether some subsequent special relationship with Australia is worked out, and what such a special relationship might be, can only be worked out in the future between the then Government of a self-governing Papua and New Guinea and the then Government of Australia.
>
> But my Government believes that the development of Papua and New Guinea as a seventh state of Australia is fraught with difficulties and that statehood as against self-government is not likely to be the outcome of Government.

If the speech was in the nature of a reluctant burial service for statehood it still left open in ambiguous terms the possibility of some relationship short of statehood. The use of the term 'special relationship' was characteristically vague. If the government envisaged throughout 1968, as the Governor-General's words implied, some form of future special relationship then why did it not say what it was? The policy announced in Lord Casey's speech was almost identical with that of Mr Barnes in 1965, more cautiously worded but essentially the same. A year later, in a statement that revealed obvious differences of opinion with both the Minister and his departmental advisers, the Prime Minister, Mr Gorton, in a television programme from Melbourne on 6 July 1969, came firmly down on the side of independence. In answer to a question on New Guinea's constitutional development he said:

'No, I don't see Papua/New Guinea becoming an eighth state . . . we do not see this as a possibility . . . we see Papua and New Guinea as an independent, self-governing state in its own right and we are seeking to develop it towards that end.' This seems to be unequivocal even though it neither raises nor disposes of the promises of a 'special relationship' at the time of self-determination, mentioned in the Governor-General's speech twelve months before. However, while independence should mean neither more nor less than what it says, namely, sovereignty, it often does mean different things to different people, whether in Port Moresby or in Canberra. The Governor-General's speech, where it deals with New Guinea was of course written for him by the responsible Minister and his departmental advisers. That of Mr Gorton's is presumably all his own work. There is a sharp difference of tone and view between the two. Mr Gorton's speech which refers to independence in unqualified terms seems to suggest that he believes that nothing less than independence will *ultimately* suit Australians, our Afro-Asian critics who would be likely to view any special relationship as disguised neo-colonialism and, not least of all, New Guineans themselves despite regionalist fears and pressures and the present desire of the majority, as expressed in the House, for continued Australian aid.

The policy contained in the Governor-General's speech, which was a formal statement to the parliament of New Guinea, in effect says that New Guinea will have independence 'if and when' its people want it. In short, if they don't ask for it they won't get it and Australia will neither force it on them nor plan it for them. This in the end is a policy of sheer drift smugly rationalised as one of flexibility in which the government supposedly leaves its options open. It ignores, as Australian policy has for many years, the need for New Guineans to be able to plan their political future within some framework of certainty. It is not enough to claim, as the Government has over New Guinea for many years, that it will not force the pace or seek to 'impose' solutions upon New Guineans because, in the fullness of time, New Guineans might arrive at their own solutions. How? New Guineans have no way of arriving at solutions because they have been given no alternatives. The prototype Westminster government which now operates in New Guinea was 'imposed' in any case. However, a much more serious implication of a policy of drift is that as the politics of independence start to gather speed the Australian government has failed to create in New Guinea either a workable political structure, or a political élite, with which it can deal in the pre-independence and post-independence period. If the proposition is accepted, and it can hardly be rejected, that New Guinea is going to be independent, perhaps a great deal sooner than we have imagined, then positive policies to regulate Australia's relations with an independent New Guinea must be created now. This must mean, in the first instance, whether the Westminster system is persisted with or alternatives are sought and proposed, that New Guineans start to govern themselves and with quickening pace assume powers of decision. The results will not be according to our best hopes let alone our preconceptions but this is now beside the point which is that there is an urgent need to consider flexible target dates.[11] They will probably, but not necessarily be shortened by events unless they are totally unrealistic. In this respect United Nations opinion cannot be entirely ignored even though it has failed to prove the irresistible force that many thought it a few years ago.

The results of drift, rationalised as policy, were brought sharply home to Australians in 1968. The UN Visiting Mission Report was, all things considered, extremely mild, urging a name, flag and anthem for the country, further political educa-

---

[1] For a Territorian view see 'Target Dates Now!', *New Guinea*, No. 1, 1968, by H. L. R. Neall, a former District Commissioner and a former speaker of the House of Assembly.

tion for the people and abolition of the 'T' schools. All in all, innocuous. This was partly due to the fact that Liberia's permanent representative at the United Nations had been changed. The new representative, Mr Fahnwalu Caine was eminently more reasonable than his predecessor, Mr Nathaniel Eastman. But if the Visiting Mission's report was fair, the reception to the Report, as expressed in the Afro-Arab resolution in the General Assembly calling not only for early, fixed dates for independence but for United Nations supervised elections in New Guinea, was however unrealistic or insulting, the shape of things to come. The resolution for all its misplaced venom exposed the basic weakness and uncertainty of Australian policy. The Australian Permanent Representative to the United Nations, Mr Patrick Shaw, in a speech to the General Assembly on 20 December 1968, in rebuttal of the Afro-Arab resolution (carried 72 to 19 with 17 abstentions including Indonesia), very properly rejected the call for new elections but, on direction from Canberra, could only fall back on the old routine of reasserting the rights of New Guineans to self-determination:

To set a target date for independence now, would have to be based on today's circumstances. This timetable could be proved by events to be unacceptable to the people. In a very short time they may see things differently. Their wants may be different. They may want to shape the future of the Territory in ways not thought of today.

A timetable imposed now would deprive the people of choices on their own future which they might otherwise wish to exercise.

To turn from the ambiguities of past Australian policy over New Guinea's political future, indeed from the sheer uncertainty of present ones, what are the principal conditions that will face an independent New Guinea government? One of the most consistent elements in Australian gradualist policies over New Guinea, forming a large part of the early statehood and later close association arguments, has been the stubborn notion that New Guinea is essential to the defence of Australia. In the

new strategic conditions of the world, New Guinea is no longer
Australia's first line of defence although an astonishing number
of Australians, Territorians and New Guineans continue to
imagine that the conditions of 1942 still prevail when the Japanese Army, protected by one of the world's largest and most
powerful navies, landed on the island preparatory to invading
Australia. There is currently, despite Soviet interests in the
Indian Ocean, only one naval power of consequence in the
area today and that is the United States. More importantly, it
operates in an area which is no longer a political vacuum, as
it was in 1942, but comprises sovereign, independent, South
East Asian states, which, despite precarious political structures,
are interlocked with each other in a common front against
hostile, outside pressures. There now seem only four possible
types of war that can, at this stage and in the foreseeable future,
affect New Guinea and in not one of them can New Guinea be
considered essential to Australia's continental security.[12]

The first contingency is a nuclear war in which New Guinea
will be irrelevant. The second contingency is a large scale con-
ventional war in South-East Asia, with Australia as an ultimate
target—a war in which it is reasonable to suppose US involvement in Australia's defence, probably under the provisions of
ANZUS, with US air and naval forces operating between New
Guinea and the main theatre of war. Even if the US were not
involved New Guinea's relevance to Australian continental
defence remains dubious. The third contingency is large scale
subversion in New Guinea externally promoted and sustained.
The fourth contingency is internal rebellion which would be
entirely Australia's affair.

In the case of externally induced subversion, United States
obligations to Australia under ANZUS might not apply or might
prove difficult to invoke. American responses would depend on
numerous factors such as whether New Guinea alone was

[12] See J. R. Kerr, 'From the Defence Angle—No Great Prize' in *New
Guinea*, No. 8, 1966, and also for an extremely prescient view, a decade
earlier, on New Guinea's changing strategic value to Australia, J. Andrews,
'New Guinea and Australia', papers read to the AIPS 24th Summer School,
Canberra, 1958.

threatened or parts or the whole of South-East Asia, with New Guinea forming the last and weakest domino. At the same time the possibilities of large scale, foreign-inspired subversion in New Guinea are probably not as great as many Australians fear. Whence is the subversion to come? And who is to succumb to it? The most probable sources since Indonesia's counter-coup are the Soviet Union or Communist China and to neither of these powers is New Guinea likely to prove a rich strategic prize. The island is not easily accessible and is poor in resources. Neither its forbidding terrain nor two million preponderantly subsistence people are valuable acquisitions compared with the people and resources of Thailand, Malaysia, Singapore, or Indonesia. New Guinea has no bases and no technology. Even an independent New Guinea, governed by those prepared to hazard Australian aid and friendship by pursuing pro-Communist policies, is not likely to prove inviting, in terms of cost-effectiveness, to Soviet or Chinese penetration either for the purpose of a Cuba-type operation directed against Australia or as the easternmost conquest in the subversion of South-East Asia. Contemporary Indonesia and neighbouring countries would in any case regard Chinese or Russian penetration of New Guinea with active hostility. If Indonesia itself became Communist, improbable under present conditions, Soviet or Chinese naval, air and rocket attacks could be launched more efficiently against Australia from eastern Indonesia than from New Guinea. It seems doubtful that either a pro-Communist Indonesia or New Guinea would make themselves vulnerable, inviting targets for retaliatory strikes—one assumes US intervention under ANZUS or, possibly in the very long term in response to a gathering threat, an independent Australian nuclear capacity—by providing facilities to either the Soviet or China to launch attacks against Australia in the first place. In any case, this sort of process would involve a complicated and lengthy escalation in which New Guinea would be scarcely worth the effort.

None of the foregoing denies that Australia will prefer and strive for a friendly, independent New Guinea. An unfriendly New Guinea could refuse Australia air space and cut its normal lines of communication to the north by denying it staging facilities in the event of South-East Asian commitments. But even if this should happen it would prove militarily and commercially embarrassing rather than pose a grave threat to Australia's continental security.

Nevertheless it would be unwise to dismiss the possibility of future Chinese or Russian meddling in an independent New Guinea but it only seems probable under rather unlikely circumstances where either country wishes to bring direct pressure of one sort or another on Australia, and is willing to risk the hostility of neighbours, by having a calculated 'presence' in New Guinea even if it is a non-military one. Today the Soviet seems far more pre-occupied with helping to maintain economically viable, sovereign South-East Asian states as part of a Peking containment policy than in subverting and alienating the countries of the area of which New Guinea is the last and strategically least important. In any case a Soviet or Chinese presence also assumes an independent New Guinea willing to risk Australian aid subsidies for dubious Russian or Chinese credits. It assumes, in fact, a more 'irrational' or determinedly anti-Australian New Guinea government than seems probable. The very assumption nevertheless points to the unwisdom of seeking any 'special relationship' between Australia and an independent New Guinea involving automatic Australian guarantees of New Guinea's internal security.

If Indonesia again becomes hostile to Australia, West Irian might well be used as a source of subversive activities against East New Guinea. Given the present regionalist, anti-Communist disposition of Indonesia's government, the scarcity of its resources, its dependence on western aid, its run down military machine, and its general logistic incapacity, this seems highly improbable. Nevertheless, the character of Indonesia's government is not immutably fixed and it is worth remembering that while East New Guinea remains a dependency of Australia, armed rebellion against the Administration for any reason, including that of external subversion, would have the character of sedition demanding Australian military intervention. The effect throughout the world, particularly in the Afro-Asian and

Communist worlds, of white Australian troops possibly being obliged to kill, in Papua for instance, those who are technically brown Australian citizens, would create serious political problems. Avoiding situations like this, however improbable, is yet another argument for ensuring ultimate independence for New Guinea. The history of anti-colonialist attitudes over the past fifteen years seems clearly to suggest in timing and response that it may be very much easier to answer a call for help from the sovereign government of an independent, neighbouring country than to take automatic action in that country because it is a dependency.

What then are likely to be the most important conditions in New Guinea's independence? There seem to be four: New Guinea's continued dependence on an Australian subsidy and investment for an indefinite period of time after independence; the continued presence of American power in the western Pacific if not on the mainland of South-East Asia; the uncertain course of New Guinea's relations with West Irian, its Papuan neighbour, which in turn must involve its own and Australia's relations with Indonesia as well as those of New Guinea itself with Indonesia: and a highly unstable internal political situation in New Guinea itself. An independent New Guinea will remain an indefinite charge upon Australian goodwill and concern. Australia's increasing aid to New Guinea— the annual grant is almost twice that of Australia's foreign aid expenditures—is inevitably creating rational New Guinean expectations that even though the Australian grant must one day diminish, it will remain substantially high in the years immediately following independence. It is probable that Australian sentiment will agree to this while United Nations and anti-colonialist pressure will seek to enforce it. While New Guinea will undoubtedly attract foreign investment capital, in particular, Japanese, for extractive and other industries, the bulk of its foreign aid, both in direct grants and in the private investment field, must inevitably come from Australia as both New Guinea's economic productivity and strategic value will remain relatively minor in a world scale. Therefore, even an 'anti-Australian' independent New Guinea government will have to

consider carefully its domestic and foreign policies in the light
of its dependence on Australian aid, capital and skills. Nevertheless its foreign policy will be carefully geared to take
account of its powerful neighbour, Indonesia, as well as that
of Australia. In the long run its greatest concern will be Indonesia, with which it shares a border, and any shifts in Indonesian foreign policy, any changes in Indonesia's domestic politics, will be a matter for careful analysis and careful response
by an independent government in Port Moresby. If Australia,
with its relatively advanced technology and rapidly growing
capacity, finds it wise to tread carefully with Indonesia, as well
as promote harmonious and constructive relations between
Canberra and Djakarta, the government of independent New
Guinea will find it much more so. This will mean central government firmly discouraging attempts by, say, frustrated, regionalist or uninformed New Guinean politicians, to meddle
in the affairs of West Irian for these are by definition the
internal affairs of Indonesia.

It will be surprising, in fact, if at the time of independence
the New Guinean government does not seek a Treaty of Friendship with Australia embodying such matters of concern to both
countries as the annual Australian grant, guarantees for continued Australian investment security and special provisions
covering immigration, customs and tariff arrangements between
the two countries,[13] and presumably also the vexed problem
of citizenship for Australian residents in the Territory. While
some will unhesitatingly opt for New Guinea citizenship most
will seek to retain Australian citizenship as well, or special
arrangements whereby they can freely move between the two
countries. This would be impossible unless Australia granted
New Guineans the same rights of double citizenship or free
movement—a most unlikely development. It is also unlikely
that a Treaty of Friendship will include even general Australian guarantees for New Guinea's defence while confiding the

[13] It will also presumably re-arrange the Queensland border which in
part runs only a mile or so off the Gulf of Papua. An oil strike in the area
might become a matter of future contention. See Jeremy Beckett, *New
Guinea*, No. 4, 1965.

conduct of New Guinea's foreign policy to Australian hands for some unspecified period. United Nations, Afro-Asian and Communist bloc opinion will demand that an independent New Guinea not only be independent but appear to be independent. New Guinea will have to maintain an independent foreign service and an independent foreign policy—however closely tied in with Australia's. Defence arrangements might include a Defence Agreement (quite separate from a Treaty of Friendship) under which Australia, in carefully defined circumstances, would accept certain defence obligations to New Guinea solely at the request of the New Guinea government of the day. One can imagine the caution with which Canberra would approach this problem. The defence 'power' as such could not stay with Australia. The arrangement might well cover Australian aid in maintaining New Guinea's army and police forces which will be necessary for New Guinea's post-independence internal security, the greatest of New Guinea's post-independence problems and a matter of great concern to Australia.

The general tribal village nature of New Guinean society, the absence in it to date of any viable nationalism—due to lack of cultural cohesion and as much to the failure of Australian governments to try and create it—will almost certainly make it liable to post-independence fragmentation. For this reason many New Guineans will want a continued Australian security 'presence' after independence and it will be in Australia's interests, and no less in Indonesia's in view of its West Irian problem, to provide it. This begs the question as to how big a defence establishment New Guinea will be able to afford when independent. Currently, defence costs are a charge against the Commonwealth Government and are hard to extract from overall Commonwealth expenditures. One estimate for total defence expenditure in 1967-68 is $36 million, an improbably large sum unless it comprises very heavy expenditures on the completion of the Moem Barracks at Wewak and maintenance of other military establishments in addition to those on RAAF and RAN operational costs in the Territory. However, the maintenance of a Brigade of Infantry, even two battalions, headquarters and Corps troops, Navy patrol boats and shore facilities and air transport would amount to a very considerable charge against the revenues of an independent New Guinea even allowing for a continuing, substantial Australian grant-in-aid. Considerations of this sort also open up the question, already canvassed, of whether in the time remaining between now and independence it is possible to create a disciplined Army, loyal to central government and imbued with a nationalist spirit. At the present moment the PIR has eight indigenous officers, four of them captains and one of them likely to reach the rank of lieutenant-colonel within the next six years. But it is still largely a white Australian officered force, pledging loyalty to the Queen of Australia and oriented to the standards and political outlook of the Australian Army than to a role which it clearly sees for itself. Therefore the composition of an independent New Guinea's security force will require careful thought well before independence. Should there be in effect only a few, if any, Australians physically attached to such a force? Should internal security be left entirely to (Australian) trained indigenous forces with the promise that Australians would come to their help from the mainland only if the going got really rough? And if it did just how far would Australians physically intervene in view of Afro-Asian attitudes? These matters would require careful decisions, the most difficult of which to make would be whether or not Australia should actively intervene if an alternative New Guinea government of anti-Australian character appeared to have substantial local support in a situation of rebellion against the established regime. Should, or even can, it intervene in post-independence secessionist situations? New Guinea's national unity as an independent state is likely to be extremely precarious as we have seen.

As suggested in Chapter 5 there may be practical benefits for Australia, and ultimately for New Guinea, in deliberately promoting secession with a view to a form of federation, if it is possible, of the eastern islands of Manus, New Ireland, New Britain and Bougainville, to which because of its ethnic ties with the latter, the Solomons could eventually adhere. The practical benefits are simply those of greater political stability through the amalgamation of areas with more mutual interests, however minimal, than differences. It is not the purpose once again to argue here the advantages or otherwise of the suggestion but rather to make the point that if secessionism is in any case eventually inevitable, as it may well be, it is very much easier for Australia as administering power to promote or accede to secessionist pressures before independence than for a sovereign New Guinea government to contain them after independence when it might look unavailingly to its great and powerful neighbour to help it do so. But whether at independence there is a single, united Papua and New Guinea comprising its present territorial borders or two, separate, independent political units, either will entail special Australian responsibilities and concern (however reluctant) in the exercise of which Australia will seek and need considerable flexibility of action. In some fundamental respects an independent New Guinea while continuing to confront Australia with very considerable problems will at least afford it a very much greater selectivity of response than is the case with a dependent colony.

In terms of broader strategic considerations New Guinea is sandwiched between Australian power to the south and east and by the US defence umbrella of the Strategic Trust Territory to the north—a huge area of Pacific Ocean and Micronesian islands where the US flag is sovereign. While the United States has stated it will wind up the Strategic Trust Territory by 1972, it is likely it will offer US citizenship in one form or another to the 90,000 Micronesians scattered throughout the area. In this event United States power will be formalised in perpetuity in the western Pacific in groups of islands immediately north of New Guinea and as far west longitudinally as Adelaide. This seems to imply that the only unguarded approaches to New Guinea lie west of the border between Australian and Indonesian New Guinea. Even if Indonesia shows no inclination to meddle in East New Guinea's affairs, over a period of time there are other strains that could arise from the interaction of the two sides of the island. It is the unsettling effect of East New Guinea on West Irian, rather than the reverse, that may prove an unsought, uncomfortable catalyst of Australian-Indonesian relations. The future relationship between East and West New Guinea has yet to be worked out and is one of the incalculable factors of the future. Because it has already been dealt with in the preceding chapter, it is sufficient to summarise the apparent difficulties.

A combination of continued Indonesian repression of West Irianese political activities, Indonesian incapacity to institute and maintain minimal economic activity, East New Guinean sympathy for their less fortunate 'brothers' in the West, a rapidly accelerating disparity in economic development on the two sides and East New Guinea's comfortable, subsidised march to independence—these may produce political tensions in the island involving Canberra and Djakarta in opposing positions that neither metropolitan power may find it easy to control.

This possibility seems to suggest as do other considerations that from the viewpoint of Australia's national interests, Australian governments will find in early rather than later independence a much greater flexibility in their dealings with New Guinea and more importantly with Indonesia, despite the fact that Djakarta will have grave misgivings over the political effects on West Irian of East New Guinean independence. To sum up: An independent New Guinea is likely to prove a weak, client state greatly dependent for its continued development on Australian aid, technical skills and private investment. This must to a large extent limit its relations with other countries around it. It may even have special ties with Australia by Treaty. The generosity and extent of the Treaty provisions, will depend primarily on the political complexion of the two governments at the time of independence as well as upon the general political stability of the South-East Asian area including Indonesia. There is no reason why New Guinea, like Australia itself, should not fit ultimately into some framework of South-East Asian political and economic regional co-operation if initiatives like ASPAC and ASEAN (Association of South-East Asian Nations) develop fruitfully—or perhaps into some new Australian-Pacific regional grouping.

In addition, it must be remembered that Australia's indus-

trial and military potential are growing rapidly. Its annual
GNP is now greater than that combined of all nations that lie
between it and Japan, China and India to its distant north.
An independent New Guinea will be regarded by Australia's
Asian neighbours as a sphere of Australian national interest.
Nevertheless, none of this necessarily spells out permanent
Australian commitment to New Guinea or the Australian electorate's enduring endorsement of the high costs of a semi-
permanent New Guinea subsidy even though the Australian-
New Guinean relationship will inevitably be close at the time
of independence. However, in circumstances of regional Communist takeovers (less likely now than before) or of dramatic
changes of ideological direction in Indonesia (unlikely but
not impossible) an Australian government at the time of New
Guinea's independence will probably view any suggestions of
automatic defence guarantees to its former colony with extreme caution notwithstanding history, sentiment or expatriate
pressures. This is not to suggest an inevitable Australian desertion of New Guinea for the spread of Australian government,
private and institutional interest is now very wide and growing
wider. Quite apart from the direct personal engagement in
New Guinea of expatriate residents in the Administration, in
the missions and in commercial enterprise, New Guinea is becoming a subject of increasing preoccupation, and concern, to
mainland Australians in a broad institutional spectrum—in the
churches, universities, political parties and in industrial, commercial and professional organisations. The number of New
Guineans now visiting Australia on sponsored tours, on courses
and as employee apprentices is evidence of this growing
interest.

Once so distant, Port Moresby is today only four hours by
jet from Sydney. Mainland government and commerce conduct
daily business there by telex and by telephone. While Sir Robert
Menzies' famed dictum 'We are here to stay' will not prove
true in the sense in which he used that phrase it is certainly
true to the extent that Australian involvement in New Guinea
is now more ramified and, in some ways, more binding than
most Australians realise. But it is not indefinitely so. At this

stage involvement is unavoidable. Later it may prove painful even if it differs from that of the Europeans in Africa and Asia in one highly important respect. The whites who went to Asia and Africa so long ago eventually made their homes there over several or more generations and established in their own interests what they hoped would prove permanent political domination. The Europeans who settled in the Netherlands East Indies, for example, were relatively few in number but came to regard it as home and themselves as permanent settlers. White Rhodesians today neither want, nor can afford, to return to distant Britain.

For all but a handful of Australians, New Guinea has never been home. It is not even today when easy jet access to Australia, more comfortable living conditions and the modern amenities of town life in an exotic setting make it more attractive to permanent settlement. While many Australians have loved New Guinea, and some its people, it has primarily remained a place to earn a living or a pension. If at some future date New Guineans post 'Australians, go home!' signs or indulge in race riots in Port Moresby or Madang, then Australians *will* return home, not only because they will want to but because they can. In the absence of necessity there will be little disposition to remain, for in the end Australia offers them personal security, economic opportunity, a future for their children and an agreeable climate. It always has.

Hopefully unlikely, an enforced retreat from New Guinea would prove a cruelly disheartening experience profoundly affecting Australian attitudes to the area in which we live. In subtle and diffuse ways yet to reveal themselves, New Guinea will not only test an old legend in which Australians appear as model colonialists but a new one, just emerging, in which Australians play the role of sympathetic regionalists. At present we think of regionalism only in the glamorous context of South-East Asia. We will have to be regionalists, if we are going to be, not only in South-East Asia, which now includes West Irian, but in our off shore islands. New Guinea is not, after all, the only island in the region to challenge our political imagination, although it is the chief one, any more than the 141st

K

meridian is the only border of concern to us. There remains the British Solomons with its looming implications of future Australian responsibilities.

Some of the problems besetting our future relations with New Guinea apply equally to the whole of Melanesia. No one can predict what course Melanesian nationalism will take, or even that in any forceful form it will ever arise, although it is vaguely stirring throughout the western Pacific from New Guinea to distant Fiji where there is a growing conflict between indigenous Melanesian and immigrant Indian in a situation in which Australian companies control seventy per cent of all foreign investment. In the long run it seems inevitable that Australia's Melanesian outliers must, like Fiji, come increasingly within the orbit of burgeoning Australian power, resources and influence. Equally Australia will find itself involved with the economic, social and political development of a near chain of weak, sparsely populated islands of relatively poor resources. While none of these islands may appear as important strategic prizes to hostile Communist forces they could logically become areas of political and economic penetration just as they will almost certainly appear attractive to future Japanese economic exploitation—to the political and other consequences of which we will have to adjust in a number of ways.

Under these conditions the political foresight and resolution by which Australia seeks to define and maintain its interests in the area, and to stabilise it politically, will be the degree to which it meets its challenges as a Pacific and regional power. This will demand some nice political judgments of Canberra in the not too distant future. One of them may nevertheless be a cool, tough conclusion that having discharged its Trusteeship obligations, Australia will not feel politically or morally compelled to undertake binding commitments to half an island which, despite its proximity, is vital neither to the defence nor the economy of the mainland.

# Appendices

# APPENDIX A

## Table I—Papua and New Guinea—Value of Imports by Standar

| Year | Food | Beverages | Tobacco | Mineral fuels, Lubricants and related materials | Drugs and Chemicals | Clothing and Footwear | Textiles and related products (except clothing) |
|------|------|-----------|---------|------------------------------------------------|---------------------|----------------------|-------------------------------------------------|
| 1947 | | | | | | | |
| 1948 | | | | | | | |
| 1949 | | | | | | | |
| 1950 | | | | | | | |
| 1951 | | | | | | | |
| 1952 | | | | | | | |
| 1953 | | | | | | | |
| 1954 | 8,037,108 | 717,444 | 1,064,158 | 1,562,612 | 1,486,962 | 900,430 | 1,633,47 |
| 1955 | 9,408,422 | 669,442 | 1,238,020 | 1,822,660 | 2,199,052 | 1,243,192 | 1,635,53 |
| 1956 | 8,871,832 | 800,980 | 1,264,054 | 1,873,262 | 2,790,170 | 1,083,746 | 2,060,92 |
| 1957 | 9,813,634 | 755,418 | 1,277,340 | 2,105,356 | 2,785,960 | 1,317,506 | 1,859,02 |
| 1958 | 9,885,844 | 797,746 | 1,349,978 | 2,060,118 | 2,535,790 | 1,336,074 | 2,273,54 |
| 1959 | 10,274,500 | 794,168 | 1,353,306 | 2,055,598 | 2,729,238 | 1,347,802 | 1,943,55 |
| 1960 | 10,684,476 | 666,290 | 1,204,284 | 2,279,400 | 2,713,768 | 1,678,556 | 2,323,99 |
| 1961 | 12,760,494 | 802,840 | 1,396,038 | 2,484,308 | 3,292,032 | 2,210,734 | 2,919,96 |
| 1962 | 13,117,214 | 909,408 | 1,390,042 | 2,503,388 | 3,598,176 | 2,473,618 | 2,392,73 |
| 1963 | 13,506,560 | 1,173,478 | 1,362,022 | 2,992,846 | 3,859,254 | 2,460,304 | 2,440,14 |
| 1964 | 16,218,588 | 1,286,722 | 1,597,958 | 3,175,372 | 4,494,254 | 3,440,914 | 3,054,77 |
| 1965 | 18,986,554 | 1,254,896 | 1,635,522 | 3,515,122 | 5,358,208 | 3,970,872 | 3,126,76 |
| 1966 | 22,635,450 | 1,472,576 | 1,988,854 | 3,934,015 | 6,125,122 | 4,905,703 | 3,689,7 |
| 1967 | 24,817,007 | 1,870,977 | 1,835,410 | 4,549,577 | 6,785,862 | 5,931,389 | 3,730,04 |
| 1968 | 29,987,577 | 2,387,854 | 1,941,692 | 5,366,194 | 7,641,081 | 6,156,402 | 3,663,4 |

Note: Prior to 1953/54, the dissection of total value of imports into value of commodities is
Source: Compendium of Statistics for Papua and New Guinea. Department of External Territori

ernational Trade Classification—Year ended 30th June ($)

| ransport quipment | Machinery | Base Metals and Metal Manufactures | Other Manufactured goods | Crude Materials (inedible) | Oils and Fats | Miscellaneous | Total (excl. Outside Packages) |
|---|---|---|---|---|---|---|---|
| | | | | | | | 5,239,220 |
| | | | | | | | 9,997,444 |
| | | | | | | | 13,765,742 |
| | | | | | | | 17,228,776 |
| | | | | | | | 19,690,286 |
| | | | | | | | 25,476,954 |
| | | | | | | | 21,988,876 |
| ,065,388 | 3,665,986 | 2,331,142 | 3,364,784 | 391,582 | 42,296 | 312,622 | 27,575,986 |
| ,276,972 | 4,699,830 | 3,050,508 | 3,880,654 | 646,122 | 52,260 | 273,946 | 34,096,616 |
| ,526,164 | 5,328,264 | 4,297,156 | 4,975,000 | 471,028 | 24,410 | 1,144,740 | 38,511,726 |
| ,816,996 | 5,837,994 | 3,668,752 | 5,412,084 | 251,248 | 25,804 | 1,242,346 | 39,169,466 |
| ,408,264 | 5,971,132 | 3,901,942 | 5,360,554 | 342,188 | 32,900 | 1,221,470 | 40,477,540 |
| ,395,222 | 5,217,798 | 3,947,346 | 5,519,860 | 256,388 | 38,728 | 1,263,488 | 40,136,996 |
| ,996,694 | 5,624,444 | 3,944,110 | 5,758,072 | 185,540 | 41,544 | 1,515,474 | 41,616,642 |
| ,600,830 | 7,267,922 | 5,654,456 | 7,563,640 | 190,874 | 45,170 | 1,738,748 | 52,928,050 |
| ,667,610 | 6,202,738 | 4,417,130 | 7,447,782 | 172,186 | 58,788 | 1,933,168 | 51,283,982 |
| ,863,940 | 7,595,934 | 5,184,602 | 8,116,270 | 222,790 | 57,282 | 2,701,038 | 56,536,464 |
| ,785,836 | 9,659,216 | 6,930,620 | 10,753,138 | 237,516 | 73,620 | 3,308,980 | 70,017,510 |
| ,996,404 | 13,710,090 | 9,612,582 | 11,932,788 | 263,736 | 75,378 | 4,347,778 | 85,786,696 |
| ,461,063 | 19,471,233 | 12,130,628 | 15,250,363 | 335,353 | 108,108 | 4,574,921 | 109,083,104 |
| ,791,971 | 21,118,550 | 14,216,158 | 18,972,160 | 503,424 | 128,248 | 5,571,121 | 125,821,896 |
| ,341,240 | 23,698,984 | 11,831,224 | 20,095,529 | 854,132 | 150,066 | 8,394,892 | 143,510,338 |

dily available.
nberra, June, 1969.

Table II—European and Indigenous Plantings Actual and Estimated
Plantings of Major Tree Crops ('000 acres)

| Crop | Actual | | Estimate | Programme | | | | |
|---|---|---|---|---|---|---|---|---|
| | 1965-66 | 1966-67 | 1967-68 | 1968-69 | 1969-70 | 1970-71 | 1971-72 | 1972-73 |
| *Coconut* | | | | | | | | |
| Indigenous | 11.6 | 16.6 | 17.8 | 19.0 | 19.9 | 21.8 | 23.1 | 23.9 |
| Non-Indigenous | 5.5 | 5.2 | 5.0 | 10.0 | 10.0 | 10.0 | 10.0 | 10.0 |
| Total | 17.1 | 21.8 | 22.8 | 29.0 | 29.9 | 31.8 | 33.1 | 33.9 |
| *Cacao* | | | | | | | | |
| Indigenous | 1.5 | 1.2 | 3.5 | 3.9 | 4.2 | 4.2 | 4.5 | 4.8 |
| Non-Indigenous | 8.4 | 5.0 | 7.0 | 7.0 | 7.0 | 7.0 | 7.0 | 7.0 |
| Total | 9.9 | 6.2 | 10.5 | 10.9 | 11.2 | 11.2 | 11.5 | 11.8 |
| *Rubber* | | | | | | | | |
| Indigenous | 0.5 | 1.1 | 2.1 | 2.4 | 3.0 | 3.6 | 4.5 | 5.2 |
| Non-Indigenous | 1.8 | 1.3 | 1.0 | 1.0 | 1.0 | 1.0 | 1.0 | 1.0 |
| Total | 2.3 | 2.4 | 3.1 | 3.4 | 4.0 | 4.6 | 5.5 | 6.2 |

|  |  |  |  |  |  |  |  |  |
|---|---|---|---|---|---|---|---|---|
| Indigenous | 0.1 | 0.2 | 0.3 | 0.6 | 0.8 | 1.2 | 2.1 | 2.1 |
| Non-Indigenous | 0.4 | 1.9 | 2.6 | 2.9 | 1.6 | 2.6 | 2.8 | 2.5 |
| *Total* | 0.5 | 2.1 | 2.9 | 3.5 | 2.4 | 3.8 | 4.9 | 4.6 |
| *Oil Palm* |  |  |  |  |  |  |  |  |
| Indigenous | — | — | — | 0.9 | 1.7 | 2.6 | 2.7 | 2.9 |
| Non-Indigenous | — | — | 0.5 | 1.0 | 1.0 | 1.0 | 2.0 | 3.7 |
| *Total* | — | — | 0.5 | 1.9 | 2.7 | 3.6 | 4.7 | 6.6 |
| *Total* |  |  |  |  |  |  |  |  |
| Indigenous | 13.7 | 19.1 | 23.7 | 26.8 | 29.6 | 33.4 | 36.9 | 38.9 |
| Non-Indigenous | 16.1 | 13.2 | 16.1 | 21.9 | 20.6 | 21.6 | 22.8 | 24.2 |
| *Total* | 29.8 | 32.3 | 39.8 | 48.7 | 50.2 | 55.0 | 59.7 | 63.1 |

SOURCE: *Programmes and Policies*, published by the Administration, Port Moresby, September 1968.

## Table III—Manpower—Papua and New Guinea

| Manpower | Actual | Programme | | | | | Total |
|---|---|---|---|---|---|---|---|
| | 1967 | 1968 | 1969 | 1970 | 1971 | 1972 | 1968 to 1972 |
| **Class A** | | | | | | | |
| Arts, Law, Education and Science Graduates | — | — | — | 20 | 48 | 53 | 121 |
| Engineers, Architects and Surveyors | — | — | 6 | 6 | 17 | 33 | 62 |
| Commerce Diplomates | — | — | — | — | 11 | 17 | 28 |
| Medical and Dental Officers | 7 | 5 | 11 | 14 | 10 | 20 | 60 |
| Pharmacists | — | — | — | — | 1 | 1 | 2 |
| Sub-Total | 7 | 5 | 17 | 40 | 87 | 124 | 273 |
| **Class B** | | | | | | | |
| Primary Teachers (C. Cert.) (b) | 107 | 140 | 218 | 285 | 335 | 685 | 1,663 |
| Secondary Teachers (b) | 27 | 17 | 44 | 57 | 68 | 119 | 305 |
| Assistant Forestry Officers | — | — | 10 | 12 | 12 | 23 | 57 |
| Agricultural Officers | 9 | 16 | 23 | 24 | 26 | 36 | 125 |
| Professional Nurses | 3 | 3 | 7 | 23 | 20 | 13 | 66 |
| Other—Medical | 25 | 39 | 51 | 27 | 28 | 75 | 220 |
| Other—General | 31 | 16 | 36 | 61 | 76 | 80 | 269 |
| Sub-Total | 202 | 231 | 389 | 489 | 565 | 1,031 | 2,705 |

| | | | | | | | |
|---|---|---|---|---|---|---|---|
| Primary Teachers (A and B Cert.) (b) | 400 | 518 | 422 | 400 | 370 | 300 | 2,010 |
| Enrolled Nurses | 91 | 110 | 130 | 130 | 67 | 35 | 472 |
| Patrol Officers | — | 7 | 31 | 40 | 40 | 40 | 158 |
| Assistant Agricultural Officers | 15 | 26 | 36 | 36 | 60 | 84 | 242 |
| Co-operatives Officers | 11 | 10 | 10 | 16 | 9 | 23 | 68 |
| Artisans | 87 | 118 | 186 | 231 | 264 | 567 | 1,366 |
| Technical College Certificants | — | 22 | 24 | 4 | 36 | 39 | 125 |
| Other—Technical | 44 | 52 | 45 | 61 | 60 | 62 | 280 |
| Other—General | 20 | 35 | 42 | 57 | 47 | 49 | 230 |
| *Sub-Total* | 668 | 898 | 926 | 975 | 953 | 1,199 | 4,951 |
| *Class D* | | | | | | | |
| Medical Workers | 220 | 238 | 175 | 195 | 191 | 191 | 990 |
| Stenographers | 9 | 18 | 18 | 35 | 35 | 35 | 141 |
| Police Constables | 490 | 339 | 150 | 543 | 500 | 500 | 2,032 |
| Warders | 164 | 90 | 40 | 90 | 90 | 90 | 400 |
| Forestry Assistants | 13 | 27 | 14 | 27 | 27 | 27 | 122 |
| Other | — | 45 | 45 | 60 | 60 | 50 | 260 |
| *Sub-Total* | 896 | 757 | 442 | 950 | 903 | 893 | 3,945 |
| *Total* | 1,773 | 1,891 | 1,774 | 2,454 | 2,508 | 3,247 | 11,874 |

(a) Graduates from full-time Territory courses. (b) Includes Mission outputs.

SOURCE: *Programmes and Policies*, published by the Administration, Port Moresby, September 1968.

Table IV—Papua and New Guinea—Administrati◌

| | 1946(a) | 1947 | 1948 | 1949 |
|---|---|---|---|---|
| *Expenditure* | | | | |
| Departmental— | | | | |
| Public Health | | | | |
| District Administration (b) | | | | |
| Agriculture, Stock and Fisheries | | | | |
| Education | | | | |
| Posts and Telegraphs | | | | |
| Public Works | | | | |
| Other Departments | | | | |
| | | | | |
| Total Departmental | 553 | 2,887 | 4,234 | 5,84◌ |
| General Maintenance | 5 | 226 | 562 | 82◌ |
| Capital Works and Services | 43 | 175 | 244 | 90◌ |
| Purchase of Capital Assets | — | 1,319 | 322 | 43◌ |
| Special Appropriations | — | — | 12 | 1◌ |
| | | | | |
| *Total Expenditure* | 601 | 4,607 | 5,374 | 8,02◌ |
| | | | | |
| *Receipts* | | | | |
| Import Duties | | | | |
| Export Duties | | | | |
| Excise Duty | | | | |
| Personal Tax | | | | |
| Income Tax—Individual | | | | |
| —Companies | | | | |
| Postal | | | | |
| Public Utilities | | | | |
| Other Internal Revenue | | | | |
| | | | | |
| Total Internal Revenue | 131 | 928 | 1,828 | 2,46◌ |
| Commonwealth Grant | 505 | 4,037 | 3,734 | 6,39◌ |
| Receipts from Loan Fund | — | — | — | — |
| | | | | |
| *Total Receipts* | 636 | 4,965 | 5,562 | 8,86◌ |

(a) Period 30.10.45 to 30.6.46.

(b) Before 1964/65 known as Department of Native Affairs.

(c) Included with other departments.

SOURCE: *Compendium of Statistics for Papua and New Guinea,* Department of External Territo◌ Canberra, June 1969.

xpenditure and Receipts—Year ended 30th June—($'000)

| 1950 | 1951 | 1952 | 1953 | 1954 | 1955 | 1956 | 1957 |
|---|---|---|---|---|---|---|---|
| | 2,652 | 2,938 | 2,460 | 2,724 | 3,658 | 4,302 | 4,416 |
| | 1,798 | 2,422 | 2,036 | 1,894 | 1,802 | 2,142 | 2,240 |
| | 758 | 708 | 770 | 888 | 1,080 | 1,250 | 1,354 |
| | 786 | 876 | 818 | 940 | 1,124 | 1,372 | 1,764 |
| | 368 | 494 | 510 | 550 | 728 | 1,094 | 1,080 |
| | (c) | (c) | (c) | (c) | 58 | 248 | 956 |
| | 2,624 | 2,712 | 2,671 | 2,928 | 3,355 | 4,549 | 5,511 |
| 7,864 | 8,986 | 10,150 | 9,265 | 9,924 | 11,805 | 14,957 | 17,321 |
| 1,198 | 938 | 1,699 | 1,752 | 2,222 | 2,383 | 2,638 | 2,677 |
| 1,256 | 2,096 | 2,744 | 2,392 | 3,780 | 4,788 | 5,431 | 6,270 |
| 762 | 730 | 768 | 794 | 737 | 1,497 | 1,234 | 1,158 |
| 16 | 22 | 31 | 42 | 8 | 24 | 34 | 48 |
| 11,097 | 12,773 | 15,393 | 14,244 | 16,670 | 20,498 | 24,294 | 27,473 |
| | 1,456 | 1,903 | 1,757 | 2,518 | 2,687 | 3,479 | 3,736 |
| | 426 | 990 | 1,075 | 1,290 | 1,416 | 1,291 | 1,138 |
| | — | — | 26 | 47 | 66 | 87 | 103 |
| | — | — | — | — | — | — | — |
| | — | — | — | — | — | — | — |
| | — | — | — | — | — | — | — |
| | 140 | 190 | 316 | 254 | 269 | 283 | 490 |
| | 106 | 143 | 224 | 291 | 401 | 554 | 738 |
| | 1,604 | 1,556 | 1,471 | 1,539 | 1,470 | 2,033 | 2,102 |
| 2,801 | 3,732 | 4,782 | 4,869 | 5,939 | 6,309 | 7,727 | 8,307 |
| 8,369 | 8,709 | 10,569 | 9,314 | 10,844 | 14,257 | 16,864 | 18,893 |
| — | — | — | — | — | — | — | — |
| 11,170 | 12,442 | 15,350 | 14,183 | 16,783 | 20,565 | 24,590 | 27,201 |

Table V—Papua and New Guinea—Administrati

| | 1958 | 1959 | 1960 | 1961 |
|---|---|---|---|---|
| *Expenditure* | | | | |
| Departmental— | | | | |
| Public Health | 3,756 | 3,934 | 4,698 | 5,29 |
| District Administration (a) | 2,028 | 2,222 | 2,498 | 2,71 |
| Agriculture, Stock and Fisheries | 1,298 | 1,450 | 1,714 | 1,97 |
| Education | 2,032 | 2,452 | 3,092 | 4,08 |
| Posts and Telegraphs | 1,214 | 1,392 | 1,630 | 1,76 |
| Public Works | 1,216 | 792 | 824 | 1,03 |
| Other Departments | 7,875 | 9,137 | 10,303 | 12,31 |
| Total Departmental | 19,419 | 21,379 | 24,759 | 29,16 |
| General Maintenance | 2,892 | 3,482 | 4,134 | 4,69 |
| Capital Works and Services | 6,957 | 7,407 | 7,855 | 9,99 |
| Purchase of Capital Assets | 1,696 | 1,809 | 1,790 | 1,37 |
| Special Appropriations | 69 | 79 | 128 | 53 |
| *Total Expenditure* | 31,032 | 34,155 | 38,665 | 45,76 |
| *Receipts* | | | | |
| Import Duties | 4,268 | 4,285 | 3,912 | 4,5 |
| Export Duties | 1,069 | 2,284 | 627 | — |
| Excise Duty | 145 | 166 | 274 | 34 |
| Personal Tax | 207 | 308 | 351 | 29 |
| Income Tax—Individual | — | — | 1,885 | 2,45 |
| —Companies | — | — | 1,741 | 2,24 |
| Postal | 592 | 709 | 825 | 95 |
| Public Utilities | 907 | 1,106 | 1,182 | 1,26 |
| Other Internal Revenue | 2,262 | 2,351 | 2,391 | 2,79 |
| Total Internal Revenue | 9,450 | 11,209 | 13,188 | 14,90 |
| Commonwealth Grant | 21,593 | 22,958 | 25,617 | 29,55 |
| Loan Fund | — | — | — | 1,10 |
| *Total Receipts* | 31,043 | 34,167 | 38,804 | 45,60 |

(a) Before 1964/65 known as Department of Native Affairs.
(b) Included with departmental expenditure.
SOURCE: *Compendium of Statistics for Papua and New Guinea*, Department of External Territo
Canberra, June 1969.

xpenditure and Receipts—Year ended 30th June—($'000)

| 1962 | 1963 | 1964 | 1965 | 1966 | 1967 | 1968 | 1969 (est.) |
|---|---|---|---|---|---|---|---|
| 6,020 | 6,806 | 7,477 | 8,076 | 9,426 | 10,275 | 11,124 | 12,214 |
| 2,936 | 2,940 | 3,338 | 4,058 | 4,751 | 5,667 | 6,012 | 6,551 |
| 2,216 | 2,450 | 2,978 | 3,706 | 4,335 | 5,189 | 6,427 | 7,762 |
| 4,946 | 6,270 | 7,919 | 9,797 | 11,330 | 12,975 | 15,062 | 16,541 |
| 2,062 | 2,321 | 2,737 | 3,093 | 3,528 | 4,249 | 4,750 | 6,431 |
| 890 | 1,187 | 1,529 | 3,548 | 3,352 | 3,715 | 5,740 | 6,380 |
| 13,630 | 15,449 | 23,205 | 26,385 | 30,668 | 38,412 | 48,564 | 55,181 |
| 32,700 | 37,423 | 49,183 | 58,663 | 67,390 | 80,482 | 97,679 | 111,060 |
| 5,608 | 6,270 | 6,868 | 8,001 | 8,726 | 9,402 | 10,581 | 11,875 |
| 9,956 | 12,713 | 15,513 | 17,433 | 19,674 | 21,221 | 22,503 | 23,800 |
| 1,801 | 2,254 | 3,605 | 3,694 | 4,484 | 4,907 | (b) | (b) |
| 930 | 1,214 | 1,480 | 2,294 | 3,302 | 4,037 | 2,785 | 6,125 |
| 50,995 | 59,873 | 76,649 | 90,086 | 103,577 | 120,049 | 133,547 | 152,860 |
| 4,994 | 5,521 | 6,313 | 7,006 | 8,776 | 10,589 | 11,421 | 12,364 |
| — | — | — | — | — | — | | |
| 355 | 579 | 742 | 1,309 | 2,315 | 3,565 | 4,556 | 5,250 |
| 222 | 190 | 105 | 131 | 67 | — | — | — |
| 2,711 | 3,070 | 3,713 | 4,792 | 6,080 | 8,365 | 8,133 | 10,238 |
| 1,713 | 2,087 | 2,799 | 3,871 | 4,036 | 5,537 | 5,831 | 6,642 |
| 1,162 | 1,317 | 1,561 | 2,053 | 2,548 | 3,201 | 3,543 | 4,040 |
| 1,347 | 1,576 | 522 | 432 | 556 | 629 | 905 | 970 |
| 2,908 | 3,709 | 6,999 | 8,335 | 10,942 | 12,304 | 13,377 | 14,211 |
| 15,412 | 18,049 | 22,754 | 27,929 | 35,320 | 44,190 | 47,766 | 53,715 |
| 34,587 | 40,000 | 50,499 | 55,999 | 62,000 | 69,784 | 77,594 | 87,295 |
| 994 | 1,797 | 3,396 | 6,318 | 6,157 | 6,194 | 8,397 | 11,500 |
| 50,992 | 59,846 | 76,649 | 90,246 | 103,477 | 120,168 | 133,758 | 152,510 |

# APPENDIX B

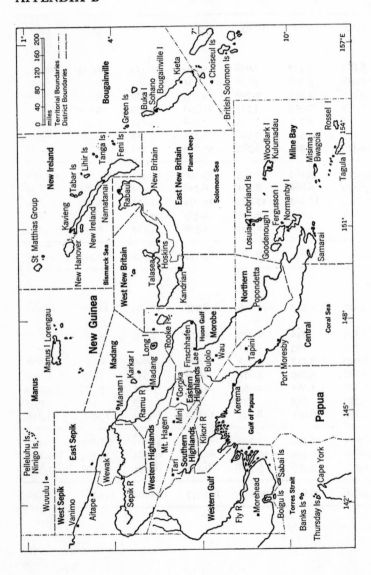

## APPENDIX C

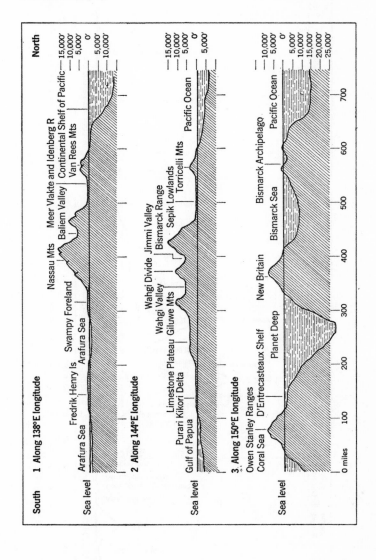

# APPENDIX D

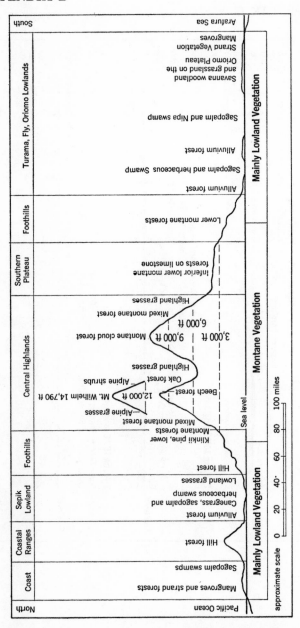

# APPENDIX E

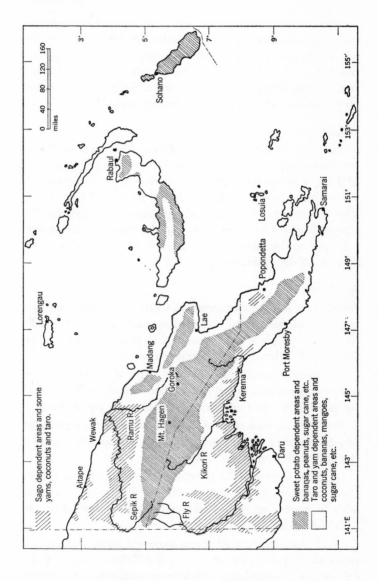

## APPENDIX F

The important articles of the 1962 New York Agreement between Indonesia and the Netherlands were those describing the act of free choice, the role of the Secretary-General's representative before, during and after the act, the eligibility of those participating in the act and the report of the Secretary-General on the conduct of the act to the General Assembly.

Article xvii

Indonesia will invite the Secretary-General to appoint a Representative who . . . will carry out the Secretary-General's responsibilities to advise, assist and participate in arrangements which are the responsibility of Indonesia for the act of free choice. The Secretary-General will, at the proper time, appoint the United Nations Representative in order that he and his staff may assume their duties in the territory one year prior to the date of self-determination. . . .

Article xviii

Indonesia will make arrangements, with the assistance and participation of the United Nations Representative and his staff, to give the people of the territory the opportunity to exercise freedom of choice. Such arrangements will include:

(a) Consultations (*Musjawarah*) with the representative councils on procedures and appropriate methods to be followed for ascertaining the freely expressed will of the population;

(b) The determination of the actual date of the exercise of free choice to be determined within the period established by the present Agreement;

(c) Formulation of the questions in such a way as to permit the inhabitants to decide (a) whether they wish to remain with Indonesia; or (b) whether they wish to sever their ties with Indonesia;

(d) The eligibility of all adults, male and female, not foreign nationals, to participate in the act of self-determination to be carried out in accordance with international practice, who are resident at the time of signing of the present Agreement and at the time of the act of self-determination, including those residents who departed after 1945 and who return to the territory to resume residence after the termination of Netherlands administration.

## Article XIX

The United Nations Representative will report to the Secretary-General on the arrangement arrived at for freedom of choice.

## Article XXI

1 After the exercise of the right of self-determination, Indonesia and the United Nations Representative will submit final reports to the Secretary-General who will report to the General Assembly on the conduct of the act of self-determination and the results thereof.

2 The parties to the present Agreement will recognise and abide by the results of the act of self-determination.

APPENDIX G

## FUNDWI PROJECTIONS—WEST IRIAN

Sectoral Budget Proposals—Investments, Experts and Fellowships—(in missions of US $)

| Sector or Activity | Investment Costs | Technical Assistance | Fellowships | Total |
|---|---|---|---|---|
| I. *Primary Emphasis* | | | | |
| Coastal and River Transport | 6.48 | .47 | .05 | 7.0 |
| Vocational Training | .80 | .94 | .04 | 1.7 |
| Education | .62 | .72 | .14 | 2.0 |
| Forestry | 2.48 | .5 | .02 | 3.0 |
| Fisheries | 2.1 | .4 | — | 2.5 |
| Joint Development Commission | — | — | — | 4.5 |
| II. *Secondary Emphasis* | | | | |
| Utilities (Power, Water) | .68 | .1 | .02 | .8 |
| Minerals | — | .5 | — | .5 |
| Agriculture & livestock | .5 | .3 | .2 | 1.0 |
| III. *Other Sectors* | | | | |
| Land Transportation | 1.16 | .3 | .1 | 1.5 |
| Air Transportation | 3.7 | .2 | .1 | 4.0 |
| Telecommunications and meteorology | .67 | .1 | .03 | .8 |
| Public Health | .4 | .2 | .1 | .7 |
| *Totals* | 19.59 | 4.73 | .74 | 30.0 |

The figures above are subject to alteration to include slightly different estimates as to sectoral costs; to include contingency reserves for project costs and previous FUNDWI expenditures including Mission costs. The Joint Development Commission will administer some funds allocated for specific sectors on either grant or loan basis and possibly in some instances on an equity basis.

SOURCE: *Design for Development of West Irian,* FUNDWI Report, U.N., 1968.

## APPENDIX H

## Text of Netherlands-Australian Co-operative Agreement on New Guinea, November, 1957

1 The Netherlands and Australian Governments base their policies with regard to the Territories of New Guinea for which they are responsible on the interests and inalienable rights of their inhabitants in conformity with the provisions and spirit of the United Nations Charter.

2 The Territories of Netherlands New Guinea, the Australian Trust Territory of New Guinea and Papua are geographically and ethnologically related, and the future development of their respective populations must benefit from co-operation in policy and administration.

3 The Australian and Netherlands Governments are therefore pursuing, and will continue to pursue, policies directed towards the political, economic, social and educational advancement of the peoples in their territories in a manner which recognises this ethnological and geographical affinity.

4 At the same time, the two Governments will continue, and strengthen, the co-operation at present existing between their respective administrations in the Territories.

5 In so doing the two Governments are determined to promote an uninterrupted development of this process until such time as the inhabitants of the Territories concerned will be in a position to determine their own future.

APPENDIX I

Undoubtedly taking its cue from Mr Barnes' speech of August 1965, the Papua and New Guinea House of Assembly Select Committee on Constitutional Development in November of the same year tabled its interim report which amounted to a request to the Australian Government to tell the people of New Guinea what constitutional options were open to them before any final choice on the constitutional status of New Guinea was made. The Select Committee asked that 'If Papua or New Guinea, or both of them, wish to move into closer relationship with Australia, the Australian Government will have to say whether Australia will accept such a relationship. When the Australian Government's attitude is known the Committee will be able to tell the people what the real choices are.' A valid enough request on any count but a significant hint as to the hopes of the Committee, evenly divided between black and white members, was contained in an important clause of the resolution's draft, but not final, form, which read: '... if Papua or New Guinea, or both of them, wish to join Australia as the seventh state, the Australian government will have to say whether Australia would accept another state.'

The Select Committee visited Canberra in the second week of April 1966, to discuss the report with the Ministers for Territories and Immigration, the Attorney-General and the Treasurer. The upshot was a statement to Parliament by Mr Barnes on 21 April reading in part: 'Ministers agreed that it would be compatible with the Government's position for the Committee to ask the Territory people their opinion on' the fact that 'the Committee felt that it would be of value if the people of the Territory were asked to say whether they wished their constitutional development to take a course directed towards separation from Australia or whether they wished their constitutional development to take a course towards evolution of an association or relationship with Australia which will endure after self-determination, recognising that the form of any such association or relationship would, so far as it affected Australia, be a matter to be decided by the Australian government of the day.' It was an ambiguous statement. It promised nothing and hinted at everything. It certainly encouraged the official journal of the influential Highlands' Farmers and Settlers' Association to editorialise in part that, 'From these statements it will be clear that the way has been cleared for a special relationship to be established between New Guinea and Australia when self-determination is attained.' Had it? These sentiments had already been contradicted by the retiring Administrator, Sir Donald Cleland, who was reported as saying in a farewell press conference that statehood was not 'practicable' and that any constitutional relationship between Australia and New Guinea would have to follow after 'independence'. He was in turn contradicted by his own Minister and, five days later, by Mr John Ballard, Assistant Secretary (Government) in the Department of Territories who said at a seminar on New Guinea organised by the Australian National University, that '. . . the Government has not precluded the possibility of New Guinea being the seventh state.'

The situation was made even more bewildering by the fact that the Minister in his statement to Parliament on 21 April had uncompromisingly set forth conditions for future New Guinean immigration into Australia. They were to be the same as those applying to Asians wishing to settle in the Commonwealth—in short no special concessions. He said that 'ministers foresaw no difficulty' in Papuans and New Guineans entering Australia for the purposes of education. Mr Barnes then pointed out that in so far as Papuans and New Guineans might want to stay here they would have to possess skills required by Australia. However these sorts of skills 'would, in the foreseeable future, be even more strongly required by the Territory itself. . . . However, should Papua and New Guinea at some time build up a surplus of skills which were short in Australia, then the entry of Papuans and New Guineans would be given special consideration within the recently advised policy.' This plain embargo on immigration meant the end of any possibility of seventh statehood for New Guinea, at least on terms of equality with the other states, and yet the implications of other kinds of relationship between Australia and New Guinea were left open.

It was a picture of complete confusion on all sides as to New Guinea's end constitutional status. But it was also indicative of the persevering paternalism of a small but powerful group, amid the enduring indifference of most, in seeking some special and always undefined relationship with the Territory. Mr Barnes returned to his paternalistic theme in Melbourne on 5 March 1967, when he told a public meeting that 'Independence for Papua-New Guinea will not be achieved for very many years, if at all'. He vehemently denied in subsequent press statements that he used the words 'if at all'. Pressed in the House of Representatives by Mr Clyde Cameron (ALP, South Australia) the Minister in obvious embarrassment refused to confirm or deny the 'if at all' qualification. At the January, 1968, Australian Institute of Political Science Summer School in Canberra, at which New Guinea was the subject, speaking without notes, after concluding his address, and in reference to New Guinea's economic development problems he said 'it is hard to see how it can be independent'.

The ALP has been no better in promoting public debate over the future of New Guinea than the government for the reason that there are considerable differences of opinion within the party as to what its future should be and what policies the ALP would adopt if it came to power. Under Dr Evatt as Leader it was largely indifferent. Under Mr Calwell, it was, if possible, even more paternalistic than the government although its 1965 platform, and those of successive years, state that the ALP favours 'the establishment of independence as early as possible'. In the same year, in April, at a seminar held at Goroka by the Council on New Guinea Affairs the then Deputy Leader of the ALP, Mr E. G. Whitlam, told a dismayed audience of both natives and Europeans that it would 'not be to Australia's or New Guinea's advantage to prolong . . . [political control] after 1970.' Influential members of his own party disagreed with him. In May 1968, Mr Whitlam—now Leader of the Party—described amending legislation providing for native Ministers in the new House of Assembly as 'excessively moderate'. He made other, and justifiable, criticisms of the Government's failure to encourage private industry to join in partnership with the

Government to develop New Guinea's resources so that 'an *independent* New Guinea could later succeed to the Australian Government's interest and immediately play a full role in the economic development of that country.' Mr Barnes predictably described Mr Whitlam's reasonable criticisms as being in line with those of the 'Afro-Asian group and the USSR.'

The ALP is certainly committed to independence for New Guinea, and so now, apparently, is the Government. However, whether Labor in power would be able, or would want, to move as swiftly as either Mr Whitlam or its own platform suggests is another matter. The more left wing elements of Labor have frequently been more paternalistic than the right over New Guinea matters.

# Bibliography

The following select bibliography is arranged according to chapter headings in this book. Obviously, however, many of the books and periodicals are of wider interest and cover more subjects than the one under which they may be listed.

CHAPTER 1: GEOGRAPHY, PEOPLE AND CULTURE

*Geography*

J. Andrews, *New Guinea*, Longmans Geographies, No. 7

E. Ford and B. Rowe, *Landscape Geography for New Guinea*, Angus and Robertson, Sydney, 1966

Diana Howlett, *A Geography of Papua and New Guinea*, Nelson, Melbourne, 1967

*Notes on the Territory of Papua and New Guinea*, Australian School of Pacific Administration, Sydney, 1968

*People and Culture*

H. I. Hogbin, *Transformation Scene*, Routledge and Kegan Paul, London, 1951

Peter Lawrence, *Road Belong Cargo*, Melbourne University Press, Melbourne, 1964

Peter Lawrence and M. J. Meggitt, *Gods, Ghosts and Men in Melanesia: Some Religions of Australian New Guinea and the New Hebrides*, Oxford University Press, Melbourne, 1965

B. Malinowski, *Argonauts of the Western Pacific*, Routledge and Kegan Paul, London, 1922

Margaret Mead, *Growing Up in New Guinea*, Pelican, Harmondsworth, 1942

C. D. Rowley, *The New Guinea Villager*, Cheshire, Melbourne, 1965

Colin Simpson, *Adam in Plumes*, Angus and Robertson, Sydney, 1954; *Adam with Arrows*, Angus and Robertson, Sydney, 1956

W. E. H. Stanner, *The South Seas in Transition*, Australian Publishing Company, London, 1955

P. Worsley, *The Trumpet shall Sound: A Study of Cargo Cults in Melanesia*, Macgibbon and Kee, London, 1957

CHAPTER 2: A BRIEF HISTORY

*Annual Report (British New Guinea) 1886-1906/7*, Government Printer, Brisbane and Melbourne

*Annual Report of the Lieutenant-Governor* (Papua), 1906/7 to 1908/9, 1910/11 to 1940/41

*Annual Reports on Papua and New Guinea*, 1946 to date, Government Printer, Canberra

B. Essai, *Papua and New Guinea*, Oxford University Press, Melbourne, 1961

J. G. Hides, *Papuan Wonderland*, Blackie, London, 1936

J. D. Legge, *Australian Colonial Policy: A Survey of Native Administration and European Development in Papua*, Angus and Robertson, Sydney, 1956

J. Lyng, *Our New Possession (late German New Guinea)*, Melbourne Publishing Company, Melbourne, 1919

L. Mair, *Australia in New Guinea*, Christophers, London, 1948

J. H. P. Murray, *Papua; or British New Guinea*, Fisher Unwin, London, 1912; *Papua of Today*, P. S. King and Son, London, 1925

*Official Handbook of the Territory of New Guinea*, Government Printer, Canberra, 1937

S. W. Reed, *The Making of Modern New Guinea*, American Philosophical Society, Philadelphia, 1943

*Report to the Council of the League of Nations*, 1914-21, 1921-22 to 1941, Government Printer, Canberra

C. D. Rowley, *The Australians in German New Guinea 1914-21*, Melbourne University Press, Melbourne, 1958

*Royal Commission (Of inquiry . . . into the Territory of Papua)*, J. Kemp, Melbourne, 1907

John Ryan, *The Hot Land; Focus on New Guinea*, Macmillan, Melbourne, 1969

CHAPTER 3: THE ECONOMY

*Annual Reports on Papua and New Guinea*, 1946 to date, Government Printer, Canberra

D. C. Bettison, E. K. Fisk, F. J. West and J. C. Crawford, *The Independence of Papua-New Guinea—What are the Prerequisites?*

CHAPTERS 4, 5, 7: ASSUMPTIONS, POLITICAL DEVELOPMENT AND THE FUTURE

C. S. Belshaw, *Changing Melanesia*, Oxford University Press, Melbourne, 1964

D. G. Bettison, P. W. van de Veur and C. A. Hughes (eds), *The Papua New Guinea Elections 1964*, Australian National University Press, Canberra, 1964

Hugh Foot, *A Start in Freedom*, Hodder and Stoughton, London, 1964

I. Grosart (ed.), *A New Guinea Brief*, Australian Institute of Political Science, Sydney, 1967

P. Hasluck, 'Australia's Task in Papua and New Guinea', seventh Roy Milne Lecture, Australian Institute of International Affairs, 1956; 'Australian Policy in Papua and New Guinea', George Judah Cohen Memorial Lecture, Australasian Medical Publishing Company, Sydney, 1956; *Australian Policy in Papua and New Guinea*, statement in the House of Representatives, 23 August 1960, Government Printer, Canberra; *The Legislative Council for Papua and New Guinea, Opening Session, Port Moresby, 17 October 1960*, Government Printer, Port Moresby; 'The Economic Development of Papua and New Guinea', address to Economic Society of Australia and New Zealand, NSW branch, *Australian Outlook*, No. 1, 1962; *Justice in Papua and New Guinea*, statement in the House of Representatives, 24 October 1961, Government Printer, Canberra; 'The Future in Papua and New Guinea', address to the Council of Adult Education, 6 January 1964, roneoed copy

Donald Hogg, *New Guinea*, A. H. and A. W. Reed, Sydney, 1969

*House of Assembly Debates, Port Moresby*, from June 1964 to date, Government Printer, Port Moresby

J. K. McCarthy, *Patrol into Yesterday*, Angus and Robertson, Sydney, 1964

*New Guinea and Australia, the Pacific and South-East Asia*, quarterly since March 1965, published by the Council on New Guinea Affairs, Sydney

*Reports of the United Nations Visiting Missions to the Trust Territory of New Guinea*, 1950-1968, United Nations Trusteeship Council, New York

J. Wilkes (ed.), *Australian Institute of Political Science Summer School, Canberra, January 1958*, Angus and Robertson, Sydney, 1968

E. P. Wolfers, *New Guinea Newsletters*, Institute of Current World Affairs, New York, from April 1967 to date; other political articles published variously in the quarterly *New Guinea*

CHAPTER 6: WEST IRIAN AND INDONESIA

*A Design for Development in West Irian*, Fund of the United Nations Development of West Irian, United Nations, New York, 1968

R. C. Bone, *The Dynamics of the Western New Guinea Problem*, Ithaca, New York, 1958

Arnold C. Brackman, *Indonesian Communism: A History*, Frederick A. Praeger, New York, 1963

Herbert Feith, 'The West New Guinea Conflict: Some Political and Ethical Aspects', paper to the New Guinea Society, Canberra, 28 June 1961; *The Decline of Constitutional Democracy in Indonesia*, Cornell University Press, Ithaca, 1962

Clifford Geertz, *The Religion of Java*, The Free Press of Glencoe, Illinois, 1960

Bruce Grant, *Indonesia*, Melbourne University Press, 1964

G. McT. Kahin, *Nationalism and Revolution in Indonesia*, Ithaca, New York, 1952

J. M. van der Kroef, 'Toward Papua Barat', article in *Australian Quarterly*, No. 1, March 1961; 'Pan-Papuanism', article in *New Guinea*, No. 4, 1969

J. A. C. Mackie, 'The West New Guinea Argument', article in *Australian Outlook*, No. 1, April 1962

James Mossman, *Rebels in Paradise*, Jonathan Cape, London, 1961

Soedjatmoko, The 1967 Dyason Memorial Lectures, in particular 'Indonesia: Problems and Opportunities', Australian Institute of International Affairs, Melbourne, 1967

Soetan Sjahrir, *Out of Exile*, John Day & Co., New York, 1959

Statements on the West New Guinea Conflict:

J. van Balluseck, First Committee, UN General Assembly, Ninth Session, 23 November 1954

Sir Garfield Barwick, House of Representatives, Canberra, 21 August 1962

*Handbook on Netherlands New Guinea*, New Guinea Institute, Rotterdam, 1958

Sir Percy Spender, First Committee, UN General Assembly, 9 November 1961

Dr M. Subandrio, UN General Assembly, 9 November 1961

*The United Nations in West New Guinea: An Unprecedented Story*, United Nations, New York, 1963. Contains text and resolution of Agreement between Indonesia and Holland concerning West Irian (1962)

P. W. van der Veur, *West New Guinea: Irian Barat or Papua Barat?* New Guinea Society, Canberra, September 1962

*The United Nations in West Irian: A Critique*, International Organisation, No. 1, 1964

*Western New Guinea and the Netherlands: The Dutch Case*, State Printing Office, The Hague, 1954

*West Irian, an Essential Part of Indonesia: the Indonesian Case*, Indonesian Embassy, Canberra, 1963

*Questionnaire Survey Among the Potential Papuan Elite in 1962 West New Guinea*, 'S-Gravenhage, Martinus Nijhoff, 1964

Documents relating to Pepera or the Act of Self Determination. These are many, varied and scattered. A roneoed guide to the procedures of, and names of all delegates to, each of the Pepera held at the administrative centres of each of the eight West Irian regencies was published by the Indonesian Administration, Djajapura

The Office of the United Nations Representative in West Irian (UNRWI) published, from Djakarta, occasional press releases between November 1968 and August 1969. A general information booklet on West Irian, describing Indonesia's historical links with West Irian, was published by the Indonesian Embassy, Canberra, 1969

The West Papuan Government-in-exile, *Fadjar Melanesia*, an occasional broadsheet in Dutch, English and Indonesian, Delft, since 1966

# Index